D1134667

Multinational Corporations and the North American Free Trade Agreement

Multinational Corporations and the North American Free Trade Agreement

Michael J. Twomey

PRAEGER

Westport, Connecticut
London

Library of Congress Cataloging-in-Publication Data

Twomey, Michael J.
 Multinational corporations and the North American free trade
agreement / Michael J. Twomey.
     p.   cm.
 Includes bibliographical references and index.
 ISBN 0-275-94617-7 (alk. paper)
  1. Investments, Foreign—Mexico. 2. Investments, Foreign—Canada.
3. Investments, Foreign—United States.   I. Title.
HG5162.T88 1993
332.6'73'092—dc20   93-6767

British Library Cataloguing in Publication Data is available.

Library of Congress Catalog Card Number: 93-6767
ISBN: 0-275-94617-7

First published in 1993

Praeger Publishers, 88 Post Road West, Westport, CT 06881
An imprint of Greenwood Publishing Group, Inc.

Printed in the United States of America

The paper used in this book complies with the
Permanent Paper Standard issued by the National
Information Standards Organization (Z39.48-1984).

10 9 8 7 6 5 4 3

This book is dedicated to my wife,

Terry Kihara,

on our tenth anniversary.

CONTENTS

FIGURES AND TABLES

FIGURES

TABLES

ACKNOWLEDGMENTS

Parts of the research for this book were carried out while the author held a Fulbright lectureship at the Center for Economic Studies at the Colegio de México. The gracious hospitality of Dr. Adalberto García Rocha and his colleagues is greatly appreciated. It was both a pleasure and an honor to be associated with the fine group of economists and other social scientists at the Colegio.

Helpful comments from presentations at CIDE, the University of the Americas, and the 1992 LASA meetings are also acknowledged.

Multinational Corporations and the North American Free Trade Agreement

1

INTRODUCTION

This book analyzes and compares the experiences of Canada, Mexico, and the United States with regard to foreign direct investment. The ultimate goal is to sketch out possible scenarios for movements in capital among the three countries as a result of the signing of a free trade agreement. Preparatory to that, some of the major theoretical paradigms treating foreign investment will be reviewed. A major part of our effort is devoted to discussions of these countries' differing experiences with foreign direct investment (hereafter, FDI). The United States has been the major source of FDI, and Canada and Mexico are among its most important recipients. A substantially historical perspective is required to put into context the rapid economic changes presently occurring. The effort is made to use the same methodological approach for the analysis of the three countries. Frequently, greater attention will be focused on Mexico; at any party there is always more interest in the newcomer.

As the subject of an academic study, this is a rather unusual mixture, given the different levels of economic development among these three countries, their radically different histories, and the corresponding dissimilarities in the published literature. Moreover, approaches to the topic of foreign investment are highly polarized. The major justification for the study is, of course, the likelihood that these three countries will soon be joined together in a free trade agreement that will substantially increase trade and investment flows.

Additionally, their histories are intimately tied together—at a minimum, all commentators would agree with Michael Hart (1990: 31), "Although Mexico is unlike Canada in most respects, the two countries do share a long history of trying to live in harmony with, but distinct from, the United States." Furthermore, the three countries present markedly distinct models of foreign investment; Canada's has been an import substituting FDI attracted by protective tariffs, Mexico is gearing up to host FDI for the manufacture of exports, while the United States is currently receiving vast amounts of new types of FDI oriented towards services. While a number of gaps remain in the analysis, our purposes will have been attained if the book serves as a useful benchmark for analysis of the impact of the free trade agreement while promoting further cross-country comparisons of FDI.

After this brief introduction, Chapter 2 begins the analysis by reviewing some major theoretical approaches. Everyone knows that the theme of multinational corporations is among the most politicized in the field, a situation that makes it difficult for one to claim to have chosen an approach that is not biased. The model chosen to do so, referred to as the OLI paradigm, is presented, along with comments relating it to its predecessors in international economics and industrial organization. Two other important bodies of writing on FDI are then discussed. Kiyoshi Kojima has provided perhaps the only alternative viewpoint on foreign direct investment from a position compatible with Anglo-Saxon economics; in addition, the writings he has produced or inspired provide an introduction to FDI from Japan, certainly the most important off-stage player in this hemisphere. Finally we review some of the vast literature critical of FDI, passing quickly from the anti-imperialism classics to the Latin American dependency school and some of its current writings.

Chapter 3 offers a series of descriptions of major policy trends towards FDI in our three countries as well as comments on major intellectual/academic schools of analysis. First comes a review of the new Canadian political economy, judged to be the most representative and refined analysis critical of MNCs in that country and also a helpful bridge to Mexican thinking. The coverage of policy in Mexico will note that it has undergone the largest swings in orientation, reaching a peak of hostility with the nationalization of oil in 1938 but now presenting a very open door. The United States has not had much of a formal policy toward either inward or outward FDI; the topic is also reviewed not only to relate that policy to those of the country's two neighbors but more importantly to discuss the possibilities of new orientations inside the country.

Chapter 4 presents a statistical description of the experience of the United States with foreign investment both outward and inward. A complementary survey is that of the next chapter, which does the same for Canada and Mexico. This leads to some interesting comparisons of the historical experiences of these countries, revealing some unsuspected parallels.

The links between economic growth and FDI are explored in Chapter 6. Although FDI will affect nationwide levels of investment and exports, it is argued that the major impact is on technological change. Placing primary emphasis on the extensive Canadian literature, we ask how multinational corporations facilitate the process of technology transfer, thereby affecting the options available to a nation's science policymakers.

Chapter 7 first discusses the bilateral free trade agreement between Canada and the United States and then proceeds into more detail on the trilateral accord in terms of the events leading up to Mexico's request for the negotiations and then with regard to some of the specifics of the subsequent agreement. These are complemented by a general description of certain areas of the Mexican economy and how they might be affected by the agreement.

Chapter 8 explores empirically some aspects of trade liberalization. In the first case it is argued that Canada's current deep recession is not predominantly attributable to the free trade agreement with the United States. Mexican production has been more severely affected by its unilateral trade liberalization of the late 1980s, although in this case it is also true that the more severe causes of declining production are related to the debt crisis. Some estimates are then presented of the potential flows of foreign direct investment into Mexico and their impact on employment at home and abroad as a result of the free trade agreement. The last chapter reviews and summarizes what has gone before and suggests issues for future research.

To complete this introduction we review some of the most important statistical indicators for the three countries in Table 1.1. Most of the message is quite familiar; the economy of the United States is ten times as large as that of Canada, and some twenty-five times that of Mexico. On a per-capita basis, the difference between Canada and the United States practically disappears, while Mexico's level is one-tenth that of its northern neighbors. Turning to Table 1.2, Canada and the United States are each others' most important export trading partners; as is the United States for Mexico. Less familiar to many is the fact that Mexico has been trading more with Canada than it has with all of Latin America.

A few words on terminology are in order before beginning the analysis. Foreign capital flows can either be portfolio or direct. The dividing line between these two is sometimes hazy, as we discuss in Chapter 4, but the concept that

Table 1.1
Comparative Data: Canada, Mexico, and the United States

		Canada	Mexico	United States
GDP/cap	(U.S.$)	19030	2010	20910
Population	(million)	26	85	249
GDP	(billion U.S.$)	489	201	5156
Value Added. Mfg.	(billion U.S.$)	NA	47	866
Exports	(billion U.S.$)	114	23	347
Imports	(billion U.S.$)	113	22	492
Investment/GDP	(percent)	23	17	15
Relative Wage	(U.S.=100)	103	16	100

Sources: World Bank *World Development Report,* 1991. Wages (index of hourly compensation costs for production workers in manufacturing) from the *Statistical Abstract of the United States,* 1991, Table No. 1468

Note: Data refer to 1989 except for value added in manufacturing, which is 1988.

Table 1.2
Foreign Trade Matrices: Canada, Mexico, and the United States, 1989

Percentage of Exporting Country's Total:

Exports Into:	Canada		Mexico		United States	
From: Canada	—		<1	(12)	74	(1)
Mexico	12	(6)	—		70	(1)
United States	22	(1)	7	(3)	—	

Percentage of Importing Country's Total:

Imports Into:	Canada		Mexico		United States	
From: Canada	—		2	(5)	18	(2)
Mexico	1	(8)	—		6	(13)
United States	65	(1)	70	(1)	—	

Source: Author's calculations, using data from United Nations, *International Trade Statistics Yearbook*, 1989, vol. 1.

Note: Rankings in parentheses.

foreign direct investment is meant to represent is control of decision making of the firm and is usually measured as some percentage of control of the voting stock of a corporation. Firms that engage in foreign investment will be referred to as Multinational Corporations (MNCs). Although the terms *foreign investors* and *transnational corporations* will also be used, no distinction is implied. There will be occasions when it is necessary to distinguish between inward foreign direct investment—IFDI—and that going outward, or OFDI. The Free Trade Agreement between Canada and the United States will be indicated as FTA; that among the three countries as NAFTA. While both the popular and the technical literature provide alternative acronyms, this usage follows that of the one official public document of the three governments (Governments of Canada, et al. 1992).

2

THEORETICAL PERSPECTIVES

ECLECTIC OLI

Any economic analysis presupposes a model, however informal. The treatment of a controversial issue such as foreign direct investment (FDI) virtually demands an explicit statement. The major theoretical approach to be followed in this book considers FDI to reflect primarily microeconomic decisions taken by firms in imperfectly competitive markets. This should be considered a working hypothesis, one that frames our mode of analysis while also being subject to testing and modification. The approach has had a number of key innovators; the names Dunning, Casson, Buckley, and Caves are at the forefront. Without denying the insights of the Heckscher-Ohlin model of comparative advantage and international production and trade, this model asks a different question—why is there FDI—and answers it focusing on a number of factors that indeed are assumed away in the Heckscher-Ohlin model, such as transport costs, scale economies, and differing technological levels. Perhaps the key breakthrough in the development of this approach was the 1960 Ph.D. thesis of Stephen Hymer (published in 1976), who first explained FDI combining the classic idea of Coase of internalization with Bain's concept of barriers to entry.[1] Although he died at a relatively young age, Hymer's ideas were later championed by Charles Kindleberger and now have widespread admiration and acceptance in the field of economics.[2]

Our brief description of this approach will follow that of Dunning (1980, 1988a), who describes it as an "eclectic paradigm" of multinational investment. This model affirms that there will be foreign investment when there are ownership or locational advantages for a firm to produce overseas, which can best be captured by internalization of production via FDI. These considerations, Ownership, Location, and Internalization, lead to its being referred to as the OLI model.

Ownership advantages can include patents or trademarks, production or management techniques, special organizational methods, and particularly the existence of economies of scale, which are said to be specific to the firm. In contrast, the locational advantages are ascribed to the host country and include factors such as resource availability, low wages or taxes, transport costs, language or cultural issues, and so forth. Finally, the internalization consideration looks for a key reason why the other two advantages cannot be utilized indirectly from afar, such as via some form of licensing, by pointing to such reasons as insecurity of patent laws, lack of knowledge of the potential local licensees, avoidance of other search and negotiation costs, special tariff rates for imports from branch plants, and the advantages allowed by intrafirm pricing, among others. One way of summarizing this approach, responding to its emphasis on sectoral specific barriers to entry and other advantages, is to label it *international industrial organization.*

The earlier analysis of FDI was a direct application of the Heckscher-Ohlin model, which explains the direction of international trade by focusing on countries' differing allocations of primary factors of production. This model was extended to the case of foreign investment by asserting that because capital is internationally mobile, foreign investment reflects a movement of this factor from the abundant to the scarce country, attracted by higher returns—the interest rate—in the receiving country. A variant of this approach looked at FDI as a response to differences in the prices of final products caused perhaps by some sort of exchange-rate rigidity. While making some contribution, this approach is generally regarded as insufficient. A last mention to "other" literature on FDI, based on neoclassical economics, is that which explains FDI as risk aversion, as managers avoid exchange rate fluctuations. While derived outside the OLI milieu, this approach is clearly subsumable as an organizational advantage of MNCs.

Heckscher and Ohlin were Swedish economists, the latter a recipient of a Nobel prize, and the theoretical paradigm that evolved from their writings, particularly advanced by the work of Paul Samuelson, has dominated international trade discussion for more than half a century. The intellectual dominance of the Heckscher-Ohlin model has been challenged recently by empirical regularities that it does not explain easily, such as the importance of intraindustry trade and foreign investment and the growth of services, and which appear to be explainable by the other factors alluded to above.

Two other heuristic explanations of FDI might also be included here, representatives of earlier thinking that has been incorporated into today's more-complex paradigms. One crude version of the product cycle asserted that a firm initially became familiar with a foreign country's market via exports and subsequently produced in that country upon accumulating sufficient knowledge of the demands of the market. This story now has less relevance for manufacturing FDI because of the contemporary degree of homogenization of consumer culture. Similarly, writers from business schools as well as many

Marxists used to emphasize the expansionist nature of FDI, as if these firms had an excess supply of managerial ability. While the OLI paradigm may incorporate this factor more subtly, the earlier statements may have given it the more accurate flavor.

While it is the case that many of the authors in the OLI perspective have published together and have been associated with the University of Reading in England, one notes different emphases in their approaches. Casson and other writers on the determinants of FDI give priority to the firm's internalization of market imperfections, showing the direct influence of Ronald Coase.[3] One of the attractions of the OLI paradigm is its inclusiveness, especially if one is willing to avoid the temptation of establishing an a priori hierarchy of the influence of the three OLI factors. So, rather than attempt the elaboration of potentially artificial differences among these authors, we are led to remark that this is a school in the process of formation; so that, there has not yet been much theoretical formulation, at least in its contemporary form as mathematical formulae. In this regard, the parallel with the "life cycle" of the Heckscher-Ohlin theory is particularly strong, and while one might wish more-visible guideposts in terms of what the OLI approach says theoretically and how to measure it empirically, one might also find relief when pondering the gap that exists between the original writings of Heckscher and Ohlin and the contemporary mathematical descendants of their model.[4]

Of particular importance to a study including Canada is the work of Richard Caves and his collaborators, which is sympathetic to the OLI approach but self-depicted as a combination of industrial organization (I-O) and international economics. Caves (1982) can serve as a textbook for the study of MNCs. A very important forerunner is the study of Canada by Eastman and Stykolt (1967), which emphasized these I-O factors (nonachievement of economies of scale, the importance of tariff protection in lessening competition), which are now seen to characterize so many host countries and which are viewed by some analysts as much more fundamental than the presence of foreigners themselves.

Although this international industrial organization school was heavily influenced by the empirical work done on FDI in Canada, it is also the case that the same combination of considerations—industrial organization and international trade—is proving to be a hotbed of research on a new approach to trade policy. Often referred to as strategic trade policy (Krugman, 1986), this writing asks whether considerations of increasing returns to scale and other assumed violations of the perfectly competitive model might justify protectionism. One part of this literature has tended to be highly theoretical, particularly incorporating insights and modeling techniques that industrial organization has filtered in from game theory. Key to many models is policy towards FDI, inward or outward. FDI may be affected directly by tariffs or trade-related requirements, or indirect measures may be utilized, such as subsidizing R&D or other inputs. Business economics literature has been drafted into explaining predatory or defensive foreign investments. Once again, many of the most important contributors are Canadians.

While the OLI approach has filtered up, so to speak, its microeconomic insights to the broader policy arena, the strategic trade models have up to now not generated a significant set of results independent of assumed initial conditions. The widespread discomfort in industrial countries caused by their productivity slowdown and the growing fear of competition from newly industrializing developing countries are creating enormous pressures for some sort of industrial policy, one component of which would be trade policy. Thus the major contribution of the strategic trade policy literature has been to restrain essentially prejudged policy conclusions by facilitating a cooler analytical approach to them. These questions will continue to command attention for the foreseeable future.

The link between the OLI paradigm and the writings on the product cycle is also very important. This approach, particularly associated with Raymond Vernon of Harvard, places emphasis on the impact of technological diffusion in determining where a product is produced and most pointedly on the role of multinational corporations in determining that diffusion. As will be remarked below, the OLI/International Industrial Organization approach has little explicit dynamic analysis, which of course is the essence of Vernon's product cycle. Many economists—including, it would seem, Vernon—now believe that the product cycle analysis is quite out of date if not simply obsolete (Vernon, 1979). If it is, that is because of oversuccess of the processes it highlighted. The traditional centers of technological advancement have lost their hegemony so that, for example, Hong Kong and South Korea are the initiators of new techniques in textiles (UNCTC, 1987). Furthermore, there are differing rates of loss of organizational advantages compared to those that are locational, and in both cases the speed of international diffusion is rising. What is obsolete is the vision of the United Kingdom or the United States as the major developers of products and processes such as mechanically spun cotton thread or mass-produced automobiles, which they then are able to dominate for decades.

It is curious to note that neither the scholars at Reading, England, nor those in Cambridge, Massachusetts, appear to have consolidated a school of researchers in Third World countries, although Dunning's close collaboration with the United Nations Center on Transnational Corporations has left a clear OLI imprint on its publications.[5]

Empirical Support

There have been a number of general reviews of quantitative studies of FDI, such as Agarwal (1980) and Hood and Young (1979). We will concentrate on key works relating to Canada both to save space and to prepare for further discussion below. The Canadian research was recently reviewed by Safarian

(1985), and an excellent treatment appears in the I-O textbook of Green (1990).

A convenient point of departure is Eastman and Stykolt (1967), who argued that economies of scale in production are not realized in Canada due to the protection that tariffs provide to factories inefficiently operating on a small scale. This book, so clearly a forerunner of today's free trade proponents in Canada, explicitly rejected an interest rate-cost of capital explanation for foreign investment, preferring to view it as a response to the advantages of multiplant production.[6] While Hymer (also a Canadian) utilized an industrial organization framework, the major contribution in this framework is the work of Richard Caves. A model for much subsequent work is Caves (1974), in which foreign investment's share of sales (as a sectoral average for two-digit industries) is the dependent variable in a regression with advertising expenditures, research and development levels, measures of minimum efficient scale, importance of multiplant production, dominance by large firms, and entrepreneurial resources, tariff levels, and wages. The results were judged to be highly supportive of both explanations of FDI based on I-O and locational variables. A follow-up book-length treatment, Caves et al. (1980), more thoroughly treated these issues with much more sophisticated statistical techniques and effectively guaranteed the I-O perspective a central spot in the FDI analysis.

Oversimplifying for the sake of exposition, we can use the work of Caves as a point of reference for reviewing other contributions. One issue is the potential limitation of using industrial averages instead of individual firm data. Horst (1972) used the data from the Harvard Business School's massive study of individual companies and obtained results less favorable to the I-O approach, a negative result that Grubaugh (1987) claims to have reversed.

A major problem endemic to I-O research relates to the handling the simultaneous determination of the percentage of foreign ownership, concentration, productivity levels, R&D and advertising expenditures, and so on. The two-stage least-squares results of Saunders (1980, 1982), are consistent with those from simpler OLS approach, and indeed one of the contributions of Caves et al. (1980) was the routine presentation of simultaneous equation alongside OLS estimates.

Another basic question is whether or not the preferred specification of a variable is its level in one country or the difference between its values in two countries. For example, for the case of advertising expenditures by U.S. and Canadian firms, Meredith (1984) demonstrated the feasibility of using their arithmetical differences as an independent variable. Caves et al. (1980) present a number of regressions utilizing as the dependent variable differences between countries—concentration (p. 51); expenditures on R&D (p. 191)—and as independent variables—relative size of markets (p. 64); rate of return to capital (p. 191); and cost of labor (p. 267). The influence on relative foreign ownership of the variable for concentration was positive from both countries, while no results are reported for the intercountry difference, although the high correlation between concentration ratios in the two countries was noted.

Finally, mention can be made of the efforts of Orr (1974) and Gorecki (1976) at concentrating directly on the effects of barriers to entry by nationality of firm, finding that indeed foreign firms were less deterred. This has been the subject of a number of recent articles, as longitudinal data have become available, and, indeed, as exit behavior—particularly of U.S. firms—also becomes of importance to Canada (Davidson and McFetridge, 1984; Baldwin and Gorecki, 1991; McMechan et al. 1992).

Having reviewed this impressive list of research on industrial organization topics, it is worth noting some that have not been subject to such close analysis but may safely be regarded as generally accepted. The higher propensity to import of foreign firms was clearly laid out in the Gray Report (Government of Canada, 1972). That the profitability (return on equity or total assets) and productivity of foreign firms are higher is portrayed each year in graphs of the CALURA reports. The interesting research has been on the causes of that higher productivity as in Baldwin and Gorecki (1986), or the possibility of technological spin-offs from foreign to domestic producers, as in Globerman (1979). The theme of R&D will be discussed in detail in Chapter 5.

The effect of taxes on foreign investment has not received much attention in the empirical literature on Canada that is consciously OLI. The subject has received some attention, of course—Murray (1982) argued that unusually low corporate income taxes in Canada led to excessive U.S. investment in that country's industry, while Damus et al. (1991) present a CGE model of the welfare effects of tax changes in an open economy, in which FDI plays a key role. One subject we do not see is careful analysis of tax breaks given to firms to entice their investments in specific communities, with a view of evaluating overall costs and benefits. It is easy to understand that data problems impede the study of tax rates and transfer pricing.

There are a couple of other areas of importance to this study, on which the literature on Canada has not advanced significantly. There appears to be next to nothing on FDI from a time-series perspective, which is particularly lamentable in light of the greater availability of data. There are few hints in the Canadian literature of how to capture the supposed simultaneity of the internalization criteria with what we are referring to as organization and location effects. A particular application of these two considerations would be the study of how the mode of foreign participation in Canada has evolved over time, relying less on complete ownership and more on joint ventures.[7] Finally, the literature on Canada has not treated the issue of political stability as a determinant of IFDI. Although one would not expect this to be important for Canada, it probably is for most third world countries. An empirical study along these lines, of OFDI from Germany, is Agarwal et al. (1991).

Policy Implications

The implications of the OLI paradigm can be analyzed on three levels; national welfare, sectoral performance, and theoretical issues.

A standard practice for theorists of international economics is to ask how foreign trade affects the national welfare of a country, contrasting in principle a before-and-after analysis in which for the prior case trade had been prohibited. The same procedure is valid with regard to international investment, although not much has been written in this vein. Nevertheless, we can assert that the OLI approach fundamentally views FDI as beneficial to both the host and the home country. This response is not surprising coming from a theoretical model focusing on microeconomic factors in an environment that is competitive, even if imperfectly so. Moreover, FDI is inevitably a "second best" solution (Dunning, 1988a: 19), where the first-best option would involve no tariffs nor barriers to entry, widespread diffusion of technology, and generally, no market distortions.[8] Thus, a more useful approach to the welfare issue is to stress the importance of specifying the changing context that gives rise to the growth of FDI. Some of these are basically positive, for instance, lowered cost of information or transportation, while others may be harmful to welfare, such as increased tariffs or tax changes facilitating fraudulent intrafirm pricing.

With regard to income distribution, FDI will benefit the possessors of ownership advantages, who by definition reside in the home country. The assumed limited degree of diffusion of those advantages implicitly suggests that their macroeconomic impact would also be small. A similar comment pertains to those who control the location advantages in the host country. While the OLI authors tend to stay away from political analyses, it is clear that a quite valid response to their approach is to look for political (or political economy) reasons for tariffs, barriers to entry, or special locational advantages.[9] Where these exist, an attitude hostile to FDI might well be appropriate, because the "first-best" response would clearly be to eliminate the artificial barriers.

The implications of the OLI analysis that have most-immediate application are at what might be called the sectoral level, reflecting the industrial organization basis of this writing. There is a very strong expectation that firms with FDI presence or sectors with above-average foreign participation will be characterized by relatively high profit rates and concentration, advertising ratios, import propensities, and R&D levels, and may well be more capital intensive and otherwise more "modern." From an operational point of view, this cannot say how much higher these variables ought to be, and finesses the implied line of research which would ask if they are too high.

Another issue of significant contemporary relevance is whether or not outward FDI reduces trade and local employment. As indicated above, the proponents of OLI would prefer to rephrase the question, asking first which factor caused the change that led to the FDI, because in some cases FDI and trade will be complements, and in others, substitutes. Suppose increases in domestic costs of production (wages, profits, taxes) or declines in foreign costs (due to technology transfer) make overseas production more profitable. Defenders of FDI indicate that it has simply accompanied a reduction of domestic employment that was to occur in any event, while perhaps some production and management jobs will be maintained in the home country due to sourcing arrangements and centralization of administrative and executive tasks. If FDI is a response to a tariff in the host country, then it similarly saves some of the jobs that were going to be lost from the investing country. Critics of FDI respond that the firms could maintain local production by reducing profits, and, perhaps more tellingly, that the organizational advantages are quite often the result of the home country's social expenditures on R&D and education, whose benefits the broader community loses because of the FDI. One version of an anti-FDI position from labor's perspective, with potential theoretical validity, would argue that since the jobs would eventually be lost to foreign producers, why not discourage FDI to maintain more employment in the home country during that short transition period?

International economists often ask what economic interest groups are benefited by tariffs; a similar question is appropriate here. The Stolper-Samuelson theorem, explained in any textbook, argues that free trade benefits the factor of production that is relatively abundant in each country and hurts the scarce factor while providing enough benefits that all might be better off than under autarchy. Because FDI is not a policy variable but a response both to different production conditions as well as to changing restrictions on capital flows, the analysis cannot be straightforwardly parallel. Undoubtedly, there will be circumstances in which one country's owners of capital will be benefited by a reduction of capital controls overseas, while that country's workers will be hurt. However, the OLI paradigm does not merely argue for a diversity of causes for FDI. The emphasis in this approach on economies of scale and technological transfer rejects the standard conditions under which the Stolper-Samuelson theory holds true. We will see below that many economic simulations of different free-trade scenarios do indeed argue that all sides benefit.

Another standard policy-oriented question is, does FDI increase industrial concentration? The appropriate response, similar to that given above, would be that it depends on what gives rise to the FDI. Note also that the OLI perspective implicitly trusts the market mechanism with regard to intellectual property rights, which is an approach that is frequently out of favor in many corners of the globe.

A comment can also be made with regard to the frequent practice of looking at a country's net FDI position as an indicator of competitiveness. Many such discussions in international economics often trail off into mercantilistic nonsense; with regard to foreign investment, technological superiority is only part of one of the factors motivating FDI. Thus, great care would be needed in making any such inferences.

Finally, the OLI literature has a number of implications at the level of theory.

In principle, this paradigm challenges the standard neoclassical model because its point of departure is that markets are not perfect, technology is not evenly diffused, and economies of scale and strategic considerations may be important.[10] Another revisionist aspect of OLI writing is the lack of emphasis given to adaptation of production techniques for different host-country situations.[11] In a more positive vein, the OLI paradigm enriches theoretical discussion particularly by facilitating the investigation of the determinants of the location of production and of the hierarchical structure of organizations. Work on the determinants and effects of FDI is particularly promising with regard to services, specific factors of production, and intraindustrial trade, especially of intermediate products.

KOJIMA AND THE HITOTSUBASHI SCHOOL

While it may be argued that the Reading, internalization, and international I-O schools are fairly closely related intellectually, there is a third body of writing on FDI that is separate from them geographically and methodologically. The most prominent writer in this tradition is Kiyoshi Kojima of Hitotsubashi University in Tokyo. In a much cited early publication, Kojima (1973) studied the circumstances under which FDI would be trade creating or trade reducing. He argued that the former would occur when a firm that possesses superior technology but lacks resources invests abroad in countries with opposite endowments. Similarly, antitrade, or domestically biased investment, will arise when a host country raises tariffs, attracting overseas investors. From a methodological point of view, this work is clearly compatible with the "Anglo-Saxon" tradition; it is based on a principle of comparative costs, with frequent citations to Hymer, Vernon, Harry Johnson, and others. However, the discussion became controversial when that author went to what many consider excessive effort to separate his model from those of the other schools and identified the beneficial investments with that of Japan and the non-beneficial type with that of the United States. We believe that any theoretical difference between Kojima and the OLI approach is terribly exaggerated, and that his theoretical contribution can easily be fit under a broad umbrella of the OLI paradigm.[12] His major contribution was to have focused on the issue of whether FDI increases or decreases trade.

As with so many innovative works, Kojima's writing has stimulated much important research, especially empirical analyses of Asian host countries. While Lee (1980) found this to be an accurate description for Korea, Chou (1988) was less positive with regard to Taiwan. Other recent articles (Hiemenz, 1987; Tai and Mehta, 1988; Sazanami, 1988; Komiya and Wakasugi, 1991) have pointed to a convergence of investment patterns from Japan and United States, the growth cycle element of FDI from the latter, the importance of investment by smaller

Japanese firms and the growth of service sector FDI from Japan. With regard to the latter, we are fortunate that there are a number of descriptions of the Japanese trading companies, Sogo Shosha (Kojima and Ozawa, 1984; Yoshihara, 1982), not so much for the analytical sophistication of the writing but because it is a useful introduction to this type of investment, that, as will be discussed below, appears to be the new cutting edge of FDI.

Kojima's earlier work, oriented towards industrial and extractive investments, missed the bigger contrast, which is in regard to services. It is rather striking that these trading companies have not been thoroughly analyzed in some version of the OLI paradigm. Rugman (1987) presents the argument that trade in services can be conceptualized in terms of transaction costs, but his data refer to Canada and the United States. The UNCTC has published studies on transnationals and services (e.g., UNCTC, 1989), but there is a need for an academic treatment focusing specifically on the Sogo Shosha.[13] Very briefly, the argument would be that the organizational advantages that allowed U.S. FDI to surpass European FDI in the early part of this century seem to be giving way to other types of organizational advantages, exploited particularly by Japanese FDI today.[14] The immediate example is management styles; Alfred Chandler has long argued that the professional managerial system of U.S. firms gave them an advantage over their family-owned and managed counterparts from England, and of course today one constantly hears of the numerous advantages of Japanese management.[15]

DEPENDENCY THEORY

Foreign investment has long played a key role in the theoretical constructs of those critical of the twentieth-century capitalist system. In the early years of the century, Hobson and Lenin asserted that a major economic force behind imperialism was the search for new markets overseas. Its cause was the condition of oversupply and a falling rate of profit at home due to the ever-larger production capacity outpacing a continually diminishing domestic purchasing power, itself squeezed by a steady worsening of the distribution of income. The Hobson-Lenin analysis was influential for its emphasis on economic as opposed to military or political explanations of imperialism. Moreover, Lenin expanded the traditional Marxist analysis with his description of imperialism as the highest stage of capitalism. Note that foreign investment and foreign trade played parallel roles in these writings and that the typical form of foreign investment at that time was bonds, not direct investment. As remarked elsewhere in this text, the distinction between the two in terms of foreign control was much less important at that time than it became at mid-century.

The very different world order that emerged after World War II found the attention of writers in this tradition refocused while remaining antagonistic towards capitalism and foreign investment. Concern with empire had evolved into rejection of neocolonialism. The United States was now the undisputed leader of the capitalist side of a bipolar world. People such as Paul Baran, Paul Sweezy, and Harry Magdoff continued to analyze critically the roles of MNCs in monopoly capitalism.

Complementary to analyses focusing on industrial countries, Latin America produced a series of works investigating its role in the international economy. Already in the 1950s, Raúl Prebisch and others at the United Nations Economic Commission for Latin America (ECLA, or CEPAL in Spanish), had developed an interpretation that emphasized the special disadvantages the region faced in its trading relations, a viewpoint that contradicted the normal reading of the international trade literature. During the latter 1960s, there evolved an extension of that analysis commonly known as dependency theory. "From the economic point of view a system is dependent when the accumulation and expansion of capital cannot find its essential dynamic component inside the system" (Cardoso and Faletto, 1979: xx). One of the key works of this school affirmed that the external dynamic was one in which "underdevelopment" increased with "development," i.e., growth inside the capitalist system, and demonstrated this hypothesis by pointing to what was considered more genuine growth, obtained by peripheral regions relatively isolated from the world system or when the core industrial countries were weakened by recession or war (Gunder Frank, 1966). For many writers the solution was autonomous development outside of the capitalist sphere, for which a prerequisite was socialist revolution.

In principle, the economic policy most consistent with dependency thinking was import substituting industrialization.[16] National industrialization was necessary to avoid the stagnationist tendency inherent in reliance on raw material exports. Tariffs and other controls on imports were the key policy to foment industrialization. Much effort in the dependency tradition was devoted to analyzing the specific class alliances that would be necessary to provide industrial growth and development, to counteract situations in which the local bourgeoisie was too allied to semifeudal landed interests or to international groups with contrary interests.

In cases where neither the domestic entrepreneurs nor the state were willing and able to generate sufficient manufacturing investment, foreign investment was the only other option. The experience of Brazil epitomized the situation of rapid growth led by multinational firms or dependent development. Mexico was widely seen as converging onto that same path in spite of its revolutionary tradition and nationalist ideology.

At its worst, dependency is merely an empty political slogan; at its best, it is a central hypothesis around which have been organized and written numerous case studies of a multidisciplinary nature about a particular country, region, social class, or industry, with emphasis on the deleterious effects of international linkages. We may honor this second aspect without necessarily doing full justice to it by focusing on what dependency writers have emphasized as the key economic issues relating to MNCs. In so doing we do not forget decades of gunboat diplomacy and its successor policies, especially, most recently, the support and participation of U.S. multinationals in, most egregiously, the coups in Guatemala and Chile. Those examples are the tip of the iceberg; we are reviewing why ice floats.

While there is no way to prioritize the components of this analysis, perhaps we should begin with profits, central to most criticisms of capitalism. MNCs are associated with concentration, use their greater power to lower wages, have better technology, and manipulate transfer prices to avoid taxes. Their production has a higher-than-average imported content; in addition, its utilization of factors of production does not respond well to the host country's profile because the technology is imported.

Two paths in which the dependency writers link economics to broader social concerns relate to the host country's development strategy and advertising. MNCs, the argument goes, provided a certain guarantee of successful achievement of certain macroeconomic goals such as GNP growth, which gave policymakers an excuse for not confronting more-fundamental issues such as realigning income distribution or caring for the environment. Another example of the distortions associated with MNCs is their role in introducing and adapting advertising, promising the "American way of life," which corrupts the social fabric while strengthening social classes more closely linked to it and eliminating from popular consideration an ideological alternative.

The main methodological approach of dependency writers was a multidisciplinary case study. An overall evaluation of the empirical validity of the literature is necessarily not feasible. One example of statistical work more comparable with others mentioned in this book is Bornschier and Chase-Dunn (1985), who studied the effect of the penetration of foreign investment (roughly, the foreign-owned percentage of the domestic capital stock) on average growth rates. Their cross-section regressions, including over 100 countries, resulted in a negative coefficient for the stock of FDI and a positive one for FDI flows. These coefficients were highly significant. The authors interpret the change in signs as reflecting a nonlinear relationship. Although a number of issues of an econometric nature could be raised, the reader must be impressed by the strength of these results. Along those same lines, Hammer and Gartrell (1986) claim to demonstrate a "mature dependency effect" of a reduction in Canadian growth rates due to greater U.S. ownership of Canadian capital, for the post-World War II period.

Another work that links the dependency tradition to our interests here is the collection edited by Newfarmer (1985). In the introductory chapter the editor asks, "Do TNCs exert an independent influence on development or is their behavior neutral and no different from other firms?" (p. 4). A decidedly industrial organization framework is adopted, with numerous citations to Caves, Hymer, and Dunning, among others. The book's summary argues that while the rules of the game often bias the distribution of gains towards MNCs away from host country governments, both groups benefit, and indeed these latter are able to affect that distribution.

The multidisciplinary scope of dependency writings, true to their Latin American heritage, frequently included a political component. Indeed, it is politics, not economics, that best distinguishes the ECLA structuralists from the dependency school. In a related vein, a much-cited review asked if dependency was a formal theory of underdevelopment or a methodology for analysis of concrete situations, concluding in favor of the latter (Palma, 1978). Moreover, it was the political plane that Gunder Frank referred to when he declared in 1972 that dependency theory was dead (Gunder Frank, 1992). A long decade of possibilities that opened with the Cuban Revolution, ended with the overthrow of the Allende government in Chile. Subsequent world events can only have strengthened that viewpoint. In particular, the Mexican request for the opening of negotiations on a free trade agreement is a leading example of the rejection of virtually all that dependency theory implied.

What new writings have come from the dependency school? Three areas of debate will be mentioned; that relating to the NICs, a reconsideration of international dependency, and a reevaluation of class struggle.

The strong growth and development of the so-called newly industrializing countries, or NICs, especially the "four tigers" of East Asia—South Korea, Taiwan, Hong Kong and Singapore, have redefined the list of options available to developing country policymakers. Their growth has accompanied rapid growth of industry and strong exports based on manufactured goods. On the face of it, these experiences appear to contradict the major thrust of the dependency school. Additionally, the World Bank and other international policy advisers have continually pointed to the export openness of the NICs, contrasting it to the protectionism and antiexport bias of Latin American countries.

The dependency writers have not avoided the debate; indeed, they have used these cases to bolster their own positions. As sketched out in Evans (1987), the rebuttal centers on the different historical experiences of the two groups. Because Hong Kong and Singapore are island economies, their experiences are rejected out of hand, and the comparison is restricted to Korea and Taiwan. First and foremost, the role of MNCs has been radically different. These were active in Latin America throughout this century, growing particularly in the 1950s and 1960s, when the two Asian countries received practically no FDI but were beginning their growth phase.[17] Also consistent with dependency writing is the effective role of the much stronger state in Korea and Taiwan.[18] One might add that in those countries the state more severely restricts the activities of labor unions and dissident voices. Thirdly, both Korea and Taiwan experienced dramatic land reforms at the end of World War II; this "prerequisite" has still not been achieved in Latin America. A final note would highlight the protectionism of the two Asian countries, carried out using subsidies and other transfers in such a way as to minimize a bias against exports.

As befits a broad, vibrant school with many adherents, Marxism has always been characterized by strong internal debates. This is particularly true today as a result of changes in Eastern Europe and the defeat of or disillusionment with socialist regimes elsewhere. As reviewed by Chilcote (1990), a common theme in much writing of what he terms "Post-Marxism" is a "retreat from class" in Latin America (and elsewhere) as the focus of analysis or political organizing. Important roots to this thinking can be found in the Eurocommunist and Eurosocialist developments of recent years that reflect a perception of greater possibilities for a socialist transition under democratic regimes, combined with a disillusion with popular movements based strictly on class conflict.

One version of those themes, pertinent to our general interests here, is the line of analysis known as Post-Imperialism (Becker et al., 1987). While denying the accusation of being "old liberal wine in new Marxian bottles" (p. 54), this corpus criticizes "the erroneous premise that international capitalist expansion is necessarily and ineluctably imperialist" (p. 60). Specifically, the impact of MNCs is being re-evaluated and "the attitudes and policies of 'third world' leaders clearly are converging around a satisfying, nonideological middle course of 'assertive pragmatism' toward direct foreign investment" (p. 10). Some writers have pointed to an increased bargaining power of nation states because of the weakened hegemony of U.S. MNCs vis-à-vis those of other countries (McNally, 1990; Pitelis, 1990). One result is the growth of a transnational bourgeoisie, a technocratic-industrial elite without national allegiance that contributes to and benefits from the internationalization of capital. Thus, dependency analysis is shorn of some of its nationalist elements and attention refocused onto class conflict in which the role of MNCs is more subtly complex.

An important question that literature from a Marxist tradition has just begun to confront is the changing role of labor in industrial countries as their MNCs become more welcome abroad. Writing from a dependency perspective, Barnet and Müller (1974) criticized the impact of MNCs on Third World countries while also noting the resulting "obsolescence of American labor." Should that analysis be modified as new production techniques evolve us into a brave new world of "post-Fordism"?

One discussion along these lines, quite apropos for our interests here, is McNally (1990). From a perspective rooted in Marxist analysis, he criticizes what he refers to as the "left protectionism" of the nationalist project of the Canadian labor movement, the basis for its opposition both to the FTA and to NAFTA. After reviewing data on the growing internationalization of Canadian capital—both banks and commodity producing MNCs—he rejects dependency or neocolonialist depictions of Canada, preferring to interpret the pursuit of the FTA as a coherent response by the Canadian bourgeoisie to growing world trade blocks. Referring back to the classic writings of Bukharin, he calls for greater international solidarity among labor movements.

FDI in Mexican Agriculture

One of the classic cases of foreign domination, to which dependency writers frequently refer, is agribusiness in Mexico. In certain specified regions of the country, blessed by natural conditions and ease of marketing, foreign companies have precipitated a rapid modernization of agricultural production and processing, destined for export. A number of components of this situation deserve attention.

Central to the Mexican Revolution was the agrarian movement that distributed land to peasant communities known as *ejidos*. While that land has not been (officially) sold to the MNCs or private Mexican interests, in some cases it has been rented or otherwise committed to them under contract. The production of domestically consumed foodstuffs inevitably declines. The resulting loss of food self-sufficiency and control by farmers over the use of their land is seen as an especially serious reverse of revolutionary gains; one author dubbed this "Strawberry Imperialism" (Feder, 1977). The leading role of MNCs in this process is analyzed in Rama and Vigorito (1979); an extension of this criticism to the experience of various Latin American countries is developed in Burbach and Flynn (1980). An associated complaint is the environmental harm that this high technology production is causing.[19] The increased incorporation of Mexican farm production to U.S. needs is not limited to vegetable products; large numbers of calves are exported to the United States for fattening; the increased absorption of Mexican production to U.S. needs has given rise to the phrase *agromaquila*—agricultural *maquilas*, or mills (Sandoval Godoy, 1992).

Although these effects occur in the countryside, the source of the change is industrial and perhaps urban. The MNCs are registered in the statistics as manufacturers and traders. While they may have tremendous impact at the farm level, their weight in industrial totals, for example in concentration ratios, is minimal. As foreign investments in the agribusiness sector has been permitted for a number of years, it is unlikely that recent changes, either NAFTA itself, or more specifically the liberalized laws on FDI and the constitutional reforms relating to the *ejido*, will affect it significantly.

Finally, note should be taken of the recent growth of outward FDI from Mexican agricultural interests. The investment has been directed toward securing access for specific crops in the U.S. market. Mares (1987) highlights the assistance provided to local growers by Mexican officials at the state and national levels. While too small in magnitude to receive much attention from official statistical agencies on either side of the border and clearly smaller than the amount of FDI in agribusiness in Mexico, this phenomenon further challenges researchers to expand the dependency model in the search for a comprehensive understanding of the role of foreign investment.

NOTES

1. A glance at Hymer's 1960 dissertation reveals numerous references to a 1958 book of Dunning on U.S. FDI in England. The convention of ascribing to Hymer the merging of the concepts of internalization and barriers to entry should probably be qualified. Hymer's work on the Gray Report will be noted below; additionally, his overall position on FDI apparently moved considerably to the political left in his later years.

2. However, one can distinguish differences in acceptance of this model and the subject itself between business economists and more-traditional international trade theorists. The corresponding article in the *Handbook of International Economics* has few citations to works in the OLI orientation and a lengthy discussion on how capital exports affect the terms of trade (Ruffin, 1984).

3. Important examples are Rugman (1987) and Galbraith and Kay (1986). The felicitous phrase of Ethier (1986) is that internalization is the Caesar of the OLI triumvirate.

4. Some interesting comments contrasting early and later versions of the Heckscher Ohlin model are available in the forward and introduction to recent translations of two of their early works, published as Heckscher and Ohlin (1991). While the sophisticated mathematical elegance of later versions of this model due to Samuelson, Jones, et al. led to its increasing popularity, perhaps some credit is also due to the empirical study that challenged its major prediction, became known as the Leontieff paradox, and by inspiring so many attempts at its explanation, tremendously enriched this body of analysis.

5. This influence is quite noticeable in those economic/business journals that devote considerable attention to the subject of FDI, such as the *Journal of International Business Studies,* and *Weltwritschaftliches Archiv.* To put it more strongly, there currently is no economic approach to FDI that does not utilize some version of the OLI paradigm, even though writers such as Aliber and Kojima might not welcome this broadly cast analytical net. Preference for the OLI approach is especially evident in Graham and Krugman (1989).

6. The issue of economies of scale has been most thoroughly studied by Baldwin and Gorecki (1986).

7. For outward investment from the United States, see Agarwal and Ramaswami (1992). Aside from that work, empirical studies of FDI have not focused on minority ownership and joint ventures, presumably because of data availability.

8. Presenting a theoretical result that recalls the decades-old quip that second best may well be second worst, Brecher and Findlay (1983) showed that when FDI is motivated by tariffs, the resulting growth may well be immiserizing, essentially because it encourages an inefficient allocation of resources. See also Tsai (1987).

9. References to publications on the political economy of tariffs and to more recent work in the same vein on FDI appear in Bhagwati et al. (1992).

10. The analysis of the "gains from trade" is much more complex under increasing returns to scale. See Grinols (1992).

11. More precisely, studies of the technology used in MNC affiliates shows that, after accounting for industrial organization factors, these affiliates are slightly more adaptive to local conditions than their domestic counterparts. See Helleiner (1989), Section 6.1.

12. An example is Kojima (1989), which illustrates some of his distinctions about internalization using a fixed/variable cost model. Lee (1990) also argues for their compatibility while urging a more dynamic version of both, utilizing the "flying geese" metaphor of K. Akamatsu (also of Hitotsubashi) that Kojima (1973, p. 11) had summarized as a "catching-up product cycle."

13. Kojima and Ozawa (1984, p. 82) note that Dunning's "eclectic theory aptly fit[s] the operations of trading companies." Yoshihara asks why the trading companies continue to exist and broadly describes a transaction cost model, referring particularly to earlier insights along this line of Kozo Yamamura.

14. But not just Japan; on Korean business groups, see Chang and Choi (1988). A related question, unanswered at press time, is whether multinational companies from Third World countries will have comparatively more success in other Third World countries than in industrial countries.

15. Particularly impressive are the figures that Kojima and Ozawa (1984: 25) give on expenditures on communications in Sogo Shosha; as a percentage of sales, these range between 1.9 percent and 9.6 percent! As a barrier to entry, these compete with the highest levels of R&D.

16. The belief in the necessity of land reform is also characteristic of most Latin American structuralist thought of whatever political tendency.

17. Bornschier and Chase-Dunn (1985: 109) also highlight the different degree of penetration of FDI in Brazil and Korea.

18. An influential writer on the development and industrialization of South Korea reiterates the theme of the importance of a strong state capable of disciplining big business (Amsden, 1990). Her works share with the dependency school an emphasis on social institutions and the necessity of "getting prices wrong"—correctly.

19. Of interest is the observation of Wright (1986), who claims that, in the Culiacán Valley in northern Mexico, the primary danger to human health is not due to noncompliance with Mexican or U.S. EPA standards, but rather to the inappropriateness of those standards, the ability of the companies to devise new strategies for avoiding them, and the lack of precautions by agricultural workers or their employers.

3

COUNTRY SPECIFIC ANALYSES

CANADIAN POLITICAL ECONOMY

Tariffs and foreign investment play a central role in Canadian economic history. Conflicts with the United States over trade policy were an important ingredient in the events that led to the Confederation of the provinces in 1867. Protectionism, the "National Policy" tariff, was to epitomize the policy stance of the rest of that century—with varying emphases on different economic activities, regions, and so forth.[1] Those tariffs attracted foreign investment; that this process resulted in "tariff factories" had been recognized as early as 1904 (Rugman 1990: 18). Furthermore, as Pomfret (1981: 141) notes, for many years after Confederation all investment was welcomed into the country regardless of national origin. Although foreign investment did not arouse chauvinistic feelings, trade did, and in some important cases, elections were decided by a nationalistic vote against the party supporting lowered tariffs on U.S. products. "No truck nor trade with the Yanks" was the victorious rallying cry in 1911.

Thus, in terms of policies, a neutral stance toward FDI *per se* became one of positive encouragement when seen in the context of the tariff. However, the economic goal of expanded industrial production and employment stood in uneasy equilibrium with the political need for a definition of the country as distinct from the United States. That FDI stood at the center of these contradictory orientations was underlined most clearly in the 1965 Auto Pact. In the face of trade conflicts between Canada and the United States, this agreement provided for tariff-free exchange of automotive products between the countries under an arrangement with the terminal companies (the U.S. "big three"), in which more or less balanced trade in the sector was to be maintained. No one would deny the economic importance for Canada of the motor vehicle sector, particularly in Ontario and Quebec.[2] Nevertheless, this agreement continued to squeeze domestic firms in the sector while blatantly surrendering Canadian control of decisions on most aspects of production as well as tariffs.

The post-World War II period was one of rising foreign ownership, which will be documented in Chapter 5. It was also one of growing nationalism. Under the Liberal Party's prime minister, Pierre Trudeau (governed 1968-1984, briefly interrupted in late 1979), these changed attitudes toward FDI became translated into policy. The Foreign Investment Review Agency (FIRA) was created in 1973, and the New Energy Policy (NEP) was instituted in 1980. Along with many others, these actions were intended to increase Canadian participation especially in energy and mining but in manufacturing and other economic sectors as well. The resulting increase in Canadian ownership occurred both in the public sector (Petrocan, Canadian Development Corporation) as well as in the private sector.[3]

The Progressive Conservative Party, under Brian Mulroney, won the national election of 1984. One of the new government's earliest acts was to rename FIRA as Investment Canada; an indication of the new attitude was the prime minister's declaration at a dinner with New York business interests, "Canada is open for business again." This new position on foreign investment was accompanied by the decision to seek a free trade agreement.

What caused this rather quick reversal of policies toward FDI? It is too early to identify the relative contributions of the different factors, although the major candidates are well known. On the economic front one notes a spotty record of growth under Trudeau and a rapidly changing international environment that does not forgive chauvinistic excesses. In terms of political factors, there have been several centrifugal forces in the different provinces and a number of individual personalities whose influence undermines simplistic economic determinism. Finally, and perhaps most important, the process of redefinition is not by any means finished, and the current situation may not endure.

Therefore, instead of focusing on the most recent inversion of attitudes and policies with regard to FDI, it may be more useful to review their longer-run antecedents. What has been the "learned opinion" of Canadian academics and politicians with regard to their economic relations with their southern neighbor, and specifically, in terms of investments? What were the influences and traditions that created an ambience such that a recent article in a respected Canadian academic journal might begin, "North American economic and social integration may be undermining Canadian political integration" (McDougall 1991: 395)?

A useful start to answering this question lies in a review of the uniquely Canadian school of political economy. It is customary to distinguish two cycles in the development of Canadian political economy; the first centering around the writings and career of Harold A. Innis (1894-1952), and the second corresponding to the period of heightened nationalism in the Trudeau years (Clement and Williams, 1989). While the contributions of these two eras were quite different in content and context, it is difficult to conceive of the second without the first.

Innis was an economic historian whose major academic contribution is the Staples thesis of Canadian development, which identifies the country's pre-twentieth century history into a series of phases, each dominated by a particular product (furs, fish, lumber, and wheat). The development of each staple served sequentially to open up the country to settlement and economic growth. It was further argued that the growth of these staples created a variety of what would later be called linkages and multipliers but did not lead to a coherent development of industry. What was shown to be true for Canada provided a major model for other areas of recent settlement, such as Argentina and Australia. Many participants in the second phase of the Canadian political economy noted the parallels between the work of Innis and the Latin American dependency approach, and indeed Innis worked at the same time as the formative years of Raúl Prebisch's career, although their work was independent, and deteriorating terms of trade do not play an important role in the staples analysis. For the purposes of this book we highlight: 1) first and foremost, the academic content of Innis's contribution, a synthesis of myriad facts generating a unified interpretation of a long period of Canadian history. (He is not remembered for specific political positions, although he did have a forceful personality.); 2) the model Innis provided had a markedly different tone from the dominant analysis in the Smith-Marshall tradition of the influence of growth and trade; 3) finally, his discussion touched very little on foreign investment.

This approach to understanding the role of foreign economic relations in the country's development—a historical, regional, and institutional approach—slipped into the backwaters for two decades, in Canada as it did in most other countries. The issues surged back to the forefront in the late 1960s; among academics who tended to come from departments of sociology and political science rather than from economics, with a palpable influence of Marxism and reflecting the zeitgeist of the Vietnam War era. Another parallel between Canadian political economy and the dependency school is the undecided role in each approach of a Marxist class analysis, given that they are fundamentally critical of the operation of the international capitalist system.

The harshest book of the newer generation of Canadian political economists was Kari Levitt's *Silent Surrender: The Multinational Corporation in Canada* (1970), whose criticisms ranged across economic and political considerations, leading her to conclude "Canada may be described as the world's richest underdeveloped country" (p. 25). Surprisingly, another major contribution to the new political economy perspective was made by reports of governmental commissions; that of Walter Gordon in 1957, or that of the commission chaired by a prominent social scientist, Mel Watkins, and finally the report issued under the leadership of a member of Parliament, Herb Gray, who was subsequently head of FIRA, the foreign investment regulatory agency.

The Gray Report (Government of Canada, 1972) summarized the statistical evidence of increasing foreign control of Canadian industry, presented a sophisticated analysis of the factors determining FDI, and recommended the creation of a governmental agency to regulate foreign investment. As will be discussed below, the fraction of Canadian industry controlled by foreigners, especially U.S. corporations, began to decline after the mid-1970s, a major explanation for which is the nationalist policies adopted at this time and implemented by FIRA. The Gray Report's discussion of the MNC's "distinctive capacity" closely echoes (or foretells) the organizational advantage of Dunning's eclectic paradigm, undoubtedly reflecting the contribution of Stephen Hymer's work with Gray's committee. However, in spite of its carefully detailed exposition of data on ownership trends, R&D expenditures, and balance-of-payments impacts, the Gray Report was viewed at the time as quite controversial and as a landmark in the nationalist position.

A further step in analyzing the role of MNCs in Canada, inside the political economy framework, is provided in the writings of Clement, Naylor, and others (Clement and Williams, 1989). These authors expanded the hints of Levitt and others, going beyond an economic analysis of MNCs that focused on immediate gains or losses in terms of output, balance of payments, or R&D, to argue that indeed there is a crippling of the development of a Canadian industrial and entrepreneurial class due to the presence of foreigners in manufacturing. The result is a business economy led by merchants and financiers and an underdeveloped Canadian state which has lacked autonomy because of its dependency.

This is not the place for a full evaluation of the intellectual merits of the Canadian political economy nor of the variations presented by its numerous contributors. We note that many participants in this debate have played important roles in the government and with different political parties, and that the issue of nationalism in Canada at the time of this writing (summer 1992) is the central theme in the political debate in the country.

While the description of the nationalist position, especially by its supporters in the new political economy group, has merited some detail, less space will be devoted here to the position of those Canadian academics who welcome FDI. This position has traditionally been described as the "continentalist" case and can be simply described as the belief that FDI represents the efficient workings of the competitive market and is therefore to be encouraged. As a logical corollary, government intervention against MNCs is to be discouraged. Most Canadian economists support this position; their influence in the OLI school as well as with the negotiating teams of the FTA and NAFTA is quite apparent.

To many outsiders as well as to Young (1989), the division of Canadian academic opinion on both FDI and the Free Trade Agreement appears starkly defined along professional lines; generally speaking, economists are in favor, and political scientists are opposed. This is a reason for not attempting a more detailed description of the continentalist case; it is implicit in the analysis of much of the economic work on Canada to be presented below. Of course, as a purely technical matter, the classical liberal economic position would be to favor completely free trade, and therefore the FTA or NAFTA might be judged a step in the wrong direction. Thus, the position of "the economics profession" in Canada on NAFTA cannot be assumed, and indeed it is not the issue. More noteworthy is the existence of the "New Political Economy" school, which borrows from economics many concepts and statistical techniques while adopting policy positions often opposed to those of the typical liberal economist.[4] In contrast to the situation in the United States and Mexico, in Canada there is less dominance of a single paradigm; this school forms an important link between the dominant analysis in the United States and the nationalist position adopted in Mexico and elsewhere.

ANALYSES AND POLICY TOWARD FDI IN MEXICO

Over the years, much has been written about the policies of the Mexican government toward direct foreign investment. What we will attempt here is a brief summary of the evolution of those policies, placing that description in the context of evolving international and national economic events as well as broader economic policy. Four periods will be distinguished: up to 1910; from the Revolution to 1944, from 1944 through 1989, and the brief time since then.

Perhaps more than in most countries, opposition to foreigners has been a constant in Mexican history since the days of the Spanish conquest. We will take up the story with the regime of Porfirio Díaz, who ruled dictatorially for over a quarter century before being overthrown by the Revolution that began in 1910. Providing a classic case of liberal economics and positivism, Díaz and his *científico* advisers reversed previous policy and encouraged foreign investment in Mexico, especially in railroads, mining, petroleum, and agriculture. Subsidies to these activities, very often going to foreigners, belied Díaz's *laissez faire* image while generating much hostility to the outsiders. Historians note that Díaz manipulated the different foreign groups against each other, and that his finance minister, José Limantour, began nationalizing the foreign-owned railroads in 1906 on the grounds that their development had not been sufficiently in the national interest.

Highlights of the period between 1910 and 1940 are the Constitution of 1917 and the 1938 nationalization of the petroleum companies. The Constitution was a landmark in too many ways to summarize here; of importance for our purposes, it reverted to the state the ownership of subsoil rights, thereby reversing Díaz's policy that had intended to attract foreign investment in raw material extraction in the broader context of a reassertion of the social function of private property.

While the issue of subsoil rights dominated the government's conflict with the petroleum companies, three other issues played a role: damages to the companies during the period of fighting; the allegedly high taxes which were levied on them;

and the decline in production related to the above as well as the exhaustion of some oil fields, and the companies' investments in Venezuela. The break between the companies and the government was precipitated by labor issues; many commentators stress the arrogance of the foreign managers. A good review of the whole question is Meyer (1977).

The nationalization of the petroleum companies together with the strengthening of the agrarian reform mark the high points of the nationalistic attitudes characterizing the Mexican Revolution and the governmental structures to which it gave rise. Another action deserving mention is the establishment in 1925 of a central bank, the *Banco de México*, which fulfilled the goal of the Constitution of increasing control over the quantity of money, taking it from foreign-held commercial banks. Similarly, the Federal Electrical Company, CFE, and the national oil company, Pemex, were established before the nationalization of the petroleum companies.

While the case of petroleum in many ways defines the limits of the nationalistic surge, it is also useful to review developments in the mining sector, where that nationalism was unable to achieve its goals. As described by Sánchez Gamper (1989), President Cárdenas's policy toward mining companies in the latter 1930s was pressured by the fervor ignited by agrarian reform and strengthened by the conflict over petroleum as well as by labor mobilizations from inside the mining sector. However, the companies were not taken over. Nevertheless, these latter reacted to the generally hostile atmosphere and decided to decapitalize. Sariego et al. (1988) point to the president's support of cooperatives in mining as well as unfavorable tax laws and exhaustion of known reserves as specific contributors to the decline of interest on the part of foreigners. Incidentally, after World War II the foreign mining companies turned their attention towards Chile and Peru, thereby repeating for Mexico the post-World War I experience of the oil companies' flight from an aggressively nationalistic Mexico to a more welcoming Venezuela.

But if the late 1930s marks the apogee of nationalism, it follows that more-recent times will be seen as less nationalistic. The useful summary description of Whiting (1991) is that there were three separate policy regimes differentiated by sector. In strategic industries—certain primary exports and utilities, there was direct state ownership and control, as we have seen. Manufacturing was directed by import substitution, which permitted and even promoted FDI. Global manufacturing of labor intensive components in the maquila sector was subsequently to recreate export enclaves. We turn first to the most important and complex case, that of manufacturing.

The period after 1940 initiates the era of conscious industrialization policies in Mexico. The new government, led by Manuel Avila Camacho, reoriented priorities from agriculture to industry, deemphasized land redistribution, and instituted tariffs for import substitution. Given that there still existed fears of a supposedly socialistic orientation of the government, there resulted an uneasy relation between the government and the private sector in which the latter was not sure it welcomed the government's intervention. The growing presence of foreign investors completed a three-part distribution of and competition for power: the government, Mexican entrepreneurs, and foreign companies. On any given issue two sides of the triangle would ally against the third: the government and the local private sector against the foreigners over issues of national sovereignty; the local and foreign businesses against the government on questions of state intervention; the government and the foreign companies against domestic entrepreneurs on issues of competition. Very broadly, our description of the period from the 1940s to the 1980s is one in which the two Mexican sides of the triangle, although starting from quite different positions, gradually converged to a consensus on the need for regulation and control of the foreigners.

Looking first at the government, there was an important redefinition of its policy toward direct foreign investment in a decree of 1944. Basically, new firms were to have majority Mexican ownership except with the permission of the Secretariat of Foreign Relations. While this act was initially described as an emergency step toward controlling the significant quantities of flight capital that had entered the country as a result of the World War, it nevertheless established a precedent for the entire postwar period. This policy, referred to as "Mexicanization" was praised by some for its flexibility and condemned by others for its arbitrariness. With the intention of reducing that uncertainty, the new president (Alemán) published in 1946 a list of key industries to be Mexicanized, and an investment commission was created. However, that list was to be revised repeatedly in the years that followed, as indeed were the procedures for application for permission to invest. Some areas that were initially reserved were radio, cinemas, domestic airlines, autobuses, soft-drink bottlers, publishing, domestic shipping, and tires; fertilizers and insecticides were particularly prone to redefinition of status.

Conflicting with the apparently nationalistic attitudes of the 1944 decree, was the government's desire to industrialize the country. For a number of years a major public relations effort was used to convey the government's message that foreign investors were welcome, especially in industry. As the world's major flows in direct foreign investment were now to be coming in industry and from the United States, there began a relatively long period of peaceful coexistence.

Overall, with regard to government policy, this period was characterized by a strong reaffirmation of a nationalistic orientation in 1944, followed initially by a phase of relaxation of regulations towards FDI and then a gradual strengthening of restrictions, culminating in the Law of 1973. In contrast to this apparent reversal of policy with regard to manufacturing were a number of governmental actions that reflect a continuity of orientation with regard to utilities and basic exports. Telephones were Mexicanized in 1958, as were electric power companies in 1960. Mines were affected by a 1961 law with a clearly parallel intent and similar results. A 1965 law reasserted the prohibitions against foreign ownership in banking and finance. The country thereby secured national ownership of extractive activities and basic services at the same time that foreign investment was increasing in the most dynamic sector, manufacturing. This has led some commentators to suggest that the Mexicanization—51 percent local ownership—of basic activities was pushed by a government needing to strengthen its nationalist and revolutionary credentials, which were being weakened by events in many other areas of the economy and society.

In addition to actions taken with the specific intention of affecting foreign investment, other policies were evolving that inevitably affected the foreigners. The 1954 Law on New and Necessary Industries encouraged import-substituting industrialization via tariffs and subsidies. While designed to help domestic entrepreneurs, it inevitably attracted FDI, as we have seen. In 1962 a program was initiated requiring automobile assemblers to achieve a certain percentage of national content in purchased inputs. This measure predominantly benefited foreign firms by squeezing out the smaller, less-powerful local producers. The maquila program was established in 1965, under which firms would import free of taxes on inputs that would then be assembled and reexported. This early version of an export- processing zone generated significant foreign exchange and employment, although it has been criticized for its inability to incorporate more national inputs than unskilled, low-wage labor. While these measures were intended to help the national economy, it became increasingly clear that foreign investors were benefitting, which was made even less palatable by the fact that the mode of entry increasingly became one of takeovers of existing firms, which was judged to have smaller impact on technology, capital inflow, and employment.

The Mexican government's gradual movement toward a stronger regulatory environment became concretized in 1973, with the approval of the Law to Promote Mexican Investment and Regulate Foreign Investment. This measure established Mexicanization as the norm for new investments in industry, while still allowing for exceptions, when approved by the National Commission on Foreign Investment, or CNIE. Consistent with Mexican legal practice, existing firms were not obliged to submit to majority ownership, although pressures were inevitably brought to bear. At the same time, a law on patents and trademarks was approved, whose intent was to increase technology transfer. While to a considerable extent the 1973 law simply formalized existing practices, nevertheless it also highlighted the increasing regulatory environment.

Let us turn now to the private sector, where the attitudes of leading business groups also underwent transformations during this period. In the 1940s, FDI was widely welcomed as furthering industrial development while strengthening the hand of the private sector against the state. However, there were some incidents in the 1950s in which different business groups began to criticize FDI. In the mid-1950s the CNIT (a national association of small manufacturers founded in 1941, forerunner of CANACINTRA), published a series of pamphlets urging the restriction of foreign investment, specifically, calling for a general application of the 51 percent rule associated with Mexicanization in the law of 1944. Sánchez Gamper (1989: 75) also sees in a 1955 position paper of the CONCANACO (Mexican Chambers of Commerce) the beginnings of limitations to their traditionally liberal attitude towards FDI due to the competition of foreign marketing chains. Finally, in 1957 the Cámara Textil del Norte (Northern Textile Association) sponsored a study that criticized FDI on both economic and political terms and recommended to an industrial congress a series of steps that would oversee foreign investments. While this position was not to be accepted by the majority at that industrial congress, the group did approve a motion reaffirming the notion that foreign investment should be complementary to the development of the country and stay within the boundaries set by exiting laws and regulations. Bohrisch and König (1968) observed a gradual strengthening of the nationalistic, antiforeign investment position on the part of a wide cross section of business groups that they attribute to the strengthened position of national entrepreneurs as well as the influence to the positions expounded by the CNIT. However, Sánchez Gamper (1989: 120) perceived a moderation of the critiques of FDI on the part of the CNIT during the 1960s, attributing it to: 1) the realization of certain goals—Mexicanization of mining, electricity, and telephones, as well as a general acceptance of the position of complementarity of FDI; 2) strengthening of the position of small enterprises in the economy; as well as 3) the association of many of these entrepreneurs with foreign investors, indeed the sale of their factories to the foreigners. Nevertheless, it would appear that this attitudinal change was limited, so that Whiting (1981) could cite numerous opinion surveys indicating that the average Mexican welcomed foreign investment, but in a complementary, that is, nonmajority role.

It would be difficult to summarize the evolution of the position of Mexican academics on foreign investment. There has always been a vast number of social scientists opposed to it, with only a numerical minority in favor. These positions cannot be more closely measured, much less can we specify the actual influence of these different groups. Two well-known Mexican economists, Raúl Ortíz Mena and Victor Urquidi, participated in a World Bank project (Ortíz Mena et al., 1953), which concluded that the country did not have the resources necessary to finance its own development and would have to resort to foreign investment. While our study will cite a number of important works by Mexican economists on FDI (Sepúlveda and Chumacero, 1973; Fajnzylber and Martínez Tarragó, 1976; Casar et al., 1990), these works are more noteworthy for their empirical analyses of new data than for the authors' broader policy stances. Indeed, the description of those positions using categories such as "in favor" or "nationalistic opposition" would be much affected by historical circumstances. The task of tracing learned opinion is further complicated by the fact that, as we saw in the previous chapter, one of the principal sources of writings critical to foreign investment comes from the dependency school, but its arguably best-known writers (Gunder Frank, Cardoso and Faletto, Jaguaribe, Sunkel) have not been Mexicans. Of course a number of Mexican authors have made key contributions to this school, but disentangling the national contribution to an essentially hemispheric analysis is not a fruitful exercise.

Having looked at the attitudes and actions of major national groups—government, business, intellectuals—we should note that both Whiting (1981) and Sánchez Gamper (1989) also emphasize the importance of changing external factors in the evolution of Mexican policy, leading to the greater regulation of the 1970s. Examples include concrete historical experiences (Guatemala, Cuba, Chile; the Andean Pact; the OPEC countries) as well as changing attitudes in international fora (UNCTC, UNCTAD). It is a logical extension of the arguments presented elsewhere in this work to postulate that evolving economic conditions also contributed to such changes. To the degree that there are increasing numbers of multinational companies competing to invest in a country, and/or as the existing companies lose the OLI advantages that they previously had, it may well be in the host country's interest to attempt to extract greater benefits from MNCs. Such an outcome was indeed foreseen by Vernon (1963: 173). Of course, as Whiting (1981) points out, it is incorrect to view this situation as one of a zero-sum bargaining arrangement between two unique actors in a well-defined game; agreements with regard to technology transfers or import content by an MNC automobile company are very different from agreements as to the purchase price of an electrical company.

The focus on international factors as contributors to changing policies towards foreign investment highlights the advantages of the comparative approach in this study. Just when Mexico was attempting to strengthen its control of multinationals, so was Canada, utilizing the same sort of arguments and proposing similar policies. The controversial work of Servan Schreiber, *The American Challenge*, was stirring up similar attitudes in Europe. Fundamentally, the rapid expansion of U.S. direct investment was a worldwide phenomenon, not simply limited to Mexico and Canada.

RECENT REORIENTATION OF POLICY

The regulatory tide changed in many parts of the world during the 1980s, and in 1989 a new decree drastically liberalized foreign investment in Mexico. Later in that year, regulations on banking and finance were also liberalized, while those affecting intellectual property were brought closer to those of industrial countries. While this decree was a significant opening to foreign investment, it has its limits, which can be seen by noting the activities in which some restrictions still hold, as listed in the following excerpt from the annual report of the Central Bank.

The approval system for economic activities included in the "Catalogue" [i.e., subject to restrictions] is divided into the following six regimes:

1. Activities exclusively reserved to the State (12 activities), include extraction of petroleum and natural gas, petroleum refining, the generation, transmission and supply of electrical energy, telegraph systems, railways, minting of coins, etc.

2. Activities reserved to Mexicans (34 activities), include private broadcast of radio programs, broadcast and repetition of television programs, auto-freight transportation, ground passenger service, etc.

3. Activities in which foreign investment up to 34 percent of the capital stock is permitted (4 activities); include carbon mining, extraction and/or refining of sulfur, of phosphatic rock and of ferrous minerals.

4. Activities in which foreign investment up to 40 percent of the capital stock is permitted (8 activities), include secondary petrochemical products and the automotive industries and related activities.

5. Activities in which foreign investment up to 49 percent of the capital stock is permitted (25 activities), include fishing, mining (excluding those listed in groups 1 and 3), telephone services, insurance and finance leasing companies.

6. Activities in which the Mexican Foreign Investment Commission's prior approval is required for foreign investors to hold a majority interest (58 activities), such as agriculture, livestock and cattle; printing, editing and associated industries; industrial; and other construction and educational services. Foreign investment may be permitted in up to 100 percent of the capital stock of companies engaged in activities listed in group 6, subject to the Mexican Foreign Investment Commission's prior approval.

(Banco de México, *The Mexican Economy 1991*, pp. 148-149)

For unrestricted activities, said to account for 66 percent of Mexico's GDP, direct foreign investment up to 100 percent is permitted, subject to some minor constraints, the most important of which is that permission must be granted if the investment amounts to more that US $100 million.

The above list does not mention banking, and currently (1992) automobile assembly is wholly foreign owned, and much of mining is completely open to foreigners. In addition, certain sectors do not effectively become open until the government's dominance over them is ended via privatization; that is the case of steel, the companies of FERTIMEX and CONASUPO, as well as banking. Furthermore, it has been noted that these changes were obtained by means of a decree—which is not voted on in Congress; some argue that a stronger invitation to foreigners would be made in the form of a law, which would have to pass the Congress. Most importantly, Mexico neither has a completely open-door policy with regard to foreign investment, nor are the rules fixed. Of course, that is why the negotiations for the Free Trade Agreement were so important.

In light of our earlier analysis, let us examine the background for the shift in attitudes towards foreign investment. In the economic sphere, the country had experienced, since the mid-1970s, a roller coaster propelled by international oil prices and newly discovered petroleum reserves, which resulted in 1981 with the need for a declaration of the country's inability to pay its foreign debt obligations. The decade of the 1980s was one of unprecedented austerity measures. The policymakers who pursued these measures were economists who firmly believed in free market economic principles. In point of fact, the effects of this neoliberal tendency were evident throughout the sexenio of President De la Madrid; the restrictions on foreign investors had been relaxed de facto during that regime, and de jure in 1984 and 1988. Indeed, the decontrol of foreign investment may well be less important for the country's future than the decision in 1985 to enter the GATT, which has been followed by reduction of tariffs and discretionary import controls. With regard to political currents, most observers would agree that the economic failures associated with the populist measures of the 1970s severely damaged the credibility of that orientation. This was certainly true of the technocrats who are currently running the country and may well characterize the population as a whole. It is clear that there were significant international pressures for the kind of liberalization that has occurred in Mexico for which renegotiation of the country's external debt burden was utilized as the major pressure point. Whatever the relative importance of these factors, Mexico is currently at the forefront of economic liberalization among developing countries.

U.S. POLICY TOWARD MNCs

It is frequently asserted that the United States is very open towards foreign investment, inward or outward. Increasing globalization of the world's economy has created pressures on that position, but with the exceptions to be noted, the various administrations have successfully resisted significant control, certainly of the sort practiced by the country's two neighbors. It is certainly the case that no formal school of analysis has arisen in the United States with regard to either inward or outward FDI, unless the free market, noninterventionist position is considered a school.[5] We will first discuss issues related to outward FDI, then discuss inward investment, which will lead to some general comments with regard to consistency and appropriateness.

Outward Investment

As will be indicated in the next chapter, two broad phases of outward FDI can be distinguished for the United States, the first one in the early years of the century, primarily directed towards natural resource extraction, and the current one, more concentrated in manufacturing. Apparently, government economic policies neither helped nor hindered that first wave by design or by default. There are broader issues, of course, in terms of the political/military support given the U.S. MNCs, but we will stay with those identifiable as economic, believed to be an important building block of the bigger picture.

In spite of the overall hands-off orientation, there currently are some ways by which economic policy does affect U.S. OFDI. With regard to taxes, the very useful summary in Bergsten et al. (1978) distinguishes two policies, foreign tax credit and tax deferral. The foreign tax credit reduces taxes payable in the home country on a one-to-one basis, avoiding "double taxation." Tax deferral allows a company to postpone payment of taxes on income and profits until those profits are returned to the home office. The obvious result is to encourage firms to finance further investments by transferring funds among overseas affiliates. Both of these policies increase OFDI.

During the 1960s and 1970s, there was a growing impact on FDI of macroeconomic policies designed to affect interest rates, balance of payments, and the exchange rate. Under the administrations of both Democrats and Republicans, capital exports were discouraged for balance of payments considerations. The opposite effect on FDI was attributed to the overvaluation of the exchange rate.[6] A final policy worth noting is the minimal impact of the few attempts at applying antitrust laws to the global operations of MNCs.

Tariff policy usually is mentioned for its impact on inward oriented FDI. However, the U.S. tariff code, in its sections 806.30 and 807, reduced import tariffs on goods processed in U.S.-owned plants overseas, by limiting the taxable part to the foreign value added. The U.S. dominated maquila industry in Mexico was the principal beneficiary.

Can anything be said about technology policy? That some U.S. firms have organizational advantages due to domestically subsidized R&D is widely accepted, although few would argue that those R&D programs were specifically designed to help U.S. firms abroad. The one area in which policies on technology and outward FDI did intersect was in terms of trade with communist countries. Here there was conflict because governments of countries host to U.S. affiliates did not share those anticommunist attitudes. For our purposes here we judge these restrictions as quantitatively not very important; they affected a small part of total sales, were difficult to enforce, and became obsolete with political developments.

On a vaguely defined borderline between economic and political policies affecting outward FDI is the Overseas Private Investment Corporation, a governmental entity that sold insurance to MNCs against expropriation and losses due to currency controls. One suspects that the subsidy element has been much weaker than the political influence that the government has brought to bear on these cases.

The overall evaluation of the economic impact of these policies is that they have been slightly favorable to outward investment (Bergsten et al., 1978).

The U.S. labor union movement has often opposed outward FDI. Bergsten et al. (1978: 46) note that in the 1920s the American Federation of Labor spurred a public policy debate on job loss due to branch plants overseas, without eventually obtaining concrete relief. We might speculate that the earlier wave of outward investment did not create as much domestic opposition because that investment was concentrated in raw material-producing sectors in which little or no domestic production existed, such as bananas and rubber, or (foreign) public utilities. Petroleum investments did not threaten many workers' jobs. The opposite was true of products such as copper as well as manufacturing. In the early years of the century the labor movement predominantly worked to stop the southward flow of investment inside the country.

Actions on the part of organized labor to reduce outward FDI gained force in the 1970s. The unsuccessful Burke Hartke Bill of 1971 would have eliminated both the foreign income tax credit and the tax deferral. A stronger break with past policy would have been the requirement of licensing of outward FDI.[7] As has often happened in the United States, these proposals hostile to OFDI were part of a larger set of measures that attempted to help U.S. production by restricting imports.

Inward Investment

The United States is currently the recipient of the largest amount of IFDI in the world; this was also the case before World War I. While the economic factors characterizing these two periods were very different, we might benefit by noting how certain contemporary attitudes had predecessors a century ago.

Wilkins (1989) describes the widespread involvement of foreign investment in the United States before 1914, providing a number of sectoral and individual case studies. In the epilogue of her massive book she broadens the prospective to ask questions about the general policy-making and political context. While she does note cases of attempts by foreigners of influencing the domestic decision-making process in the United States, she believes that "The dependency [on foreign sources of finance and technology, as well as political] proved not to be oppressive" (p. 617). Furthermore, "The large quantity of contemporary negative responses in America to foreign investment here seems to have been more visceral than rational" (p. 625). Those negative responses were strongest in the west and related to land for mines or for farms and grazing, much of which had been in federal hands. Another commentator notes: "By 1884, all the national parties adopted platforms opposing foreign land ownership. Altogether, 13 states passed legislation restricting or prohibiting additional foreign acquisition of land" (Zagaris 1980: 5). These populist attitudes reappear with frequency.

Unease with the current wave of foreign investment inside the United States began to surface in the 1970s. The criticisms are quite familiar—inordinate control of banks, farmland, and real estate; high import propensities; the draining of profits; and tilting the political balance of power against unions. A number of recent commentators have pointed out the direct analogy with anti-FDI writings, similar to the Dependency orientation, which we have already seen in other countries.[8] Also familiar is the extremism of what is hopefully only characteristic of the fringes; "Spiritually, [foreign investment] breaks down the barriers of the nation state, race, religion, and culture. Conversely, it brings [an] insidious attack on the free enterprise system through investment by foreign governments" (Crowe, 1978: 8). These complaints frequently have a palpable ethnic tinge; the "buying of America" has been blamed on Arab oil sheiks, South American dictators, and hard-working Japanese businessmen, not the British, Canadian, and Dutch who the data indicate are the dominant investors.

While generally neutral towards inward FDI, U.S. government policy is not completely laissez faire; restricted sectors include radio, television, airlines, nuclear energy, banking, and maritime transport. In 1975 the Committee on Foreign Investment in the United States was established as a watchdog agency, although the subsequent administrations deprived it of any impact (Laney, 1991). In 1988, the Exon-Florio Amendment gave the president power to limit foreign investments by merger, acquisition, or takeover when these are judged to be a threat to national security. Additionally, there are a few examples of policies towards IFDI being determined by technology considerations, for instance, no foreign company is a member of Sematech, and foreign participation in space projects such as Comsat is limited, but these have been infrequent.

While the federal government had only these relatively minor incursions, much more active were the "subnational" levels of government. Cities as well as states actively lobbied overseas for FDI and attracted it with tax benefits and other subsidies (Fry, 1980). An interesting example of public policy at the state level, affecting both inward and outward FDI, was the unitary tax. This measure levied taxes on the worldwide sales of an MNC, not simply those attributable to the home office. An intense lobbying effort by MNCs from the United States and elsewhere had succeeded by 1988 in getting these weakened or repealed in all states—California has been one of the most resistant to change (Graham and Krugman, 1989: 107).

Consistent Responses?

Of our three countries, the United States is the only one where the size of inward FDI is similar to that of outward FDI. Moreover, the relative importance there of inward and outward FDI has changed twice during this century. An intriguing exercise is to analyze the government's policy towards both OFDI and IFDI, looking for patterns whose consistency might be explained by a theoretical model of FDI. Two general categories of responses to FDI can be distinguished: neutral or nonneutral. The latter reaction can be either uniform—always in favor or against—or nonuniform. The nonuniform response can be further subdivided into symmetric and nonsymmetric, where the symmetric response would be favorable to FDI in one direction and opposed to it in the other. These options are indicated in Figure 3.1. The point of the exercise is to highlight the variety of logically consistent responses while suggesting that policy positions in the United States have typically been inconsistent.

An application of these categories to traditional international trade theory may be useful; let us consider taxes on traded goods. Laissez faire economists who are in favor of free trade consistently desire a neutral trade regime, rejecting both import taxes and export subsidies. Similarly, some farm groups symmetrically favor restrictions on food imports and subsidies on exports. The Stolper-Samuelson theorem is a consistent response to trade intervention that we have labeled symmetric.

The nominal policy position of the U.S. government has always been uniform neutrality towards FDI in both directions, based on direct acceptance of free trade market principles. Recent works by influential U.S. economists reflecting that position include Graham and Krugman (1989) and Bergsten et al. (1978).

Figure 3.1
Policy Positions on FDI

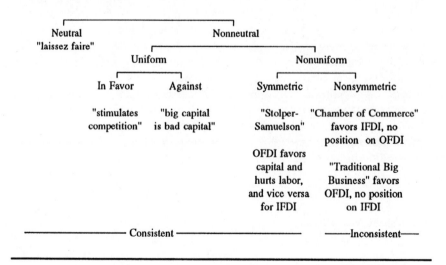

Similarly, any number of business-sector commentators push for a neutral policy because of their distrust of the government's ability to intervene effectively. Furthermore, many critics of FDI quite uniformly oppose FDI whenever and wherever, either rejecting capitalism in general or perhaps reacting to the bigness associated with MNCs as a deviation from pure competition. All of these positions are logically consistent.

Recall that in the previous section we characterized the U.S. Government as encouraging outward FDI by its tax policies, while state and local entities encourage inward FDI. Similarly, in the 1992 presidential campaign, the Democratic candidate called for a tightening of the enforcement of tax laws on IFDI, making little mention of the use of intrafirm pricing by U.S. based MNCs to avoid taxes. It is difficult to label these configurations as consistent.

Equally as important are the asymmetries in the policy stances adopted by private sector groups. Traditionally, labor has opposed outward FDI but does not support inward FDI (Howes, 1991). Business groups have similarly welcomed outward FDI but not opposed inward FDI.[9]

Perhaps not surprisingly, we believe that those inconsistencies will lessen over time. The parallel with policies on protectionism is again illustrative so that in spite of the government's official commitment to free trade, import barriers are rising. The casual empiricism of newspaper reading supports this prediction of a redefinition of positions on foreign investment, where some spokespersons for labor now welcome IFDI and the hostility of certain automobile company executives towards IFDI is very public. This is the policy configuration referred to as symmetric in Figure 3.1, reflecting the Stolper-Samuelson logic. In a trivial sense, this realignment of positions is a response to the globalization of the economy; the United States did not have a policy on IFDI because it did not have any IFDI. In a broader perspective, however, the changing technological competitiveness of U.S. companies will alter the benefit-cost analysis of all forms of protectionism, and we should expect increased public debate on policies affecting all forms of FDI in the United States. The question, therefore would be whether those groups whose positions are currently classifiable as nonsymmetric will tend toward the neutral, uniform, or symmetric positions. If economic principles dominate, one outcome would be the neutral, laissez faire stance. Economic self-interest could also generate movement toward the symmetric stance. A political analysis might well argue for uniform support on the grounds that MNCs from whatever country are capable of exerting dominating pressure because of their size.

We interpret the high local-content provisions of the NAFTA—accentuating the anti-laissez faire provisions of the FTA—as an important step in the redefinition of the policy of U.S. business groups, turning towards hostility to IFDI. This position corresponds to what we called the symmetric category, and indicates an incipient alignment of U.S. capital and labor on opposites sides of the issue of openness towards IFDI.

NOTES

1. One part of the attraction of Canada for U.S. investors was tariff preference inside the Commonwealth.

2. As a result of the Auto Pact, this sector provides a quarter of industrial employment in Canada and over half of non-resource based industrial exports and is generally considered the mainstay of the country's non-resource based manufacturing industry.

3. An authoritative discussion of policies toward the very important oil and natural gas industries can be found in Helliwell et al. (1989).

4. The contradictory influences of these two traditions are nowhere more apparent than in discussions of the free trade agreements as illustrated in McNally (1990).

5. There is always great relativity in giving names to schools of thought or policy. A related example is the tendency of many commentators to characterize President Reagan's approach to governing as hands-off, lackadaisical, and distracted, and then describe his steadfast adherence to a laissez faire approach to FDI as radical and doctrinaire.

6. While these policies affect MNCs, policy debates were also stimulated by growing impact of MNCs on macroeconomics. In addition to affecting exports and imports, these companies reduced the effectiveness of monetary policy by virtue of their access to international capital markets and were perceived as major participants in exchange rate speculation.

7. Bergsten et al. judge the overall effect of U.S. government policy to be mildly supportive of outward FDI. They also estimated the effects of the AFL-CIO proposal as reducing foreign investment outflows by over 50 percent (1978: 209).

8. In addition to Wilkins (1989), this is the case of most of the writers in the Fall 1991 issue of *Annals of the American Academy of Political Science* as well as Graham and Krugman (1989). It can also be found in the writings referred to in the text as occupying the fringe. Some authors delight in stretching the analogy to encompass the support of FDI by America's first protectionist, Alexander Hamilton, who apparently was also in the pay of foreign producers.

9. An interesting case is provided by the 1965 Auto Pact, which strengthened the position of US MNCs in Canada and therefore might have been expected to have received opposition from the labor unions in the United States. It turns out that the UAW at that time was an international union representing car workers in both countries and so could not have taken a nationalist position. The same union provides a counterexample with regard to IFDI, when it opposed the establishment of VW and Volvo in the United States. One interpretation is that the leadership felt that it was still possible to hold out for a nationalist policy in favor of domestic production. Another interpretation of even more relevance in terms of investments by Japanese automakers is that the foreign companies bring

in new production techniques and styles that undermine the privileged position of established workers. See Howes (1991).

4

THE U.S. EXPERIENCE WITH OUTWARD AND INWARD FDI

GLOBAL MAGNITUDES

An overview of recent worldwide levels of FDI serves to set the stage for this chapter's detailed description of trends in the United States, followed in the next chapter by similar presentations on Canada and Mexico. A convenient comparison is the value of the stock of FDI to a country's GDP, and is presented in Table 4.1. With the exception of Japan, each of the developed countries listed on that table has sizeable flows both inward and outward. While Canada and Australia have the biggest inflows (relative to GNP), the ratios for other countries are roughly comparable. Germany and Italy became net exporters of FDI around 1980, while the United States has recently become a net importer. One noteworthy item is the atypical size of outward FDI in Switzerland and the Netherlands.

Turning to inward FDI for developing countries, we can see in Table 4.1 that the range of values of the ratio of IFDI to GDP for LDC's is similar to that for developed countries, and that Asian countries tend to have significantly less FDI than do those in Latin America or Africa. In all but one of the Latin American countries, there is an increase of FDI compared to GDP in the decade 1975-1985.

In terms of absolute amounts, the United States has been the world's major source of foreign investment since World War II, as indicated in Table 4.2. Perhaps more surprising is the fact that over two-thirds of FDI has been placed in the developed market economies, and, indeed, that the United States is now the recipient of the largest amount of FDI of any individual country as well as the recipient of more FDI than all developing countries combined. Two historical features not indicated in these tables are that at the turn of the century three-fifths of all OFDI was directed to today's developing countries and only 15 percent of FDI was in manufacturing (Dunning, 1990: 6).

Table 4.1
Inward and Outward FDI Stocks as Percentage of GNP, Various Countries

	I/Y	O/Y		I/Y	O/Y		I/Y	O/Y
	U.K.			**Australia**			**Netherlands**	
1987	12.9	22.2	1988	19.8	11.7	1982	13.2	27.1
1980	11.5	14.8	1980	4.5	0.8	1973	12.0	24.8
1970	8.2	15.3						
	Italy			**Denmark**			**Japan**	
1983	2.3	2.6	1981	6.2	3.7	1987	0.38	3.23
1971	4.7	2.0	1970	6.4	1.5	1980	0.31	1.85
			1960	2.5	1.5	1977	1.73	
	U.S.			**Canada**			**Germany**	
1989	7.7	7.2	1986	18.4	10.8	1985	4.8	7.1
1980	3.0	7.9	1980	20.4	8.9	1977	5.2	3.9
1970	1.3	7.7	1970	30.0	7.1	1965	1.8	
1960	1.3	6.2	1960	33.6	6.4			
1950	1.2	4.1	1950	21.5	5.4			
1929	1.4	7.3	1926	34.6	7.7			
1914	3.4	7.0	1914	33.6				

INWARD FDI/GDP, only

	Africa	Asia	Latin America	S.E. Europe	Turkey	
1985	12.6	5.9	13.6	3.2	0.8	
1975	15.0	4.7	8.9	2.1	1.6	
	Indonesia	South Korea	Malaysia	Philippines	Thailand	
1985	6.4	6.9	28.6	6.1	5.9	
1975	3.2	2.8	24.7	3.1	3.4	
	Cote d'Ivoire	Egypt	Morocco	Nigeria	Mexico	Peru
1985	19.1	20.3	6.0	5.4	8.9	15.4
1975	12.6	0.5	2.3	20.9	5.5	11.0
	Argentina	Brazil	Chile	Colombia	Ecuador	Venezuela
1985	12.9	13.9	14.0	11.8	8.3	15.0
1975	5.9	5.6	5.7	7.4	11.6	13.7

Sources: UNCTC (1988), supplemented by author's calculations based on the investment data in OECD (1987), and the IMF *International Financial Statistics*. For earlier years for the United States, see U.S. Department of Commerce (1975b). For Canada during 1926-1950, Urquhart and Buckley (1965). The datum for Canada for 1914 refers to direct private investment from the United Kingdom and the United States only; the U.K. total comes from Paterson (1976), the U.S. total is that of Lewis (1938). Canadian GNP for 1914 is the rough estimate of Buckley (1955).

I/Y — Inward FDI/GNP; O/Y — Outward FDI/GNP.

Table 4.2
Stock of FDI in Value and as Percentage of GDP
(Values in Billion Current U.S.$)

	1960		1975		1985	
	Value	%GDP	Value	%GDP	Value	%GDP
OUTWARD FDI						
World Total	67.7		282.0		713.5	
Developed Market Economies	67.0	6.7	275.4	6.7	693.3	8.0
U.S.	31.9	6.2	124.2	8.1	250.7	6.4
U.K.	12.4	17.4	37.0	15.8	104.7	23.3
Japan	0.5	1.1	15.9	3.2	83.6	6.3
Germany	0.8	1.1	18.4	4.4	60.0	9.6
Switzerland	2.3	26.9	22.4	41.3	45.3	48.9
Netherlands	7.0	60.6	19.9	22.9	43.8	35.1
Canada	2.5	6.3	10.4	6.3	36.5	10.5
Developing Countries	0.7		2.3		19.2	
INWARD FDI						
World Total			246.8	4.9	637.2	6.1
Developed Countries			185.3	4.5	478.2	5.5
Western Europe			100.6	5.8	184.3	6.6
U.S.			27.7	1.8	184.6	4.7
Developing Countries			61.5	6.4	159.0	8.5
Africa			16.5	15.7	22.3	10.8
Asia			13.0	3.2	49.6	5.7
Latin America			29.7	8.9	80.5	13.6

Source: UNCTC (1988), pp. 24 and 25.

Note: The totals for outward and inward FDI do not match in the source.

In this and subsequent tables, a blank indicates that the datum is not available; the NA indicates either that the source reported NA, or that a necessary calculation was not possible.

Availability of Data

The United Nations Centre on Transnational Corporations (UNCTC) has advanced very significantly the study of foreign direct investment in a number of ways. One of these contributions is the expansion of availability of statistical information. The UNCTC collects data from national sources, including some not publicly available, and publishes it in a uniform format. Selection and classification criteria for the raw data are those of the individual countries, however. Nevertheless, major advances in coverage and analysis have been made, examples of which are UNCTC (1985, 1988, 1991).

The use of a firm-level questionnaire for the elaboration of a census of U.S. inward and outward FDI by the U.S. Department of Commerce appears to have begun in the early 1940s, although the first report on OFDI with detailed breakdowns of data for affiliate sales, assets, employment, and trade dates to 1966. It and its successors will be referred to in this book as the Benchmark Studies (they are U.S. Department of Commerce, 1975a, 1981, 1986, and 1991). Prior estimates were made by embassy consular officers and are often cited even if no uniformity of coverage was obtained (Lewis, 1938; Arno Press, 1976). Although the methodology and coverage improved continually after World War II, it is unfortunate that the survey of 1955 had only a two-thirds response rate for Mexico (U.S. Department of Commerce, 1957). Benchmark surveys of FDI into the United States have been published since the early 1970s (U.S. Department of Commerce, 1976, 1983, 1989b), providing detailed information on essentially the same items as the surveys on outward investment. In addition, the Department of Commerce internally estimates a reduced set of statistics and publishes them annually for both inward and outward FDI, in the *Survey of Current Business*.

Canada presents us with two sources, a report titled *Canada's International Investment Position* and the CALURA reports. The former provides a broad outline of the ownership of equity, going back to 1926. There is much more disaggregated information on ownership, income, sales, profits, and taxes of corporations from the late 1960s in the other source, known by its acronym CALURA (Corporations and Labour Unions Returns Act), created as a response to unease over the weight in Canadian society of both U.S. firms and U.S. labor unions.

There are fewer data series on FDI in Mexico. The Banco de México has a series covering 1938 to about 1981, broken down into stocks and flows by country and industry. The industrial secretariat, SECOFI, has a series starting in the early 1970s, which is cited most frequently for current data. The SECOFI data refer to projects that have been approved, but the numbers are not adjusted for those that for some reason are postponed or canceled. The comparisons presented below of either of these two series, measured in U.S. dollars, with the country's GDP will of course be muddied by changes in the purchasing power parity of the Mexican Peso, which have been significant since around 1970.

There are several problems associated with the measurement of foreign direct investment. One initial question is the amount of control a foreign investor(s) must have to distinguish direct from portfolio investment. Another basic issue is which indicator to use for the size of the firms; fixed assets, sales, or the amount invested by foreigners. The Canadian sources are the most useful, with CALURA reporting these three items for all corporations in Canada above a certain minimum size.[1] The U.S. Department of Commerce provides detailed information on these items in the Benchmark Studies, which cover outward FDI only for the years 1966, 1977, 1982, and 1989. However, most countries do not provide data on total sales or the market value of foreign-owned firms. In these cases the investigator must work with the indicator of FDI as the stock of long-term private capital flows. Naturally enough, this ignores basic factors such as inflation and depreciation, particularly tending to undervalue those investments made when prices were lower. Furthermore, countries are not consistent in terms of inclusion of reinvested earnings from FDI, and there is even less uniformity in terms of exchange-rate changes. Finally, some countries report the amount of FDI "approved" by the authorities that may not be actualized in the immediate year. Data on Japanese OFDI suffer these last two defects.

The Department of Commerce establishes 10 percent as the minimal level for identifying an establishment in a foreign country as being an affiliate of a U.S. company.[2] More-detailed data are collected for majority-owned foreign affiliates. Globally, the majority-owned firms account for 80 percent, by value, of all foreign affiliates, and nearly 95 percent of affiliates in Canada, according to the various Benchmark studies. However, in Mexico only about half of the assets or sales are accounted for by majority-owned firms, reflecting the ownership structure imposed by regulations in that country. Another minor problem arises in terms of the country of residence of the foreign firm; the U.S. data indicate a major increase in investments into and from Panama and the tax havens of the Caribbean. The resultant bias repeats the experience of reporting the Netherlands or especially Switzerland as headquarters for overseas operations in cases where most production or sales occur elsewhere.

Comparability of Data

Another useful preparatory exercise is to check the consistency of statistics on the same variables between different countries. For the comparison of Canadian to U.S. data, the availability of U.S. Benchmark surveys limit us to the period starting with 1966.

In this book there will be a number of occasions to inquire about long-term trends of FDI. Because the original data are always reported in nominal terms, they will be deflated by price indexes. Of course this is standard procedure with regard to sales or even fixed capital in studies of domestic contexts; the variation here is to deflate totals for U.S. outward investment by U.S. prices. An additional problem is that, although our major interest is sales or perhaps total assets, data availability is normally limited to foreign equity. Thus, we ask two questions:

How close is the correspondence between the values of the data from Canada and the United States? How well do the series on equity positions reflect trends in sales or assets?

We see in Table 4.3 that the data from these two countries exhibit a high degree of consistency. The first section of that table indicates this where one country's nominal data are converted to the other currency, using average exchange rates. An alternative approach is to deflate each set of data by the individual country's price index and compare to the resulting "real" growth rates. These calculations, presented in the second section of Table 4.3, also indicate a high correspondence between the two sets of data. The series for sales and assets move more closely than does that for equity, which is a bit disheartening in light of our need of using U.S. data on equity in other countries.

With regard to the comparative changes in ratios of Sales, Assets, and Equity positions, we see in Table 4.4 that for both total investments and manufacturing the two countries provide data whose ratios move very closely. This consistency reinforces the following conclusion about overall movements in the ratios: the asset/sales ratio fell significantly between the late 1960s and 1977 in both manufacturing and nonmanufacturing sectors. However, depending on which country's data one chooses, the asset/sales ratio in manufacturing rose or fell slightly thereafter while that ratio for nonmanufacturing clearly increased.[3]

Both countries' data indicate that the ratios of either sales or total assets with respect to equity have gradually risen since the mid-1960s. One plausible explanation of this observation, which also characterizes U.S. global aggregates, is that the older data on equity is undervalued by these series, which utilize historical costs. Two items in these tables that support that interpretation are that the asset/sales ratios provide greater constancy and that the statistical offices of both countries report the same result. This subject will also be touched on in the section of U.S. OFDI.

Another related item that is important for both Canada and the United States relates to the mode of financing FDI and its measurement. As will be argued below, much of U.S. FDI has been financed by retained earnings and not new equity flows, basically for tax reasons. In cases such as this, estimates of FDI assets or equity position based on balance of payments flows are clearly very biased.[4] The importance of this omission for Canada can be demonstrated by comparison with the official data of the United States, Canada's major investor, presented in Table 4.5. As is discussed in more detail in the next chapter's section on Canada, net equity inflows from the United States to Canada were actually negative through some of the early 1980s. Fortunately, we can see in Table 4.5 that both countries' sources provide consistent numbers on the breakdown of the relative importance of equity flows and retained earnings, even for the episode of the early 1980s.

Let us now turn to a comparison of the Mexican data with the U.S. data on U.S. FDI in Mexico, presented in Table 4.6. The U.S. Department of Commerce

Table 4.3
Comparison of Canadian and U.S. Data on U.S. MNCs in
Canada, 1966-1988
(Items are Ratios of Canadian to U.S. Data)

	1977	1966	1977	1982	1988
	Ratios of Current Values in Canadian $	Indexes of Ratios of Current Values in C$, 1977=100			
U.S. MNC Sales in Canada					
Total	97	94	100	97	96
Manufacturing	114	NA	100	103	NA
U.S. MNC Assets in Canada					
Total	76	90	100	100	97
Manufacturing	118	NA	100	102	NA
U.S. MNC Equity in Canada					
Total	95	80	100	98	100
Manufacturing	128	NA	100	94	85
		Indexes of Ratios of Real Values, 1977=100			
U.S. MNC Sales in Canada					
Total		101	100	108	103
Manufacturing		99	100	115	NA
U.S. MNC Assets in Canada					
Total		92	100	100	94
Manufacturing		95	100	102	NA
U.S. MNC Equity in Canada					
Total		82	100	98	97
Manufacturing		97	100	94	NA

Sources: U.S. data from Benchmark Surveys. Canadian data from CALURA Reports. Price data from national sources.

Note: For the first set of data, the U.S. data were converted into Canadian dollars at average 1977 exchange rate. For the second set of data, each country's nominal values were converted to real terms using the country's own price index. The ratios of these numbers are presented here. The 1966 data for Canadian manufacturing was projected by this author from the reported total for 1968.

Table 4.4
Financial Ratios for U.S. MNC Affiliates in Canada, 1966-1989

Data from:	U.S. Department of Commerce				CALURA Reports			
	1966	1977	1982	1989	1968	1977	1982	1988
Total								
Assets/Sales	124	91	91	105	97	71	73	83
Assets/Equity	211	247	256	293	196	198	209	219
Sales/Equity	169	272	281	280	203	279	284	265
Manufacturing								
Assets/Sales	82	62	64	65	90	64	66	62
Assets/Equity	194	208	195	213	187	192	194	204
Sales/Equity	238	338	303	326	209	301	296	329

	Ratios of Canadian/U.S. Values, as an Index with 1977=100			
	1966	1977	1982	1989
Total				
Assets/Sales	99	100	103	101
Assets/Equity	116	100	102	93
Sales/Equity	117	100	99	92
Manufacturing				
Sales/Assets	106	100	98	92
Equity/Assets	105	100	108	104
Sales/Equity	98	100	110	113

Source: CALURA Reports and U.S. Department of Commerce Benchmark surveys. The 1989 U.S. Direct Investment Position from the August 1991 *Survey of Current Business.*

Note: All indexes reported as percentages. For the Index of Canadian/U.S. Ratios, the initial and final years did not exactly coincide.

series and the Banco de México series are in the same ballpark in terms of total investment, while the Mexican sources indicate significantly more investment in industry for the earlier years in that table. During the 1980s we note a growing discrepancy between the numbers from the SECOFI and Department of Commerce, one that suggests that the degree of overstatement in the SECOFI series around 1990 is between one-third and one-half. Apparently there are no estimates from official Mexican sources of the value of sales of U.S. MNC

Table 4.5

Annual Flows of FDI into Canada from the United States: Comparison of Canadian and U.S. Data

	CANADIAN DATA (Million C$)					U.S. DATA (Million U.S.$)				
	Canadian IFDI: All Countries	Canadian IFDI from the United States				United States OFDI into Canada				
	Increase in Book Value	Increase in Book Value	Net Capital Inflow	Ret. Earn.	Other	Increase in Book Value	Net Capital Outflow	Ret. Earn.	Inter-Co. Debt	Val. Adj.
1980	7385	5911	278	4704	929	4316	-422	3589	176	
1981	4906	3414	-3694	3162	3946	1979	-3609	1770	1135	
1982	2237	554	-2038	110	2482	-1616	-2657	852	190	
1983	4367	2872	-894	3447	319	1413	-412	3664	-1839	
1984	5626	5012	801	4171	40	2492	13	2629	-255	105
1985	3157	1812	-2925	3034	1703	377	-2573	1930	-92	1112
1986	5175	1012	-1464	— 2476 —		3072	-393	2191	866	408
1987	9891	4763	2055	— 2708 —		6885	408	4848	1102	528
1988	8527	1372	-18	— 1390 —		4827	-4	2285	307	2240
1989	8762	4051	1249	— 2802 —		2892	-1974	3287	-283	1083
1990	5758	3237	1473	— 1764 —		3114	387	235	2272	219
1991	4897	4149	3394	— 755 —		1477	1461	524	-710	202

Sources: Canadian data from *Canada's International Investment Position,* 1986 and 1991. U.S. data from various years of the *Survey of Current Business.*

Note: Ret. Earn. is retained earnings; Inter-Co. Debt is intercompany debt flows; Val. Adj. is valuation adjustment. The categories for the U.S. data were changed for the data after 1983, and the data have been subject to considerable revision.

During this period, the cost of the U.S. dollar varied between 1.10 and 1.40 Canadian dollars.

affiliates in Mexico, and indeed only very limited estimates of the sales of all MNC affiliates in the country. We do not know of Mexican data giving the breakdown of mode of financing of U.S. FDI in Mexico, so that particular comparison is not possible.

UNITED STATES

Outward Investment

The United States has had sizeable outward foreign direct investment since the late nineteenth century; indeed, especially into Mexico and Canada. After World

Table 4.6
The Stock of U.S. FDI in Mexico, 1940-1991: Comparison of Mexican and U.S. Data
(Current U.S.$ million, and percentages)

Year	1940	1950	1960	1966	1970	1977	1982	1985	1989	1990	1991
U.S. Sources											
Total	358	415	795	1,329	1,912	3,187	5,051	5,088	7,280	9,398	11,570
Industry	6	22	391	927	1,380	2,400	4,036	4,053	5,853	7,196	8,493
Mexican Sources											
CNIE — Total							3,961	7,335	9,840	16,772	19,080 21,466
BdM — Total	296	390	900	1,584	2,237	2,554					
— Industry	30	135	488	1,092	1,650	1,962					
Ratio of U.S. Total to Mexican Total,											
Using Data from:											
CNIE						80	69	52	43	49	54
BdM	121	106	88	84	85	125					

Sources: U.S. data: 1940-1950, U.S. Department of Commerce (1955); 1960 from August 1961 *Survey of Current Business*; 1966, 1977, 1982, from Benchmark Surveys; 1970, U.S. Department of Commerce, *Select Data on U.S. Direct Investment Abroad, 1966-78* ASI 80 2704-3; data for 1985-91 from various issues of the *Survey of Current Business*.

  Mexican data: Banco de México, *Inversión Extranjera Privada Directa, 1940-62*, and *Inversion extranjera directa. Cuaderno 1938-1979*, CNIE *Informe 1983-1987*, and SECOFI, "Evolución de la inversión extranjera directa en 1991" (1992).

War I investments started to take off, contrary to the experience of the United Kingdom and the continental powers, only to be interrupted by the Depression, resuming again after World War II. Some data on U.S. equity abroad, deflated by the U.S. price index, are presented in Table 4.7, and illustrated in Figure 4.1. They indicate two phases of growth of OFDI from the United States; that before 1930 (interrupted briefly during World War I), and from 1950 through 1970. Sometime in the decade after 1965 the growth rate of OFDI declined. This inference is made with regard to equity; the reader will recall that the use of historical cost inflates recent estimates of this growth; thus, the recent weakening of U.S. OFDI is larger than that indicated in Figure 4.1. In that graph, as well as

Figure 4.1
U.S. Outward FDI, 1897-1990

By Geographical Area

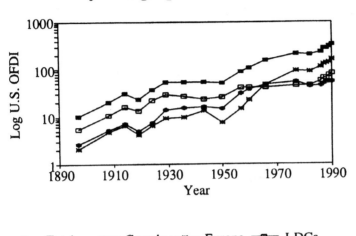

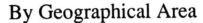

By Productive Sector

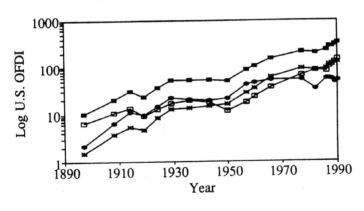

Sources: Lewis (1938), Arno Press (1979), U.S. Department of Commerce (1960), and Benchmark Studies, deflated by the U.S. GNP deflator.

Table 4.7
Indicators of U.S. Outward FDI, 1957-1989

		Sales (Billion 1982 U.S.$)					Employment (1982=100)	
	Total	Petrol.	Mfg.	Canada	Europe	LDCs	Total	Mfg.
1957	122	46	59	37	36	39	39	31
1966	316	83	155	76	133	76	77	78
1977	963	353	366	141	411	272	108	110
1982	936	329	359	120	442	231	100	100
1986	816	175	394	116	428	143	94	93
1989	1003	177	508	145	522	177	100	95

		Assets (Billion 1982 U.S.$)				
	Total	Petrol.	Mfg.	Canada	Europe	LDCs
1957	136	47	48	45	30	53
1966	368	78	253	95	246	85
1977	728	170	284	128	307	172
1982	751	195	266	110	308	223
1986	818	153	313	114	376	212
1989	1040	153	389	152	521	214

Source: U.S. Department of Commerce (1960), (1989a), and Benchmark Studies.

Note: Items for "real" values are author's calculations, deflating by U.S. GNP deflator. Employment data for 1957 and 1966 are calculated by reference to the changes for majority-owned firms; all other items are for all non-bank affiliates. Reporting employment data for 1957 was voluntary, and the Department of Commerce estimated a grand total nearly double the figures provided by the firms. It is included here only as a crude reference.

Petrol. - Petroleum; Mfg. - Manufacturing

other data to be presented below, suggest some recovery of that growth in the latter 1980s.

Historians are familiar with the fact that before 1950, Third World countries, predominantly some in Latin America, played a central role in the FDI of the United States as elsewhere, and that those investments were concentrated in nonferrous mining and petroleum. The plantation agriculture of banana and sugar did not weigh heavily in the aggregates.

More recently, one notes the rapid rise in investments into Europe after 1960, the stagnation of investments into Canada in the 1970s, and a short-lived absolute decline in total FDI stocks during the 1980s (which is even present in the nominal data). This latter is most true of petroleum. Manufacturing and other activities apparently stagnated in the early 1980s and more recently are growing at a slower rate.[5]

Beginning in the 1920s, there has been a shift of the sectoral distribution of U.S. FDI out of primary activities (agriculture, mining, and petroleum) into manufacturing. Analysis of the price adjusted values of the stock of equity indicates a decline in agriculture, which had been located predominantly in Latin America, partially counteracted by a rise in petroleum, as indicated in Table 4.8. The share of services is about the same in the 1980s as it was in the 1920s, having dipped during the early post-World War II period. Corresponding to this shift has been a similar one away from investments in Latin America toward Europe. Canada's share of the total rose and then fell after 1960.

The recent dynamism of the service sector merits a special comment. The activity that has seen the highest growth is financial services, in Europe and Latin America—essentially Panama and the Caribbean island tax havens. Wholesale trade has also increased in real terms. Other, traditionally important areas of U.S. FDI in services, such as utilities, retail trade, hotels, real estate, and construction, have stagnated along with other elements of outward FDI.

Although the data that reaches back to the first years of the century indicate strong shifts in the sectoral allocation of investment, one of the surprising results in Table 4.9 using the more detailed surveys after 1966 is the relative constancy, across countries and over time, of the distribution of U.S. outward investment among the major productive sectors, with manufacturing holding 40-45 percent of the stock of outward FDI, as well as inside the subsectors of manufacturing industry. The clear implication is that specific industrial-sector determinants of FDI differ less across countries than do the country macrocharacteristics that determine overall volume of FDI, such as size of market and openness to FDI. Basically, production of items such as automobiles and computers will receive a lot of investment, while production of shoes and pipes will not. Casual empiricism suggests a certain parallel story with regard to OFDI from Japan. Initially, that investment varied significantly, according to each country's natural resource attractions. More recently, Japanese OFDI in manufacturing has been attracted by protectionism in host countries, tending to make its profile more homogeneous.

Having noted this pattern with regard to OFDI from the United States, we turn to an attempt to measure the weight of U.S. investment inside the various host countries' economies. Table 4.10 presents these results for sales in Canada, Mexico, and Europe considered as a single entity. The comparisons are necessarily quite rough; in particular one would prefer value-added rather than sales by U.S. MNCs. In addition, as noted above, the data referring to majority-owned U.S. affiliates in Mexico reflect only about half of the corresponding totals for all U.S. affiliates in that country; in most other countries the difference is of the order of 10 percent.

Table 4.8
Equity Position of U.S. Outward FDI, 1929-1966
(Million Current U.S.$ and Percent)

	1929	1936	1943	1950	1959	1966	1929	1936	1943	1950	1959	1966
Total	7,528	6,691	7,862	11,788	29,735	54,711						
By Country/Area							**Breakdown by Country/Area (%)**					
Canada	2,010	1,952	2,378	3,579	10,171	16,999	27	29	30	30	34	31
Europe	1,353	1,259	2,051	1,733	5,300	16,209	18	19	26	15	18	30
Lat. Am.	3,519	2,847	2,798	4,576	8,990	9,826	47	43	36	39	30	18
Other	646	633	635	1,900	5,274	11,677	9	9	8	16	18	21
By Productive Sector							**Breakdown by Sector (%)**					
AgMinPet	3,182	2,588	2,869	5,108	13,943	20,520	42	39	36	43	47	38
Mfg.	1,813	1,710	2,276	3,831	9,692	22,058	24	26	29	32	33	40
Services	2,533	2,393	2,717	2,849	6,100	12,133	34	36	35	24	21	22

	As Percent of Total U.S. Investment						As Percent of U.S. Sectoral Total					
	1929	1936	1943	1950	1959	1966	1929	1936	1943	1950	1959	1966
Agriculture												
Canada	0.3	0.1	0.4	0.2	0.2		2.4	2.1	6.8	3.6	9.1	
Europe	0.0	0.0	0.1	0.0	0.0		0.0	0.0	1.0	0.2	0.2	
Lat. Am.	10.9	6.0	4.9	4.4	1.8		92.8	83.0	76.5	88.8	79.9	
Mining												
Canada	5.3	3.6	4.9	2.8	3.7		33.8	23.2	39.5	29.6	38.1	48.4
Europe	0.0	0.6	1.9	0.3	0.2		0.0	4.2	15.3	2.7	1.7	1.3
Lat. Am.	9.7	10.6	5.2	5.6	4.8		61.8	68.6	41.6	59.0	49.5	26.6
Petroleum												
Canada	0.7	1.6	2.0	3.5	8.3		4.9	10.1	11.6	12.3	23.6	22.3
Europe	3.1	4.2	4.8	3.6	4.9		20.7	25.9	26.9	12.6	13.9	24.6
Lat. Am.	8.2	6.8	7.9	11.1	11.1		55.2	42.2	44.4	38.4	31.8	17.9
Manufacturing												
Canada	10.9	11.9	12.0	16.1	15.3	14.0	45.2	46.7	41.3	49.5	47.0	34.8
Europe	8.4	9.1	11.2	7.9	9.8	16.2	34.7	35.8	38.6	24.3	30.2	40.2
Lat. Am.	3.1	2.9	4.1	6.6	4.8	5.6	12.7	11.2	14.3	20.4	14.7	14.0
Service												
Canada	9.5	11.9	10.9	7.7	6.7		28.2	33.3	31.6	31.9	32.8	
Europe	6.5	4.9	8.2	2.9	2.9		19.5	13.6	23.7	12.0	14.2	
Lat. Am.	14.9	16.4	13.5	11.1	7.8		44.3	45.7	39.2	45.7	37.8	

Sources: U.S. Department of Commerce, *U.S. Business Investments in Foreign Countries,* (1960: 93), and the August 1967 *Survey of Current Business.*

Note: The amount for Services was obtained by subtracting AgPetrolMin (agriculture, mining, and petroleum) and Manufacturing from the total. For 1966, the amount for agriculture (which was only 10% of the 1959 total) is included in Services.

Table 4.9
Disaggregation of U.S. OFDI in Manufacturing, 1966-1989
(Data Are Percentages of Country/regional Manufacturing Total)

	1966	1977	1982	1989		1966	1977	1982	1989
All Countries					**LDCs**				
Food	9	9	9	10	Food	12	11	10	10
Chemicals	19	19	22	23	Chemicals	NA	25	23	24
Metals	7	7	7	5	Metals	NA	10	8	7
Machinery	16	18	17	17	Machinery	NA	9	11	12
Electric	9	9	9	8	Electric	NA	11	12	14
Transport	19	15	13	15	Transport	12	10	11	12
Other	23	22	24	21	Other	NA	24	24	20
Canada					**Mexico**				
Food	9	10	8	7	Food	12	9	9	8
Chemicals	16	15	22	20	Chemicals	28	27	18	26
Metals	7	8	7	8	Metals	8	12	8	5
Machinery	12	10	10	10	Machinery		7	6	5
Electric	8	7	7	7	Electric		9	12	8
Transport	18	20	20	24	Transport	13	13	19	26
Other	14	29	25	25	Other		23	28	22
Europe & Other Developed Countries					**Brazil**				
Food	7	8	9	11	Food	10	9	10	7
Chemicals	NA	19	21	24	Chemicals	17	19	21	18
Metals	NA	6	5	4	Metals	5	7	11	12
Machinery				21	Machinery		16	20	20
Electric				6	Electric		11	7	4
Transport	22	15	12	13	Transport	18	12	7	14
Other				21	Other		27	24	24

Source: U.S. Department of Commerce Benchmark studies.

Note: NA or blank spaces indicate data are not available.

In general, U.S. investment into Canada is roughly three times as large relative to host country GNP as it is into Mexico or Europe. Compared to host country manufacturing, U.S. investment is half as big in Mexico as it is in Canada, with investment into Europe being half again as small. Since the early 1970s there has been a continual decline in the relative size of the U.S. presence in Canada, one also well documented by the Canadian source CALURA, as discussed below. However, there are clear indications of a strong increase in the U.S. presence in European manufacturing, which occurs even while the U.S.

Table 4.10

Comparison of Sales of U.S. Overseas Affiliates with Total Domestic Sales in Canada, Mexico, and Europe

		1957	1966	1977	1982	1989
Sales of U.S. Non-bank Affiliates as Percent of Host Country's GDP						
Canada:	Total	36.0	44.5	46.3	39.6	33.3
	Manufacturing	24.0	26.6	24.4	18.7	18.7
Mexico:	Total	10.8	12.4	13.2	12.8	14.3
	Manufacturing	7.0	9.4	10.5	10.2	11.3
Europe:	Total	[4.4]	7.9	13.0	14.4	11.7
	Manufacturing	[2.5]	4.3	5.9	5.8	5.9
CANADA Sales of U.S. Manufacturing Subsidiaries as Percent of Canadian Manufacturing Production						
	Gross Value	35.0	40.7	35.5	36.3	
	Value Added	79.0	99.4	113.7	121.4	
MEXICO Sales of U.S. Manufacturing Subsidiaries as Percent of Mexican Manufacturing Production						
	Gross Value	15.1	18.9	17.8	20.0	NA
	Value Added	33.6	45.2	48.0	47.9	46.0
EUROPE Sales of U.S. Manufacturing Subsidiaries as Percent of Regional Manufacturing Production						
Compared to European Value Added		NA	14.0	20.0	23.0	25.0
Real U.S. Manufacturing Sales ÷ European Industrial Output. Index, 1982=100						
	All Affiliates	[37]	63	108	100	121

Sources: Data on Sales of U.S. Affiliates from the various Benchmark Surveys of the U.S. Department of Commerce and *U.S. Direct Investment Abroad.* Canadian data on sales of U.S. controlled corporations from the CALURA reports. Data on industrial production and value added from various issues of the U.N. *Industrial Yearbook.* 1957 Data from Urquhart and Buckley (1965). Mexican data on GDP and industrial production from INEGI *Cuentas Nacionales,* converted at average exchange rates. Other data on GDP from the 1988 *International Financial Statistics.*

Note: The coverage for "All Affiliates" increases between 1966 and 1977. Addenda: According to CALURA reports the percentage of manufacturing sales in Canada accounted for by U.S. controlled firms was: 1968, 48.8%; 1977, 46.6%; 1982, 38.6%; 1988, 36.6%.

share of European GDP is constant, because of industry's relative decline on the continent. The U.S. presence in Mexican manufacturing also experienced a somewhat weaker growth until the 1970s, after which its relative size has remained constant.

A more complex picture emerges when we look at employment in Table 4.11. The strong relative decline in employment of U.S. affiliates in Canada is still quite evident. However, there was also a relative drop in Europe and an increase in Mexico, particularly in manufacturing. Part of the increase in the U.S. presence in Mexican manufacturing is due to the absolute decline in that country's industrial employment during the 1980s, associated with the debt crisis and trade liberalization, discussed later on. However, another noteworthy fact is the apparent changes in productivity, data on which is provided in Table 4.12.[6]

As measured by sales per employee, productivity has been rising more rapidly in European affiliates than it has either in Canada or in the U.S. parents. It has stagnated or perhaps even declined in Mexico. The more rapid growth in Europe merits further investigation; it may be a sectoral phenomenon as per OLI theory, or perhaps it is an illusion due to our use of data on total sales and not value added. Unfortunately, the few observations on assets per worker do not provide information consistent with the movements in real wages.

The different evolution indicated by the data on Mexico is quite interesting. In that country, real assets per worker have declined, as have average real wages. The growth of FDI in export processing—the maquilas—is clearly of importance. So also is the overall decline in real wages in Mexico, of the order of magnitude of 50 percent during the 1980s. The percentage gap between wages in U.S. affiliates and total manufacturing in Mexico has stayed at around 30-40 percent, as the gap between overall manufacturing and maquilas has narrowed from 50 percent to 25 percent over the last two decades.[7] Given the growing importance of maquilas in U.S. investment in Mexico, it is unfortunate that more-detailed statistics on this activity are not available.

The data in Table 4.11 indicate that the LDC share of manufacturing employment of U.S. affiliates has increased from 20 percent in 1966 to 38 percent in 1989. The growth in Mexico represents only part of that process. The comparison of these data on U.S. FDI in Canada and Europe suggests that the divestment by U.S. firms of which McFetridge (1989) speaks is rather specific to Canada. Given the constancy of U.S. affiliates' share of the European market, the observed decline of Europe's share of the distribution of U.S. affiliates' manufacturing employment is a reflection of a rise of employment in LDCs, which also came at the expense of employment in Canada as well as the United States itself.

Thus, Canada and Mexico represent two ends of the spectrum of possible future scenarios for U.S. OFDI. To the north there are declining prospects because of both the growing competitiveness of domestic firms and the inherent limits of a market secured behind tariffs. To the south there are dynamic

Table 4.11
Employment of U.S. MNC Affiliates Compared to Host Country Employment, 1966-1987

		1966	1977	1982	1989
Employment in U.S. MNCs as Percentage of National Employment					
All U.S. MNCs	Canada	[13.0]	11.0	8.6	7.6
	Europe	[1.4]	2.0	1.8	1.6
	Mexico	[1.9]	2.3	2.2	2.3
U.S. MNCs in Manufacturing	Canada	[8.3]	6.4	4.5	3.8
	Europe	[1.1]	1.5	1.3	1.1
	Mexico	[1.4]	1.9	1.8	2.0
Employment in U.S. Manufacturing Affiliates as Percentage of National Employment in Manufacturing					
	Canada	[34.1]	32.5	25.0	24.4
	Europe	[2.8]	4.3	4.0	3.5
	Mexico	[9.3]	14.8	15.2	17.8
Overseas Employment in U.S. MNCs: LDCs as Percentage of Total					
	Total	[27.8]	30.2	32.3	32.6
	Manufacturing	[20.1]	29.8	32.5	37.7

Sources: Data on U.S. MNCs from Benchmark Surveys. Data on European employment from OECD *Labour Force Statistics,* various years. Canadian employment data from Statistics Canada. Mexican employment data from various publications on the National Income accounts of SPP/INEGI, and for 1966, from Nafinsa, *La economía mexicana en cifras,* based on extrapolation of census data and therefore less comparable with later data.

Note: Data on U.S. MNC affiliates refer to all nonbank affiliates, except for bracketed data for 1966, which are calculated for majority-owned affiliates, adjusting for ratios of two series for 1977. LDCs include Africa, Latin America, and Asia except Japan, Australia, and New Zealand.

potentials in spite of a stagnant national economy due to the attractiveness of exports produced by low-wage workers.

Comparisons can also be made of U.S. OFDI and that country's domestic variables. Table 4.13 presents some basic information. When compared to domestic aggregates such as GNP and exports, sales of affiliates abroad seem to trace a long ∩ shaped pattern more accentuated than what was seen above in Figure 4.1, with a peak in the 1970s. However, this is most definitely not true for

Table 4.12
Real Wages, Sales, and Assets per Worker, U.S. MNC Parents and Overseas Affiliates, 1966-1989
(Thousand 1982 U.S.$/Worker)

	1966	1977	1982	1989		1966	1977	1982	1989
	Sales/Worker					Assets/Worker			
U.S. Manufacturing Affiliates									
Total	57	83	92	137		45	53	55	86
Europe	47	79	86	146		44	62	61	115
Canada	77	121	118	173		63	74	76	113
Mexico	46	42	45	41		56	41	36	28
U.S. MNC Parents Mfg.	NA	96	97	121		NA	80	97	147
U.S. Domestic Mfg.	80	103	104	113		60	89	110	NA
U.S. GNP/worker	34	36	35	38					

	Real Remuneration, Manufacturing			
U.S. Affiliates	10	16	15	18
Europe	10	19	19	25
Canada	17	26	24	28
Mexico	7	8	8	5
U.S. MNC Parents	NA	27	30	31
Average for United States	21	25	26	28

Source: Benchmark Studies. U.S. domestic totals from various issues of the *Statistical Abstract of the United States.*

Note: Data on employment and remuneration for 1966, and for Mexico, 1977, refer to majority owned foreign affiliates. Wages include benefits. Asset data refer to totals reported to the Internal Revenue Service; Department of Commerce data on fixed capital follow a similar trend. Data are deflated by the U.S. GNP deflator.

manufacturing, where foreign sales have been steadily rising compared to domestic sales. Curiously enough, that is not the case with employment. The ∩ pattern is present although much less marked when total affiliate employment is compared with total U.S. (nonagricultural) employment. However, this also occurs with regard to manufacturing employment, contradicting the above pattern in manufacturing production. The discrepancy results from the faster growth of labor productivity in Europe compared to the U.S. totals at home. This is true

Table 4.13
U.S. MNCs: Overseas Totals Compared to Domestic Aggregates, 1966-1989

	1966	1977	1982	1989
Overseas Affiliate Sales ÷ U.S. GNP (Percent)	15	33	30	24
Manufacturing Affiliate Sales ÷ Domestic Sales in Manufacturing (Percent)	12	22	23	28
Affiliate Employment as Percent of U.S. Employment				
Total	[8]	9	7	6
Manufacturing	[19]	27	26	23

Affiliates ÷Parents	1977	1982	1989	1977	1982	1989
	Sales			Employment		
Total	46	40	40	38	36	35
Petroleum	109	62	72	48	41	50
Manufacturing	39	43	50	45	46	45
Mining	37	38	23	63	59	47
Other	23	18	19	23	19	22

Sources: Benchmark Studies and *Statistical Abstract of the United States.*

Note: The 1966 reference group is affiliates with 25 percent ownership, biasing downward totals for that year. Bracketed employment data are author's calculations, using data for majority-owned affiliates. The corresponding data on U.S. parents do not appear in the 1966 Benchmark Study.

when the comparison is made either to the MNC parent companies in the United States, or for the nation as a whole.

A related issue, central to some discussions about the impact of FDI, is the question of the exportation of employment. It will be recalled that the OLI paradigm basically asserts that this is unimportant; crudely put, jobs lost via FDI were going to be lost anyway. Without reviewing that argument nor judging its validity here, we should at least note the order of magnitude involved. Table 4.13 shows that although employment in overseas affiliates is less than 10 percent of total employment in the United States, the ratio for manufacturing is fully one-quarter. Given the reputation of importance that manufacturing has always maintained—strategic, prestige, technology generating—such a high fraction is bound to command attention.

Another important consideration in this work is the role of export markets as an attractor of U.S. FDI; this is the key to the Mexican strategy with regard to NAFTA and productivity improvement. An average of two-thirds of the sales of U.S. affiliates stays in the local host country market. Most of the overseas sales from Canada and LDCs (including Mexico) go to the United States. This is not the result of unhindered trade in free markets; the Canadian totals are pushed by trade in the motor vehicle sector, a controlled trade, while the Mexican numbers reflect the maquila sector, primarily. Moreover, the local/total ratio has been falling, as we see in Table 4.14. This decline is widespread across manufacturing industries and host countries. The petroleum industry provides an important if isolated counterexample. More complex is the situation in Europe. According to the Benchmark studies, the fraction of the sales of U.S. MNCs located there that stays in Europe, either sold locally or to a neighboring country, has actually risen from 85 percent in 1966 to 91 percent in 1989.

Thus, although the U.S. MNCs are participating in the globalization of world trade, we should not speak of a world market for those firms, and, indeed, our picture is one of the U.S. MNCs contributing to an ongoing growth of regional trade blocks in North America and Europe. In addition, however, these data also confirm our image of the importance of the electronic and transportation sectors' exports to the United States from Mexico and other LDCs. Indeed, the largest increases in the export shares in Table 4.14 occur in manufacturing electronics, other machinery, and transport, which are growing particularly from LDCs, whose production is likely to be competitive on a world scale.

Conventional wisdom suggests that newer modes of foreign investment will tend to involve more minority-owned firms in the form of joint ventures. Although the Department of Commerce Benchmark studies do not provide sufficient detail for a thorough analysis, they do indicate that the percentage of assets or sales accounted for by majority-owned firms has been relatively constant and indeed has risen lately in Mexico.

The subject of export performance of U.S. MNCs was recently analyzed by Lipsey and Kravis (1987) as providing an indication of the competitiveness of those firms. They utilize data from the U.S. affiliates, their parent companies in the United States, and world exports; the focus is limited to manufacturing. They find a relative constancy in the share of U.S. multinational companies over the period 1957-1984, in which a decline in the share of the parents is counterbalanced by an increase in the share of the affiliates. They interpret these findings as negating alleged management failure and declining competitiveness of U.S. firms. Furthermore, they argue that changes in average export prices of goods from the United States explains a substantial part of the decline of the export performance of the country as a geographical entity.

One reason why a comparison of total sales of MNC affiliates to host country totals might suggest stagnation at the same time that exports by those affiliates

Table 4.14
Local Sales as a Percentage of Total Sales of U.S. Majority-Owned Affiliates, 1957-1989

	1957	1962	1966	1977	1982	1989
All Industries	73		75	62	65	69
Petroleum	66		79	51	65	76
Manufacturing	84	84	81	69	66	63
Food & Kindred		85	88	84	84	81
Chemicals		86	86	74	68	67
Primary & Fabric. Metals		87	90	73	74	64
Nonelectrical Machinery		79	77	63	59	57
Electronic Equipment	90	I	66	59	59	NA
Transport Equipment		86	76	61	57	54
Other Manufacturing		83	81	71	69	71
All Other			60	69	66	73
Trade		71	65	63	73	
Finance & Other			NA	88	62	75
Services			NA	78	80	75
Mining	16		25	23	18	22
Trans. & Utilities			89	98	91	70
Agr., Forest., Fish.	37		NA	42	27	22
Manufacturing in:						
Canada	84		84	70	65	62
Mexico	98		97	90	89	68

Sources: Benchmark Surveys, 1957 data from U.S. Department of Commerce, *U.S. Business Investments in Foreign Countries,* and 1962 data from *Survey of Current Business,* October 1963.

appear to be dynamic is that those exports were initially small relative to local sales and exports in general were quite dynamic. This is evidently the case for Europe and the effects there of progressive liberalization due to the Common Market.

Looking at the performance of U.S. MNCs reveals a certain loss of dynamism since the 1970s, whose magnitude varies depending on what variables are used for comparison. Is it possible to go beyond that approach and look at the fundamental determinants of the competitiveness of these MNCs? The OLI model provides a framework for such an analysis, and so the time series profiles of a number of the determinants of U.S. FDI were investigated. To the surprise of some, the various series for the United States on industrial concentration, scale, multibranch activity, R&D intensity, and advertising summarized in Table 4.15, show a decline during the 1970s, quite consistent with the observed pattern of changes in investment. It is also noteworthy that two of the variables that show the largest variation (R&D and advertising) have turned up again in the 1980s.

The results of an econometric exercise support this interpretation of the changes in U.S. outward FDI, in terms of the variables emphasized in the OLI perspective. Table 4.16 shows the results for two different specifications of the dependent variable (assets or sales), using two different means of deflating the data (U.S. GDP deflator, or nominal value of U.S. GDP), for the three benchmark years 1966, 1977, and 1982.[8] While it is clear that the high R-squareds are the result of using sectoral-specific dummy variables, almost all of the coefficients are of the hypothesized sign, which was quite gratifying for an exploratory study.

Although these results are intriguing, the limitations of this line of work are also apparent. Data from no other country are included, which means that various location considerations are not incorporated nor is the possibility that conditions in the United States no longer define those industrial organization characteristics

Table 4.15
Indicators of Competitiveness of U.S. Manufacturing Sectors, 1958-1987

	1958	1963	1967	1972	1977	1982	1987
Weighted Average of 4-Firm Concentration Ratios	33.7	34.2	35.0	34.8	36.4	34.9	NA
Percent Establishments with More than 500 Employees	1.5	1.6	1.9	1.8	1.6	1.5	1.4
Ratio of Value Added by Multiunit Firms to Total Sales by Industry	73	76	79	81	83	82	82
Advertising Expenditures ÷ Total Sales			(1970) 1.12	(1974) 0.86		(1979) 0.90	(1987) 1.27
R&D as Percentage of Net Sales		(1963) 4.5	(1967) 4.2	(1972) 3.4		(1980) 3.0	(1986) 4.7

Source: First three items; various years of *U.S. Manufacturing Census (Special Series).* Fourth item; U.S. Internal Revenue Service, *Corporation Income Tax Returns,* various years. Last item from National Science Foundation, *Research and Development in Industry,* 1985-1986, and 1987.

Note: The data for R&D as percent of net sales refers to R&D performing companies.

Table 4.16
Regression Results on U.S. FDI Assets and Sales, 1966-1982

Dependent Variable	Independent Variables					
	R&D	Multipro	CR4	Scale	AdX	R^2
Real Assets	0.08	0.12	0.07	0.06	2.68	0.96
	(0.10)	(1.02)	(1.21)	(0.16)	(2.44)	
Real Sales	-0.03	0.30	0.03	0.06	4.14	0.94
	(0.02)	(1.36)	(0.27)	(0.07)	(2.05)	
Assets/GDP	28.20	7.17	1.93	-7.73	0.15	0.94
	(0.74)	(1.19)	(0.70)	(0.38)	(2.63)	
Sales/GDP	31.80	13.20	0.52	-10.6	0.19	0.89
	(0.52)	1.38	(0.12)	(0.32)	(2.18)	

Source: Author's calculations, using the data taken from the sources listed for Table 4.15.

Note: t-statistics in parentheses. Equations are ordinary least squares estimates, pooling observations for the years 1966, 1977, and 1982. The coefficients corresponding to the dummy variables for each industrial sector are not reported.
R&D is research and development expenditures as percent of performing company sales. Multipro is the fraction of firms engaged in multiproduct sales. CR4 is the concentration index of the top four firms, using weighted averages for the two-digit classifications. Scale is the percentage of establishments with more than 500 employees. AdX is advertising expenditures as a percent of total sales.

of a sector that make it attractive for FDI. As was noted in Chapter 2, almost none of the research in the OLI tradition utilizes differences in variables between countries.

One final consideration about outward FDI from the United States is their mode of financing, in which the role of equity outflows has declined considerably. During the 1950s, 58 percent of the increase in the FDI position was due to equity flows and intercompany loans, while that ratio had dropped to 38 percent in the 1970s (*Survey of Current Business* February, 1981: 42). This change is especially marked for the 1980s, as indicated by Table 4.17, which shows that equity outflows from the United States have recently tended to be negative, so that even nominal increases in the country's investment position are due to reinvested earnings or other factors.

The importance of reinvested earnings in U.S. MNC behavior has long been recognized in the literature (see Droucopoulos, 1984). Analytical studies, especially the collection of essays in Razin and Slemrod (1990), give

Table 4.17
Financing of U.S. Direct Investment Outflows, 1983-1991
(Billion U.S.$)

	1982	1983	1984	1985	1986	1987	1988	1989	1990	1991
Direct Investment Position Abroad	207.8	207.2	211.5	230.3	259.8	314.3	333.5	370.1	424.1	450.2
Net Change		-0.5	4.3	18.8	29.6	54.5	19.2	34.2	51.7	26.1
Capital Flows		6.7	11.6	13.2	18.7	31.0	16.2	33.4	34.1	28.2
Net Equity		4.9	1.3	-2.2	0.6	4.6	-6.3	-4.5	7.4	11.7
Reinvested Earnings		13.5	17.2	14.1	10.0	19.7	12.6	22.4	20.9	18.9
Intercompany Debt		-11.7	-7.0	1.3	8.1	6.7	9.9	15.5	5.8	-2.4
Valuation Adjustments		-7.2	-7.3	5.6	10.9	23.5	3.0	0.8	17.6	-2.1

Source: various August issues of *Survey of Current Business.*

considerable attention to the "trapped equity" hypothesis, according to which U.S. tax laws provide very strong incentives to MNC managers to avoid repatriating earnings. In addition to showing that statistical sources that only report equity flows for U.S. MNCs are understating the total FDI movement; another implication of this hypothesis is that changes in the sources and uses of funds may well reflect tax regulations and not other macroeconomic variables such as profitability and interest rates. While standard economic theory would presume that a manager of an MNC attempts to maximize world profits, this theory's emphasis on taxes, loopholes, and accounting tricks gives further support to those who disdain the use of profit indicators for MNCs.

Direct Investment Into the United States

A subject that has increasingly attracted headlines in the United States is the growing presence there of multinationals from foreign countries. To place this in perspective, we might first compare the size of affiliates in the United States of foreign MNCs with domestic aggregates for the United States. These data are presented in Table 4.18. Sales by affiliates in manufacturing have grown from about 3 percent to 12 percent of total production or employment. With regard to total IFDI, sales of affiliates grew twice as fast as did GNP in the United States, while total employment overseas grew from 1 to 4 percent. In absolute terms that might well be considered small. The relative size of IFDI in manufacturing in the United States is almost half that of Mexico, as will be reviewed later.

Table 4.18
Indicators of the Size of Investment into the United States, 1974-1989

	1974	1980	1982	1987	1989
Sales of Affiliates (U.S.$ Billion)					
Total	147	436	516	799	1041
Petroleum	26	56	72	72	92
Manufacturing	31	98	141	225	347
Mining	1	3	6	6	8
Other	88	279	296	496	594
Affiliate Sales as Percent of Total Domestic Sales in Manufacturing	3	5	7	9	12
Total Affiliate Sales ÷ GNP (Percent)	10	16	16	18	20
Affiliate Employment (Thousands)					
Total	1083	2122	2435	3334	4440
Petroleum	94	101	123	115	136
Manufacturing	551	1103	1239	1543	2123
Mining	23	25	39	28	44
Other	416	893	1034	1649	2137
Affiliate Employment as Percent of U.S. Employment					
Total	1	2	3	3	4
Manufacturing	3	5	7	8	11

Sources: U.S. Department of Commerce IFDI Benchmark Studies for 1974, 1980, and 1987; *Foreign Direct Investment in the United States* for 1982 and 1989, and various years of the *Statistical Abstract of the United States.*

Labor productivity of foreign-owned manufacturing grew at the same rate as did the overall average for the country as a whole. However, productivity for all foreign investment grew more rapidly. This is the opposite of what was shown for the case of outward investment from the United States. As will be seen below, much of the sales of foreign-owned firms is in services, particularly wholesale firms. In this case, at least, the simplest explanation is that the rising productivity is simply an erroneous interpretation of sales by branches of foreign firms that import finished goods for sale; little production per se is involved.

The export propensity of these firms is quite similar to that of domestic firms in the United States. As Lipsey (1991) observes, their import propensity is higher, markedly so in the politically sensitive automotive sector. Curiously, the profit rates of IFDI in the United States are lower than that of domestic firms. The various explanations for this phenomenon analyzed in Landefeld et al. (1992) are not able to provide a convincing simple answer.[9]

One question is the relative size of outward-bound to inward-directed FDI. The overall magnitudes of this phenomenon have recently been reanalyzed by the U.S. Department of Commerce, and are summarized in Landefeld and Lawson (1991). Using the standard historical cost measure of the equity value of foreign investment, the value of FDI into the United States surpassed that of FDI from the United States in 1988. If, instead, price inflation and depreciation are taken into account, inward FDI will have surpassed outward FDI in 1990 or 1991. Their third alternative, using average indexes of stock market prices, shows the U.S. net position growing more positive because of the strong growth in overseas equity markets.

Limiting the analysis to the Benchmark series permits us to look at the values of sales and assets, which are not as subject to the biases of series on equity, and therefore facilitate both the comparison of nominal values in the same year as well as deflated values over time. The data in Table 4.19 show the value of inward investment in assets to be higher in 1989 than outward investment, and that for sales to be nearly as high. The service sector has been a net recipient for longer, although as will be discussed below, to a considerable degree this reflects establishments that import and service manufactured goods from abroad. Leaving aside the details of the estimation procedures, and indeed recognizing that the net position is primarily of symbolic importance, we can summarize this discussion by noting that there has been a large amount of investment into the United States, most of it very recently, which is worthy of some attention.

Disaggregating the data on FDI into the United States reveals the importance of wholesale trade in that IFDI, which overall averages 37 percent of total sales. For products such as consumer electronics and motor vehicles, these affiliates are the local sales representatives of foreign producers. Fully 80 percent of the sales by affiliates of Japanese MNCs are due to wholesalers. Services are relatively less important for investment from Canada, and indeed wholesale trade by affiliates of Canadian MNCs is only 10 percent of total sales in 1987. The implication that Canadian FDI is more traditional because half of it is in manufacturing is a point that will be commented on in the next chapter.

It could also be remarked that the relative importance of the different countries as sources of IFDI into the United States are different from their roles as hosts to U.S. OFDI, with especially Japan but also the Netherlands and Switzerland appearing quite important as corporate headquarters of U.S. affiliates.

Almost all investment in the United States has as its dominant market internal sales in the United States. Only about 7 percent of sales of foreign firms are exported. Again, Japan is something of an outlier in this regard, as 11 percent of that country's investments supply overseas markets in processed foods, mining, and other sectors.

While most of the discussion of the complexities of classifying and comparing data on FDI was placed above in the first section of this chapter, one additional factor could also be mentioned. The Benchmark surveys provide breakdowns by

Table 4.19
Comparison of U.S. Outward and Inward FDI, 1977-1989

		Levels			As Percent of U.S. GNP or Labor Force			Outward/Inward (Percent)		
		1977	1982	1989	1977	1982	1989	1977	1982	1989
TOTAL										
Assets:	Out	490	751	1314	25	24	25	307	159	94
	In	118	473	1402	8	15	27			
Sales:	Out	647	936	1266	33	30	24	307	181	122
	In	156	516	1041	11	16	20			
Employ.:	Out	7179	6640	6621	7	6	5	622	273	149
	In	1083	2435	4440	1	2	4			
PRIMARY ACTIVITIES										
Assets:	Out	134	213	211	7	7	4	297	279	183
	In	33	76	115	2	2	2			
Sales:	Out	248	338	235	12	11	5	456	375	230
	In	40	90	102	3	3	2			
Employ.:	Out	688	654	467	1	1	<0.5	518	378	236
	In	124	173	198	<0.5	<0.5	<0.5			
MANUFACTURING										
Assets:	Out	190	266	491	10	8	9	539	205	134
	In	26	130	368	2	4	7			
Sales:	Out	246	359	641	12	11	12	574	254	185
	In	32	141	347	2	4	7			
Employ.:	Out	4849	4429	4188	5	4	3	825	357	197
	In	551	1239	2123	1	1	2			
"SERVICES"										
Assets:	Out	165	272	611	8	9	12	209	102	67
	In	59	267	919	4	8	18			
Sales:	Out	153	238	390	8	8	8	135	84	66
	In	84	284	592	6	9	11			
Employ.:	Out	1660	1558	1966	2	1	2 ·	381	152	93
	In	409	1023	2119	<0.5	1	2			

Sources: Author's calculations based on the U.S. Department of Commerce Benchmark Studies, and *Foreign Investment in the United States,* 1982 and 1989. GNP and labor force from various years of the *Statistical Abstract of the United States.*

Note: Assets and sales are in billion current U.S.$; employment in thousands. Data refer to nonbank affiliates only. Classification is by industry of affiliate. Primary Activities include agriculture, forestry, fishing, mining, and petroleum. "Services" obtained by subtraction. The initial year for IFDI in this table is 1974, while that for OFDI is 1977. For the comparisons of OFDI to IFDI for 1977, the ratio of the data in the first column was adjusted by ratio of the two years' GNPs or employment. For 1974, IFDI sales datum was approximated by income.

activity of affiliate as well as by activity of ultimate owner. We saw above that this distinction was particularly important for Japanese investment. In addition, there is significant investment by foreign banks in nonbanking activities in the United States, amounting to some 13 percent of the total and 21 percent of the European total. Due to idiosyncracies of U.S. legislation and data collection a distinction is made between banks and other financial institutions, leading to a statistical gap because available data on the activities of banks does not reflect contemporary business practice.

U.S. Benchmark studies register some FDI in the United States from developing countries such as Mexico and Brazil. With magnitudes of less than $1 billion, these investments are of course very small in terms of overall U.S. IFDI, each accounting for about one-tenth of 1 percent of the total. Similarly, each country's FDI in the U.S. is about 5 percent of the value of the amount of FDI that they have received from the United States.[10]

What are the factors that have led to that upswell in FDI into the United States? A set of recent papers is Culem (1988), Ray (1989) and Scaperlanda (1990), each of which departs from a version of the OLI model and consciously estimates models similar to what has been done on outbound FDI from the United States. Standard variables such as size and growth of market are generally statistically significant. Notably, tariff and nontariff barriers were not shown to be important.[11] Unfortunately for our later purposes, Canada is not included in the one study (Ray) that attempts a cross-sectional study of investment from different countries. Responding to the current policy discussions in the United States, the effect of exchange rates on FDI was investigated with only minimally encouraging results. Defensive foreign investment, associated with discussion on strategic trade policy, was also not evident in the data. There were clear signs that investment in industry was attracted to high-tech sectors, which the authors, again paralleling broader policy discussions, interpret as an attempt to get access to the strong U.S. R&D base. The high level of Japanese investment in services has not been investigated systematically; two items that stand out are the importance of finance and wholesale trade of imports from Japan, in autos and electronics. An interesting paper by Woodward (n.d.) studies the locational distribution of Japanese manufacturing investments in the United States. Important determining variables are low unionization and tax rates, while avoiding the most underdeveloped parts of the country, thereby guaranteeing certain minimal educational and infrastructural levels. In the automobile industry there is a clear pattern of an automotive corridor stretching from the traditional headquarters of the industry, Detroit, south into Tennessee along the interstate highways. Outward FDI from Canada, concentrated in the United States, is discussed below.

Finally, we note that the comparison of rates of profits, trading patterns, and so forth, were studied for overseas affiliates of U.S. MNCs most thoroughly by Bergsten et al. (1978). This book, clearly the most sophisticated and thorough study of U.S. OFDI, presents an elaborate demonstration of the industrial organization explanation for sectoral differences in these performance characteristics. Unfortunately, the link to the analysis of Dunning and Caves is underplayed in the Bergsten et al. book because its early publication date put it before some of the most influential works of those other authors.

NOTES

1. The Canadian sources further differentiate between ownership and control, which we will not pursue.
2. The 1966 Benchmark used a 25 percent minimum to identify affiliates. While this creates a problem of inconsistency with subsequent Benchmarks, the bias is probably minimal when attention is focused on ratios such as sales/employee, etc.
3. We will discuss in more detail below this growth of capital-intensive service industries.
4. Some of the most-cited sources on Japanese OFDI are subject to this criticism, although this author does not know what fraction of Japanese overseas equity is financed through retained earnings.
5. An alternative calculation of sales or output results from combining the employment data in Table 4.7 with labor productivity data. Use of U.S. labor productivity suggests an increase in output of overseas manufacturing affiliates quite similar to that indicated in Table 4.7.
6. Note that all these data come from official U.S. sources, so that some of the previous tables' sources of errors, the combination of different countries' data, are avoided.
7. Mexican wages come from national income data as generated by INEGI. Maquila wage data are from Sklair (1989), citing INEGI publications.
8. The fit between the benchmark years and the census data was not exact. Unfortunately, the data on concentration corresponding to the 1987 manufacturing census had not yet been published in time for inclusion in this work.
9. Among the explanations considered by the indicated authors are an OLI-type explanation, one based directly on relative prices and exchange rates, the possibility that it arises from historical cost/market cost valuation problems. It should be noted that the question of low tax payments by foreign-owned firms was raised by the victorious candidate in the presidential election of that year.
10. Curiosity, at least, leads to the question of how this compares to Canadian historical experience. Official statistics, covering the era since 1926, indicate that Canadian OFDI was always at least 20 percent of Canadian IFDI.
11. This is inconsistent with conventional wisdom, at least with respect to certain visible sectors such as motor vehicles. See Adams et al. (1991).

5

CANADA AND MEXICO

The history of FDI in Canada and Mexico presents many complementarities to the evolution of OFDI from the United States. The Canadian case serves as the epitome of investment into a protected, friendly market. Mexico's experience encompasses various factors more common to developing countries, such as an initial concentration of FDI in raw materials and a subsequent period of a protected manufacturing sector with a highly variable welcome toward foreign investors. This chapter presents each country's analysis from the inside out, emphasizing those factors that local observers have judged most worthy of attention. Nevertheless, one of our goals is the search for the commonalities, which together with the inevitable contrasts, give life to comparative studies.

CANADA

The important historical and economic experience of Canada with respect to foreign investment is relatively well documented. A few facts should be mentioned at the start. First, during this century there was a dramatic shift in the ownership of foreign assets in Canada; the pre-World War I dominance of the United Kingdom was completely supplanted by that of the United States by the 1960s. Associated with that is a shift of the mode of investing, from portfolio to direct investment. Another aspect is the strong regional impact of FDI on the economy of Canada. Of most interest, however, is the fact that the share of foreign ownership of firms in Canada traces a long ∩ in the period since the 1920s, reaching its peak sometime in the early 1970s (see Figure 5.1).

To prepare for the discussion of this shift in ownership, we should first look at the overall stock of capital in the country. As shown in Table 5.1, about half the stock of physical capital is composed of residential housing and government and community buildings, all areas in which significant foreign investment is

Figure 5.1
Ownership of Canadian Capital Stock, 1926-1986

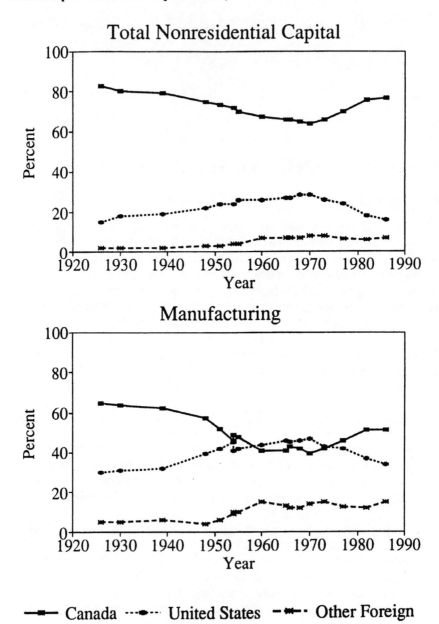

Total Nonresidential Capital

Manufacturing

——■—— Canada   ····●··· United States   —※—· Other Foreign

Source: Various years of Statistics Canada, *Canada's international investment position.*

Table 5.1
Capital Stock in Canada, 1981
(Billion C$)

Total	939		
Productive Sectors	467		
Manufacturing	108		
Other Productive Sectors	358		
Agriculture	36	Bridges & Grain Elevators	4
Forestry	3	Broadcasting & TV	32
Fishing	1	Water, Power & Gas	112
Mines & Oil Wells	62	Trade	23
Pipelines	12	Finance & Real Estate	38
Construction	7	Commercial Services	28
Transport	36		
Community Buildings and Housing	435		
Government	133	Schools, Universities	
Residential	253	and Churches	50

Source: Statistics Canada, *Fixed Capital Flows and Stocks,* 1985.

Note: Data are mid-year net stock. As in other Canadian statistical publications, petroleum refining and other processes are included in manufacturing.

GNP in 1981 was C$344 billion.

unlikely. Of the total stock a bit less than one-fifth is held in manufacturing, mining, and petroleum.[1] The remaining third is composed of utilities and other service activities, also predominantly in Canadian hands. It is in the areas of mining, petroleum, and manufacturing that the most significant changes in foreign ownership have occurred, on the order of 15 percent of those sectors, in this century. Thus we are speaking of a change of 15 percent in the ownership of 20 percent of the nation's total physical capital. Many analysts consider the attention received by this 3 percent to be worthwhile due to its dynamism and strategic importance.

The CALURA data illustrate clearly the rise and subsequent decline in foreign ownership and control of Canadian corporations (see Figure 5.2). Furthermore, the post-1970 decline is almost entirely due to a fall in the participation of U.S. firms. Finally, while the starkest changes are noted in the mining and petroleum sectors, the shift is also widely spread throughout industry.

A couple of qualifications should be noted in terms of the graph based on data from the official source, Statistics Canada. In the earlier years, up to 10 percent of corporations were not classified as to country so that when in later years the sales from these corporations were indeed attributed to companies from a particular country (apparently most often Canada), there is an exaggeration of the increase in domestic ownership. Secondly, as pointed out in Statistics Canada (1985a), during the 1970s there was a significant shift of production towards those sectors (particularly petroleum and mining) whose Canadian share was growing. This creates an index number type problem that overemphasizes the "average" shift in ownership, unless fixed weights (by share of production) are used. Our attempt to present a more precise picture is shown in Table 5.2. The Canadian ownership for 1970 and 1981 is estimated using the CALURA publications and the more detailed information for manufacturing presented in Statistics Canada (1985a). On the basis of these estimates, the Canadian share of manufacturing and mining sales increased by 16 percent, and by 12 percent if attention is limited to manufacturing. Note that most of the change occurred in the 1970s, and only 1-2 percent shifted in the 1980s. The manufacturing subsectors are arranged in the table according to a scheme emphasizing staple-based goods, which has a long pedigree in Canadian studies. In this breakdown, the largest part of the increase in Canadian ownership occurred in the staple sectors, although other sectors also gained.

These shifts have received little attention in the technical literature. Indeed, while much journalistic writing attacked the growth of U.S. MNCs in Canada, their decline has hardly been noted. A number of explanations for the changes in the weight of MNCs in Canada come to mind, classifiable most simply as political or economic factors. The former group, typified for many by the creation of the investment review agency FIRA, was discussed in Chapter 3. In analyzing the effect of these legal/institutional changes, Rugman (1980: 145) concluded that in its early years, "FIRA operate[d] in a very favorable manner toward proposed foreign direct investments [and did] not offer a substantial barrier to trade in capital. FIRA's policy was definitely not favorable to FDI in 1980-81, partially due to its leadership by Herbert Gray, but more basically reflecting the spirits of the time." (Rugman, 1990: 25). The newly elected Conservative Government in 1985 replaced FIRA by Investment Canada, which has taken a much more favorable approach to FDI. That government's initiation of the free trade discussions with the United States are in part a continuation of the reversal of those earlier nationalist policies. Of course, the same pattern occurs in Mexico.

With regard to economic forces causing changes in the weight of MNCs in Canada, the OLI model discussed earlier points to a number of potential explanatory factors: tariffs, concentration, degree of branch plants activity, R&D, advertising and other measures to differentiate products, and economies of scale. With regard to that which is of most interest in a discussion of a North American free trade agreement, there has been a clear downward trend in tariffs in Canada, widespread across economic sectors, due to the country's participation in the

Figure 5.2
Canada: Foreign Control of Enterprises, 1965-1987

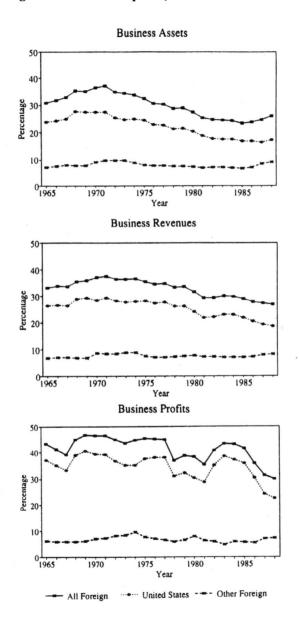

Business Assets

Business Revenues

Business Profits

——— All Foreign   ····•···· United States   -·■·- Other Foreign

Source: 1988 CALURA Report.

Data refer to nonfinancial enterprises.

Table 5.2
Domestic Control of Output of Canadian Productive Sectors, 1970-1987

	1970	1981	1987		1970	1981	1987
TOTAL NONFINANCIAL	63	70	72				
Agriculture & Forestry	93	96	98	Construction	85	89	95
				Wholesale Trade	75	73	73
Total Mining	20	52	60	Retail Trade	81	87	88
Metal Mining	33	66	71	All Utilities	89	93	95
Mineral Fuels	9	42	50	Transportation	89	93	95
Other Mining	35	62	77	Storage	92	98	99
				Communications	88	88	88
				Public Utilities	89	96	97
				Other Services	81	83	90
MANUFACTURING	39	51	52				
(Consumer Goods)	65	67	68	(Staples)	39	56	58
Food	68	74	73	Wood Industries	76	83	78
Beverages	68	65	62	Paper & Allied Ind.	55	72	73
Tobacco	18	0	0	Primary Metals	58	85	82
Rubber Products	9	11	13	Metal Fabrication	50	64	74
Leather Products	73	78	84	Nonmetallic Minerals	44	42	45
Textile Mills	50	48	54	Petroleum & Gas	1	24	26
Knitting Mills	78	82	93				
Clothing Industries	90	84	91				
Furniture	81	89	88				
(High-Tech)	25	34	35				
Printing & Publishing	87	89	91				
Machinery	22	49	47				
Transport Equipment	9	15	15				
Electrical Products	36	37	42				
Chemicals & Products	16	24	24				
Miscellaneous	40	53	65				

Source: Basic data from various years of the CALURA Reports.

Note: The identification of the manufacturing subgroups—indicated by parenthesis—is our own. Some of the ownership for 1970 and a small part of 1980 was assigned using information from Statistics Canada, *Domestic and foreign control of manufacturing, mining, and logging establishments in Canada,* 1981. That source indicates, for all manufacturing industries, an increase of Canadian control from 47.9 to 54.0% over 1970-1981 (p. 13). Averages presented here utilize fixed weights; the weights are the sectors' share of 1981 value added.

GATT (Economic Council of Canada, 1988, pp. 133-35), which should, ceteris paribus, decrease FDI. This explanation of a decline in U.S. investment in Canada looks rather weak because the tariff reductions were already occurring prior to 1970 during the period when FDI was rising. Moreover, Rugman (1990) and others tend to downplay the current importance of tariffs, basing their arguments both on direct survey questionnaires and interviews as well as more formal econometric exercises.

The issue becomes one of changing comparative OLI advantages between the United States and Canada, and may be due to an improvement on Canada's part or a decline in the United States. The latter explanation corresponds to today's conventional wisdom of the relative decline of the U.S. economy, especially in the technologically competitive areas of interest (UNCTC, 1988: 29); the political and economic implications of this for the NAFTA are discussed in Roett (1991). As an explanation for declining U.S. FDI into Canada, this interpretation is insufficient, because that decline was not repeated by U.S. FDI elsewhere in the world, as has been seen.

To the extent that this OLI shift is a relative phenomenon, specific to the United States and Canada, we should also look for the explanation in Canada. With the exception of Meredith (1984), the studies of U.S. FDI into Canada have not attempted a combined analysis of the different variables between the two countries. Moreover, we know of no study that attempts an explanation of the relative weight of U.S. FDI in Canada across time. The data on Canadian R&D in Table 5.3 could support this comparative approach, although as we will show below much of the R&D performed in Canada is due to subsidiaries of U.S. firms. An argument based on concentration immediately confronts the problem that production in Canada is much more concentrated than is production in the

Table 5.3
Canadian Industries: Intramural R&D as Percent of Sales, 1973-1988

	1973	1979	1983	1988
Total All Industries	0.9	0.8	1.2	1.4
Total Mining	0.7	0.7	0.7	0.5
Mining	0.8	0.6	0.8	0.5
Crude Petroleum & Gas	0.6	0.8	0.6	0.6
Manufacturing	0.9	0.9	1.3	1.5
Services	0.6	0.7	0.9	1.4
Transportation	0.2	0.2	0.3	0.4
Electrical Power	0.6	0.9	1.0	1.1
Computer Services	5.8	6.2	12.3	
Engineering Services	* 4.5	7.6	13.4	16.5
Other Nonmanufacturing	3.9	0.6	0.7	1.1

Source: Basic data from Statistics Canada *Industrial Research and Development,* (1982, p. 76; 1985, p. 90; 1988, p. 62).

Note: * For engineering services, the initial year was 1974.

United States. The standard explanation in the Canadian literature of this fact is that indexes such as the CR4 ratio are an inappropriate indicator in a highly open economy such as Canada's because imported products increase competitive pressure (see the discussion in Green, 1990, Chapter 4). The situation is even worse for multibranch activity, because of the presence of U.S. subsidiaries. These are clear limitations of the OLI model.

A slightly different approach investigates total factor productivity (TFP) in Canada compared to that of the United States and interprets a relative increase in Canadian TFP as causing or at least accompanying a decline in the factors that lead to FDI. The relevant work is indeed available to us in Baldwin and Gorecki (1986), who find that Canadian TFP (their TFP4 in Table 6.5) did increase significantly compared to U.S. TFP during the 1970s. However, it must also be noted that the more aggregated analyses done at the OECD such as by Englander et al. (1988) do not lead to such positive conclusions in terms of Canadian technological progress. To summarize, there are some indications that a relative improvement in technology has led to a reduction of MNCs in Canada. Technology and R&D are discussed further in the next chapter.

One explanation for declining U.S. FDI into Canada that is certainly often referred to in popular accounts is the decline in the availability of capital due to crowding out, declining savings, and other factors. While no work directly measuring this will be attempted here, it is worth noting that the United States continued to invest abroad, especially in Europe, by amounts that, if redirected into Canada, would easily have led to a growing presence there. Finally, we note once again that this process cannot be attributed to the Canada-United States Free Trade Agreement, having preceded it by more than a decade.

Outward FDI from Canada

One of the important changes in the Canadian economy in recent years has been the surge in its outward FDI. Two noteworthy characteristics of this are the strong preference for investment into the United States, and the concentration of this investment in certain sectors. Paraphrasing Rugman (1990), these are firms that are expanding due to their own firm specific (ownership) advantages, which were built up in the industries in which Canada has an inherent comparative advantage (raw materials) but which are now due to vertical integration, technological expertise, and so on. There are a few corporations whose advantages are essentially technological; Northern Telecom is the most frequently cited example.

Some basic data on outward Canadian FDI are presented in Table 5.4, in which we can see that there has been a rise in the relative importance of outward compared to inward, that the United States has consistently received over half of Canada's outward investment and that indeed the U.S. share is rising. That the ratio of outward to inward FDI has been growing since around 1960 may principally be a reflection of the decline in U.S. investment in Canada, but recall that outward FDI has also been rising compared to the country's GNP. Although the relevant data from the U.S. Benchmark surveys are not very complete, they do indicate that most of the Canadian FDI in the United States is designed for sales inside that country. Of particular importance for our interests is that the Canadian outward investment tends to concentrate in two areas, natural resource staples and finance/services. The recent review by Gorecki (1990) stresses that this is horizontal investment, that is, lumber or mining companies engaging in the same type of production in Georgia or Colorado as they do at home. Evidence also indicates that the outward FDI is highly concentrated among Canadian firms (Globerman, 1985), although that concentration is declining (Gorecki, 1990). Overall, this information suggests that the Canadian experience is consistent with a basic model of FDI driven by organizational advantages developed by firms in those areas in which Canada has an inherent comparative advantage, such as natural resources. Stretching that term to include beverage industries, this interpretation also implies that Canada has not really developed international competitiveness in a broad cross-section of manufacturing areas.

According to the U.S. Benchmark surveys, over half of Canadian investment is directed towards service and financial areas, which is actually a bit lower than the average for investment into the United States. Thus, in a sense, Canadian investment is slightly more traditional than that of other industrial countries. Some have argued that the interventionist attitudes which characterized the late 1970s in Canada had led to a certain type of capital flight; while this may well have occurred even in the categories of long-term investments under consideration here (banking and real estate, for example), the magnitudes involved in those sectors do not comprise a major part of the total.

The following emerge as tentative conclusions from this review of MNCs in Canada. First of all, there is widespread agreement among economists that MNCs have only marginal impact on productivity and a host of other performance variables such as profitability and capital/labor ratios. Secondly, there is also a widely held view that the tariff reductions implicit in the FTA will not lead to a significant repatriation of capital and entrepreneurs. There is a sizeable group who believe that Canadian R&D efforts are insufficient due in considerable degree to the presence of MNCs that foment a "branch plant" environment. Fourthly, the review of the Canadian literature supports the use of the OLI paradigm in the analysis of MNCs. Finally, the reduction of the U.S. presence in Canada as well as rising Canadian FDI abroad suggest a relative decline in the organizational advantages of U.S. MNCs.

Table 5.4
Stock of Direct Investment Abroad from Canada, 1926-1990
(Million current C$)

	1926	1950	1960	1965	1970	1980	1985	1990
Total	397	990	2,467	3,469	6,188	26,967	54,123	86,678
Manufacturing				2,111	3,207	11,750	24,808	40,054
Min. & Petrol.			543	495	870	8,231	10,316	11,709
Finance			32	165	421	3,695	12,863	24,750
Other Services				698	1,690	3,291	6,136	10,165
Percentage Breakdown								
Manufacturing			61	52	44	46	46	
Min. & Petrol.			14	14	31	19	14	
Finance				5	7	14	24	29
Other Services			20	27	12	11	12	
Investment into the United States as a Percentage of Respective Items								
Total			66	59	54	62	68	61
Manufacturing					59	72	66	
Min. & Petrol.					67	65	66	
Finance							63	48
Other Services						71	69	
Outward Investment as a Percentage of Inward Investment	22	25	19	20	23	44	62	69
Excluding Finance		21		21	25	43	57	62

Disaggregation of Manufacturing OFDI

	1970	Percent	1990	Percent
Manufacturing Total	3,207	100	40,054	100
Beverages	938	29	5,879	15
Nonferrous Metals	837	26	9,860	25
Wood & Paper Products	480	15	10,465	26
Iron & Products	593	18	4,332	11
Chemical Products	112	3	6,517	16
Other Manufacturing	247	8	2,830	7

Sources: Various years of Statistics Canada *Canada's international investment position,* supplemented by *Historical Statistics of Canada.*

FOREIGN INVESTMENT AND MEXICO

In terms of its relationship with foreign investment, this has been a long and eventful century for Mexico. Understanding where things are requires a knowledge of where they have been. In this case, our understanding of the past is evolving, as historians formulate what Florescano (1991) calls the new Mexican past. As revisionists deconstruct some of history's men of bronze, other sacred myths of the revolution are being scrutinized by a new secularism. Central to all of this is the issue of foreign investment.

Chapter Three reviewed how the desire to have Mexicans control key activities in their economy has played a central role throughout most of this century. Indeed, the prerevolutionary government had already obtained majority ownership—although perhaps not control—of the railroads via purchases of stocks at prices that were to remain a source of contention for decades. So what do the data tell us about broad trends?

Although Mexico compares favorably with its southern neighbors in terms of historical data on the stock of capital and FDI, less is known than in Canada or the United States, and so we must work with a broad, heterogeneous set of references in order to examine a significant time period. Utilizing many official and semiofficial Mexican sources as well as the two most important references in English (Reynolds, 1970; Goldsmith, 1985), estimates for a number of sectors in Mexico were assembled and are presented in a set of tables referred to hereafter as Table 5.5. There are significant differences in the underlying quality of the data on total capital stock, foreign investment, and percentage of capital owned by foreigners. Later on in this work, judgments will be made to infer one of these on the basis of the other two, or indeed to choose between different sources.[2]

The earliest point estimate of some degree of confidence is that of Alanís Patiño (1943), who for many years was the country's chief statistician as head of the Dirección General de Estadísticas. Combining information on the stock of capital from the first set of official censuses with externally generated estimates of FDI, he calculated that foreigners owned 40 percent of Mexican wealth in 1930. In order to make a similar calculation for 1902, he needed estimates for the total capital stock in electricity, mining, industry, livestock, farm machinery, commercial establishments, telephone and telegraph, ports, and household goods, for which he assumed ("en forma optimista"—optimistically) values equal to those of 1929 (Alanís Patiño 1943: 104). Using the corresponding estimates for foreign investment, he calculated foreign ownership of total wealth in 1902 at 20 percent. Table 5.5 reports our totals—15 percent for 1902 and 30 percent for 1930—which have eliminated the national debt. These numbers are frequently cited.[3]

Most other estimates of prerevolutionary foreign ownership are higher than Alanís Patiño's. While the studies vary according to coverage (whether to include

Table 5.5a
Estimates of the Stock of Capital in Mexico, Twentieth Century
(Million current pesos through 1960, billion current pesos thereafter)

	1902	1911	1930	1935	1940	1950	1960	1970	1980	1985
Total	7,558p	10,000T	9,692P	14,768p	14,011P	112,338m	428,193m	475T		64,500T
			11,600g		15,210g	78,208x	364,000g			
			19,435y							
Agriculture			3,465p		3,784p	12,868m	52,011m			
			3,422c	4,096c	4,386c	29,567c	92,787c	170c		
of which:										
Land			2,288L		2,781L	20,684L	63,444L	89L		
Livestock			754L	1,140L	6,205L	21,054L	65L			
Const. & Veh.			380L		465L	2,350L	8,289L	16L		
Mines	344z		156p	278c	634p	2,101m	4,946m			876c
							1,444b	6b		
							799B	4B	32B	221B
Petroleum	104d		120p	368c	244p	3,161m	17,334m	25k	654σ	3,626c
							6,866B	25B	384B	800B
Industry			684p	649c	914p	18,965m	83,400m			
							25,095c	58c		15,561c
							18,291B	66B	325B	1,843B
Services			4,963P		7,543P	75,243m	270,502m			21,075c
Transport						6,645m	46,135m	37c		3,526c
							34,307b	39b		
							3,467B	9B	58B	324B
RR		1,600P	1,451p		1,708p			27c		2,448c
Light & Gas		247d	296p		896p		14,720B	33B	133B	284B
							29ü	466δ		5,844c
Telef. & Teleg.	l		43p		58p	930m	4,041m	8B	84B	4,305c
							5,618b	11b		
							14B	0.1B	32B	209B
Construction						690m	3,698m	6b		2,363c
							203B	3B	13B	21B
Commerce			617p		1,019p	9,144m	24,120m	18c		4,254c
							3,221b	20b		
							6,123B	15B	44B	273B
Other Services								38c		3,144c
							3,589b	11b		
							4,407E	10B	45B	417B
Government			810p		1,191p	16,019m	77,118m			
GDPdefl.	6.8	9.3	12.8	11.1	16.6	47.7	100	141	717	7175

Note: The 1985 census gives values at replacement cost; other censuses report historical costs.

Sources: see below

Table 5.5b
Estimates of the Accumulated Stock of Foreign Direct Investment in Mexico (Million current U.S.$)

	1902	1911	1924	1929	1940	1950	1960	1970	1980	1985	1990
Total	460P	1450d 1750h	1258f	1513P	449j	556j	1,081j	2,822s	8,459i	14,629i	30,306i
Agric.		97d	200f 135a		8j	4j	19j	31s	8i	5i	86i
Mines		408d	300f		108j	112j	169j	155s	420i	278i	484i
Petroleum		52d	478f	409r	1j	12j	22j	30s	l	l	l
Industry		65d	60f		32j	148j	602j	2,083s	6,560i	11,381i	18,894i
Services		925D	220f		300j	290j	269j	523s	1,471i	2,965i	10,842i
Trans. & Com.			160f		142j	75j	31j	8s			
Railroads			383p		565d						
Light&Gas		119d			141j	137j	15j	3s			
Telef. & Teleg.	l										
Construction					0j	5j	9j	10s			
Commerce		61d	50f		16j	70j	196j	436s	755i	1,126i	2,060i
Banks		83d 105n									

Table 5.5c
Percentage Foreign Ownership of Mexican Capital, Twentieth Century

	1902	1911	1930	1935	1940	1950	1960	1970	1980	1985
Total	14P,A		30P,A	33p,A	11w,A	4M,A	3M,A			9T,A
							10s,S	13s,S		
Agric.	10z,A		9p,A			<1 M,A	<1 M,A			1T,A
			20e				<1 s,S	<1 s,S		
Mines	97z,A	98z,A	98p,A			46M,A	42M,A			11C,A
							69s,S	56s,S		8T,A
Petroleum	100d,A			99p,A		3M,A	2M,A			1T,A
							1s,S	3s,S		
Industry	29v,A			54p,A	17u,A		30C,A	45C,A		25C,A
							20s,S	28s,S		27T,A
					7M,A		9M,A	29q,S	27q,S	
							32t,A	35ö,S		
Services				42p,A						7T,A
Trans. & Com.							4s,S	1s,S		1T,A
Railroad	71d,S	79p,A								
Light & Gas	98d,S	94z,A	100p,A			49M,A	2M,A			1T,A
							1s,S	1s,S		
Telf. & Teleg.	l	l			60µ		33µ			7T,A
Commerce						7M,A	10M,A			14T,A
							7s,S	7s,S		
Construction						6M,A	1s,S	1s,S		1T,A
Banks	77n,A	40ñ,S								

Codes: A is value of assets; S is value of sales or production

Sources:

a   Aguilera Gómez (1982);

b   Banco de México (1978)—totals are adjusted for depreciation. Use of the 'B' instead of 'b' indicates data from diskettes distributed by the Banco de México, where these data were significantly different from those in the 1978 publication;

c   official census;

d   D'Olwer (1965);

e   Tannenbaum (1929: 360), referring to 1923, foreign as percent of private;

f   Dunn (1926: 91), refers to U.S. investment, which was dominant in mining, petroleum;

g   Goldsmith (1985), referring to "tangible assets";

h   Navarettte (1960);

i   Poder Ejecutivo Federal (1991)—Third *Informe* of President Salinas, reporting SECOFI/CNIE data, which as discussed in Chapter 4, is here judged to overstate recent investments;

j   Banco de México (1982);

k   SPP (1980);

L   Lamartine Yates (1978: 856), there is a minor discrepancy from his census total and the official datum for 1930;

m   Banco de México (1969);

n   Ceceña Gamez (1970: 54) using an exchange rate of 2;

ñ   Moore (1963: 44), referring to deposits.

ö   Fajnzylber and Martínez Tarragó (1976: 154);

p   Alanís Patiño (1943);

q   Casar et al. (1990);

r   Meyer (1977: 10), for 1926—he reports estimates for 1933-36 averaging 316, and for 1937 of 133;

s   Sepulveda y Chumacero (1973)—first year is 1962;

t   NAFINSA (1977), citing 1965 industrial census;

u   using m and c;

ü   Secretaría de Comercio (1977);

v   datum given by Rosenzweig (1965) for percentage of new issues, 1886-1910;

w   calculated using m and denominator of 20,000;

x   multiplying Goldsmith's (1985) datum for 1948 by the ratio of nominal GDP in 1950 to that of 1948;

y   calculated using 1940 GDP and a K/O ratio of 2.5 (Cossio and Izquierdo, 1962: 641)—note the corresponding estimate of the K/O ratio in Reynolds (1970) is 3.3;

z   Sherwell (1929)—latest date is 1926;

ß   Centro de Información y Estudios Nacionales (1983);

δ   Comisión Federal de Electricidad (n.d.);

σ   SPP (1986);

μ   Wright (1971)—first year is 1945;

     The capital letters (D,M,P,C) imply the author has made calculations based on the corresponding sources (d,m,p,c). The T indicates an estimate for which this book's author is primarily responsible. In particular, the total capital for 1911 assumes that the 1902 figure is somewhat too high, and adds to it the net capital inflow; total capital for 1970 assumed a government capital stock of 78 billion, while that for 1985 assumed agricultural stock of 10,000 billion, half land and half capital, and a government capital stock of 11,000 billion— the 1985 values are utilized below in Table 8.3. The "I" indicates item is included in the series above. Services may include "otros." Some data for 1911 is 1910, and some for 1930 is 1929. Some data for the 1920s include factories not in operation. The attempt was made to separate out from the total value of wealth that of cash and government bonds, and to separate industrial bonds from "direct" investment; this latter was not possible for the sources before 1930. The calculations for foreign ownership ratios in 1985 used the end of year exchange rate, which was 44 percent higher than the average for the entire year.

public debt or agricultural land; how to evaluate the railroad bonds), the basic cause of differences in the estimates is that no censuses had been taken. Gordon (1941: 5) speaks loosely of foreigners having one-half of total wealth. Vernon (1963: 43) roughly estimated a level of foreign ownership—outside agriculture and handicraft industries—of two-thirds. Cecefia (1970), using data for the 170 largest corporations in Mexico, presents even higher percentages for the national total (77 percent), and for certain individual sectors. However, as he noted, limiting the comparison to corporations clearly inflates the foreign percentages.[4]

When did foreign ownership of capital in Mexico reach its highest level, just before the Revolution, before the Depression, or just before the nationalization of oil? The first, traditional view, parallels present-day estimates of the ratio of FDI stocks to GDP early in the century. Alanís Patiño undoubtedly realized that his results, based on such a clearly flimsy assumption, contradicted received wisdom. Three items merit consideration. Although recent scholarship has downplayed the extent of destruction outside of agriculture during the Revolution (Haber 1991: 356), it is known that there was a decline in mining, which was predominantly foreign owned. The biggest growth in the petroleum sector, which was virtually entirely foreign owned, occurred during the second decade, after the start of the Revolution.[5] Thirdly, the high point may indeed have been reached between the two dates studied by Alanís Patiño—the inflow of FDI during the first decade was arguably sufficiently large.

One clear message from the data is that the highest level of foreign participation was reached before the 1938 nationalization of petroleum. In both mining and petroleum there had been significant disinvestment before that year. Haber (1991) argues that the accompanying decline in the stock market signals a fall in investor confidence.

In order to study the sectoral trends in FDI, we supplement the data in Table 5.5 with that of Mexico's main investor, the United States, which for these early years was estimated by the consular officers and are presented in Table 5.6. Of course the consistency between the two tables reflects the fact that the U.S. consular reports were the bases for many other estimates.

Even after acknowledging the crudeness of these numbers, several observations seem valid: 1) FDI in mining was larger in value than that in petroleum; 2) mining FDI experienced most of its growth before the Revolution, while petroleum grew during the second decade; 3) while total FDI was declining during the teens, that from the United States was rising due essentially to petroleum; 4) U.S. investment in manufacturing made up perhaps 10 percent of total capital in the industry before the Depression.

The dramatic decline of perhaps U.S.$ 1 billion in the stock of FDI in Mexico during the decade after 1929 certainly deserves further comment. Changes in the agricultural sector account for only a fraction of this change, ($100-200 million), however large individual tracts may have been in terms of absolute size or political impact.[6] The nationalization of petroleum in 1938 involved assets that the sources for our tables valued at U.S.$100 million.[7] Thus, expropriations

Table 5.6
U.S. FDI Stocks in Mexico, by Sector, 1897-1943
(Million current U.S.$)

	1897	1908	1914	1919	1924	1929	1935	1940	1943
Direct & Portfolio	200	672	854	909	1005	975	913		
Direct									
Total	200	416	587	644	735	709	652	358	287
Agriculture	NA	NA	NA	NA	12	13	8	10	14
Manufacturing	0	10	10	8	7	6	6	11	22
Mining	68	234	302	222	236	249	238	168	108
Petroleum	2	50	85	200	250	206	206	42	5
Services								116	106
Railroad	111	57	110	123	139	82	61		
Public Utilities	6	22	33	32	32	90	90		
Other								10	33

Sources: Data for 1897-1935 from Lewis (1938). Other data from American Consular reports as reprinted by Arno Press (1976).

Note: Lewis's reworking of the consular estimates for 1935/36 increased petroleum investments from 69 to 206, reduced the mining total by 25 million, and made small changes in agriculture and manufacturing.

accounted for perhaps only a third of the decline. Disinvestment was more important. This was generalized throughout the economy, as Haber (1991) notes. It was especially noteworthy in mining. As discussed in Chapter 3, this sector had suffered significant destruction during the Revolution and perceived socialistic threats from the government during the 1930s, to which the companies reacted by slow decapitalization.

The "Mexicanization"—majority ownership by Mexican nationals—of a much weaker mining sector was finally decreed in 1961. This came soon after the nationalization of electrical power in 1960, and the Mexicanization of telephones in 1958. These events are reflected in the data in Table 5.5.

Mexico's industrial sector did not undergo these extreme fluctuations between complete and null foreign ownership. The indications presented in Table 5.5 are that this sector has always been significantly in the hands of Mexicans. Any such conclusion inevitably depends on the definition of an industrial enterprise; particularly at the beginning of the century the weight of artisan shops in employment (and perhaps output) must have been high. Textiles was probably the most important sector of pre-revolutionary manufacturing industry and experienced significant foreign investment, especially from Spain and France. In the investigation by Ceceña Gamez (1969) of the 170 largest corporations in prerevolutionary Mexico, 84 percent of industrial capital was foreign owned in 1911, a finding starkly at odds with the breakdown by nationality of capital invested in corporate industry (1886-1910), cited by Rosenzweig (1965: 453) and included in Table 5.5. Further complicating the picture is the fact that many foreigners, especially Spaniards, eventually stayed in Mexico, becoming citizens. Note in Table 5.5 that the Industrial Census of 1935 stated that slightly over half of manufacturing capital and production was controlled by foreigners, which may reflect this upward bias.

The narrative of Chapter 3 indicated that policy underwent a major reorientation during the 1940s. The data for the post-World War II period in Table 5.5 suggest levels of foreign ownership significantly lower than one-half. Even for these more recent times, there remain problems with the data, particularly because of the complications caused by inflation. Note that the data based on censuses lead to an exaggeration of the weight of foreign ownership because they utilized historical cost.

That table suggests that the foreign presence fell during the middle decades of the century. As discussed above, it is not clear if that decline began around 1910 or around 1930. The percentage of foreign ownership reached a low point in the 1970s. The ratio has accelerated upward in the 1980s, recently achieving the early post-World War II levels. In many ways this is the inverse image of the experience of Canada.

An increase in foreigners' share of manufacturing assets and production is revealed by the data for the 1960s (Fajnzylber and Martínez Tarragó, 1976: 247) and contributed to the restrictive law on FDI of 1973. Such a relative increase did not occur in the aggregates for those service sectors for which data are available. Indeed, these data provide evidence for the phenomenon mentioned in Chapter 3; progressive nationalization of mining and certain services at the same time as foreign ownership of industry was rising. However, between 1970 and 1980, the weight of MNCs in sales of Mexican industry remained relatively constant at about 28 percent, according to Casar et al. (1990), repeated in Table 5.7. Those authors argue that this is the net response of conflicting pressures: the 1973 law and the expansion of parastatals, versus the continued growth and technological domination of MNCs in several areas. There is no publicly available information on more-recent levels of sales of MNC affiliates in Mexico.

Comparing Mexican data with that for other Latin American countries suggests that the share—in either total capital or GDP—of foreign capital in Mexico is currently about average for the region, while Brazil has a slightly higher rate of foreign control (Dunning and Cantwell, 1987; also Table 4.1). In addition, while the United States has always been the major source of foreign capital, the relative participation of U.S. FDI has been declining, from 70 percent in 1974 to 63 percent in 1990 (SECOFI, 1992: Cuadro 6). Although the United States is also the major source of FDI for the northern Andean countries, this is not true for major southern cone countries: Europe has 43 percent of FDI in Brazil compared to 32 percent for the United States; in Argentina the breakdown

Table 5.7
Mexico. Foreign Firms' Share of Manufacturing Production: 1970 and 1980
(Percent)

	1970	1980
Total	28.7	27.2
Foodstuffs	11.1	11.0
Beverages	29.6	29.8
Tobacco	96.8	78.0
Textiles	12.0	8.8
Clothing and Footwear	4.9	7.9
Wood and Cork Products	4.3	5.7
Furniture and Other Wooden	3.8	11.2
Cellulose and Paper	32.9	23.1
Printing and Publishing	7.9	9.7
Leather Goods	2.5	11.7
Rubber Products	66.9	66.6
Chemicals	46.8	35.2
Pharmaceuticals and Cosmetics	55.9	72.5
Oil byproducts	75.0	55.6
Nonmetallic Mineral Products	17.7	11.9
Basic Metals	46.6	14.1
Metallic Products	20.6	19.5
Nonelectrical Machinery	52.1	48.6
Electrical Machinery	50.1	57.9
Transport Equipment	64.0	68.9
Miscellaneous	33.1	40.0

Source: Peres Nuñez (1990: 19), reporting calculations of José Casar.

is 50 percent and 48 percent, and in Chile it is 41 percent and 40 percent.[8] This pattern has existed for many years.

One noteworthy example of foreign investment in Mexico is that associated with the maquila sector. As noted in the previous chapter, this program was established in 1965, after the *bracero* program was discontinued as a means to generate employment while taking advantage of U.S. provisions for special tax treatment of goods processed for reexport. Originally located on the U.S. border, the maquila (or *maquiladora*—literally, golden mills) plants spread to the Yucatán and are now allowed throughout most of the country. Major processing activities include electronics, transport equipment, and textiles. The amount invested in maquila plants is not known, although Sklair (1989: 75) cites a business study estimating that they represent one-quarter of total FDI in the country. Data on nationality of ownership is also not published; Sklair's source puts this as 90 percent from the United States. Other sources estimate this to be much lower, although most would agree that Sklair's number reflects conventional wisdom as to the major market for the products.

Employment in the maquilas has grown to nearly half a million workers, which is almost one-fifth of the manufacturing sector's work force. Most of the work done is simple, repetitive operations on partially manufactured imported items. Thus it is not surprising that the domestic value added is only one-fourth of the value of output. More important, wages and salaries are one-half of value added, and the use of locally purchased inputs is only 2 percent of total inputs. The maquilas are an important source of foreign exchange, providing U.S.$4.1 billion in 1991 out of a total current account inflow of U.S.$46 billion.[9] Given the large purchases of U.S. goods by maquila workers as well as the repatriation of profits, the net impact is surely smaller.

The initial tendency of maquila plants to concentrate hiring on young female workers has moderated recently, in the so-called second wave of maquila growth.[10] Other newer characteristics include greater use of Mexican technicians and administrators, larger and technologically more complex plants, and a modest shift away from "Taylorization"—mass production techniques. Nevertheless, labor turnover continues to average 200-300 percent per year, and the lack of integration with the local productive structure together with environmental problems partially explained by the exhaustion of local infrastructural capacities continue to be the focus of criticism of national policy.

An indirect offshoot of the maquila is the encouragement of similar processing factories in several parts of the country. Although these plants do not have maquila status in terms of taxes, they share key characteristics of being processors of materials brought into the country for subsequent export and foreign ownership. Important examples are the Ford plant in Hermosillo and the IBM operations outside Guadalajara. These plants utilize world state-of-the-art technology and have found a local labor force that is young, healthy, and eager to learn. Government officials and plant managers proudly point to the increases in domestic content of the operations.

Let us turn from this description of the growth of FDI in Mexico to some observations on its performance in the country. Naturally, there are many ways in which the economic behavior of MNCs might be different there from what it is in Canada and the United States. Nevertheless, utilization of the OLI model as the basis for a comparison of the role of MNCs in Canada and the United States did provide some fruitful insights as well as suggesting useful parallel lines of inquiry. We believe the same is true for the situation of foreign investment in Mexico.

First of all, of course, there is ample evidence that average profit rates, capital labor ratios, import propensities, foreign payments for licensing and royalties, and so on, all tend to be higher among MNCs than in national firms in Mexico (Sepulveda and Chumacero, 1973; Fajnzylber and Martínez Tarragó, 1976; Blomström and Persson, 1983; Casar et al., 1990). It is becoming clear that this responds to the industrial organization factors emphasized in the OLI paradigm. MNCs tend to be located in the more dynamic sectors, concentrating in sectors with barriers to entry, especially those created by economies of scale and by technological requirements (Blomström, 1985; Casar et al., 1990). This is consistent with the theory of MNCs described earlier.

In a series of papers, Blomström expands on the above discussion, specifically in terms of associating concentration and technological advantages when discussing the impact of MNCs. Blomström and Casar et al. further suggest that the presence of MNCs has positive effects on labor productivity even after allowance for scale, quality, K/L ratios, and similar factors, to a degree that is apparently larger than that seen in the papers referred to above on Canada, although the papers on Mexico refer to labor productivity while the Canadian work treats total factor productivity. This result has been used to argue that MNCs thereby contribute to the process of productivity convergence (Blomström and Wolff, 1989), an issue that has been receiving increasing attention of late (Willmore, 1986; Dollar, 1991). There is also some evidence that the MNCs initially speed up the concentration process inside an industry.

Some recently published data (INEGI, 1988) permit further analysis of the role of MNCs and industrial concentration. Industrial sectors specified at the four-digit level were classified by percentage of foreign ownership, and 61 percent of Mexican manufacturing capital belonged to sectors where the foreign-owned ratio was less that 25 percent. Furthermore, most of the foreign capital was in majority-owned industries. There is a strong positive correlation between concentration and percentage of foreign ownership, and, comparing the data for 1970 and 1980, that positive correlation also holds true for changes in concentration versus changes in percentage ownership by foreigners. Recalling that Meller (1978) established that a number of Latin American countries had parallel industrial concentration ratios, it might also be noted that the Mexican data look quite similar to the Canadian numbers in this regard.

An important consideration is the relationship of foreign ownership and exports, and, particularly, who will produce the new exports that NAFTA will presumably generate. A quick overview of the major export items is useful. Out of a total current account inflow of U.S.$46 billion in 1991, $27 billion were provided by merchandise exports, and the rest were mainly maquila services ($4 billion) and tourism ($6 billion). The merchandise exports break down into three roughly equal-sized categories; petroleum and derivatives, raw material intensive goods, and manufactured goods. Foreign ownership is concentrated in this last category, over half of which was automotive products ($5.8 billion). There has been no foreign ownership of oil, and very little in the other major raw material products, such as cement, steel, agricultural products, and so on.[11]

The export items most difficult to characterize with regard to nationality of producers are the "other" manufactured goods. Its value might be put at U.S.$4 billion and would cover a wide range, such as textiles, bathroom fixtures, plastics, and typewriters, as well as more maquila-type products such as computer components. Not surprisingly, this group has been the focus of a number of studies. In one of the most authoritative, Unger (1990), it is argued that Mexican owned firms dominate in the export of technologically stagnant and/or homogeneous products, and that the greater part of exports of components is in the hands of MNCs. That author, who refers to his conceptual framework as economies of scope, does see a potential for a growing role for Mexican producers in the exportation of complex manufactured products along product cycle lines. Nevertheless, his emphasis on economies of scale and MNC strategies of intrafirm pricing, suggests a certain fatalism as to the possibilities of important inroads in the short to medium term.

Finally, mention should be made of the one study on FDI in Mexico (Shah and Slemrod, 1990), which studies the importance of tax rates as a determinant of FDI. These authors report that the Mexican regulatory climate and tax rates in both the host and source countries have clear impacts on FDI flows. In their regressions, protectionism in Mexico, as indicated by the effective rate of protection, has only mixed effects on FDI inflows.

Outward Investment from Mexico

Although attention is usually focused on investment into Mexico, the country has sent FDI abroad. This author does not know of any governmental source providing relevant statistics, although we know from the U.S. sources that Mexicans have invested around U.S.$600 million in that country (compared to U.S.$11 billion in FDI from the United States into Mexico). Typical of the investing firms are Vitro and Cemex, specializing in glass and cement, respectively. As was the case with Canadian OFDI, the Mexican firms expanding abroad are natural-resource based. Part of their motive for the northbound investment is to lessen protectionist pressures. An additional comment is that these Monterrey-based firms have had little government aid in these activities and have been held up as models by governmental spokespersons for their success.

There are other dynamic areas of Mexican FDI into the United States. One is agribusiness, again partially to avoid trade restrictions in the host country, as argued by Mares (1987). Also noteworthy is the investment by the Mexican television conglomerate Televisa, which for some years has operated channels in a number of U.S. cities and recently purchased Univisión, an erstwhile competitor usually associated with other Latin Americans. In contrast to the above examples of natural-resource based FDI, these two cases represent instances where the firms' advantages were due to geographical proximity and/or cultural linkages. Their role in the integration of the border region is often overlooked by commentators from the business and political capitals of the two countries.

COMPARISONS BETWEEN CANADA AND MEXICO

In the first table of Chapter 4 we saw that the level of FDI in Canada (however measured) has been higher than that in any other developed country throughout this century. Every Mexican schoolchild knows that foreign ownership of key economic activities was also very high at the turn of the century and that for the next fifty years conflicts between the Mexican government and foreign investors cast a long shadow over all historical events. The widely different politics superimposed over roughly parallel economic situation makes comparisons of the two countries' experiences particularly interesting.

Graphs summarizing the available data on foreign investment for Canada and Mexico, are presented on the following page as Figure 5.3. We will discuss first the top pair of graphs, which leads into consideration of the other two.

In the early years of this century, the value of the stock of foreign investment was greater than GNP in both countries, with the ratio for Canada being slightly higher. Foreign investment has declined significantly with respect to GNP, with the relative decline being greater in terms of long-term loans to the private sector ("portfolio investment") than was the relative decline in FDI. Note also the decline of the position of the United Kingdom with respect to the United States.

That Canada had received a large amount of foreign investment before World War I is quite familiar in the economic history literature. The same is true for Australia and Argentina. Less well known is the fact that during the first decade of this century, the absolute size of the capital inflow into Mexico, direct plus portfolio, was about the same as what entered Canada—over U.S.$1 billion. What makes the comparison exciting is that Mexico's GDP was half that of Canada. The paths diverge most dramatically after 1910, of course, with the Revolution slowing if not stopping capital inflow into Mexico, while another billion dollars entered Canada by 1914.[12] Moreover, capital continued to flow into Canada after the world war had broken out, although much of this was capital flight from Europe. While there are good reasons to think of Canada as the classic recipient of FDI, the juxtaposition of the situation of Mexico highlights important ways in which the Mexican case was even more noteworthy.

Canada and Mexico were not unique in terms of their common experiences of a high ratio of FDI to GDP early in the century and the decline in that ratio sometime after 1930. Some illustrative data are shown in Table 5.8, for several countries for which such an exercise is not completely impossible. Although the United States had received the largest amount of foreign investment before World War I, as a fraction of GNP this amounted to less than 20 percent (Wilkins, 1989: 155). Pursuit of this topic would take us too far afield not merely in terms of recipient countries but also because the major capital exporting countries are European.[13]

While any number of political factors might be called into action to explain Figure 5.3's decline in foreign investment compared to GDP, especially in Mexico, we would prefer to concentrate on some long-term economic causes. A common element in the decline of foreign investment (relative to GDP) in both Canada and Mexico was the reduced importance of railroads—often foreign-owned or financed—due to the growing use of (domestically owned) motorcars. It might also be noted that the distinction between direct and portfolio investment

Figure 5.3
Canada and Mexico: Relative Size of IFDI, Twentieth Century

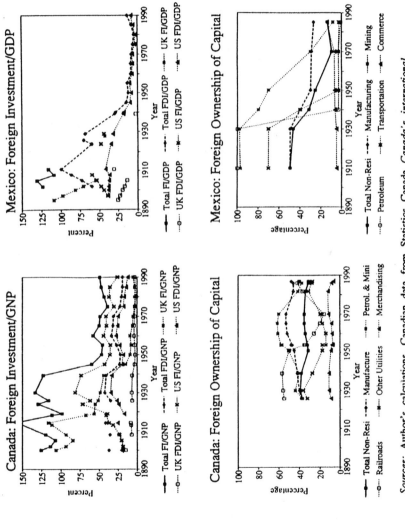

Sources: Author's calculations. Canadian data from Statistics Canada *Canada's international investment position*, and Urquhart and Buckley (1965; 1983). Investment data for Mexico from the sources of Table 5.5. GDP from Cárdenas (1987) and INEGI.

Table 5.8

Foreign Investment as Percentage of GDP in Some Latin American Countries and Australia, 1913-1938

	1913	1929	1938
Argentina	100-196	62-95	67
Brazil	64-100	65-107	48
Chile		80	136
Colombia		34	
Cuba	110	200	196
Australia	99		59

Sources: U.S. foreign investment data from U.S. Department of Commerce (1960), and Lewis (1938). For the United Kingdom, the data sources are Stone (1987), Rippy (1959), Bank of England (1950), and United Nations (1955). French investment in Argentina and Brazil from United Nations (1955). GDP estimates calculated or presented: for Argentina, Diaz Alejandro (1970); Brazil, Chile, Cuba, Mitchell (1983); Colombia UN ECLA (1957); Australia Butlin (1962).

Note: Data refer to totals near the indicated years. In most cases, the GDP total was calculated using published estimates of price and output changes with respect to a later year when official estimates were available. Different estimates of quantities in the earlier years for Brazil are the main cause of the wide range of estimates. For Argentina in 1913 and 1929, Diaz Alejandro (1970) reports UN-ECLA estimates of foreign investment which are much larger than those of the sources indicated below. Other foreign investment data refer to totals (excluding government bonds) from the United States and the United Kingdom, and, for Argentina and Brazil, from France. German investment in the region in 1914 was about U.S.$900 million, or 10 percent of the total; its breakdown by country is not available.

is particularly weak in the case of railroads[14] and that the value of motor vehicles and highways is often not included in reported capital stock totals, thus imposing a downward bias on some of the more recent estimates of capital and the capital output ratio.

Related to this but very much worth emphasizing in its own right is that in both countries there was a significant fall—a reduction by perhaps one-half—of the capital output ratio (K/O) (see Table 5.9). Goldsmith (1985) reports falling capital output ratios for a number of countries in early stages of industrialization, with increasing K/O more recently (a finding robust to different specifications of capital/assets), but he does not attempt an explanation of this phenomenon and indeed only comments on changing factorial distribution of income as a possible cause. Our results here strongly suggest an examination of evolution along sectoral lines. One example is the capital intensity of railroads and other infrastructure that had been significantly expanded during the quarter-century before World War I and would subsequently facilitate the development of other,

Table 5.9
Twentieth Century Capital Output Ratios in Canada and Mexico
(Capital and Output data are current values, in billion national currency)

CANADA

	1926	1930	1939	1951	1954	1960	1965	1970	1985
Capital	10.6	12.9	11.9	20.8	28.2	45.6	60.0	90.9	411.2
GNP	5.1	5.7	5.6	21.6	25.9	38.4	55.4	85.7	463.6
K/O ratio	2.1	2.3	2.1	1.0	1.1	1.2	1.1	1.1	0.9

MEXICO

	1902	1911	1930	1935	1940	1950	1960	1970	1985
Author's Estimates									
Capital	7.6	10.0	9.6	14.8	14.0	112.3	428.2	475.0	64,500
GDP	1.6	2.9	4.4	4.3	7.8	39.7	150.5	418.7	47,402
K/O ratio	4.8	3.4	2.2	3.4	1.8	2.8	2.8	1.1	1.4
Reynolds's estimated K/O			4.2		3.3	2.3	2.2		
Goldsmith's estimated K/O			2.9		2.4	1.8	2.2		2.6

Sources: for Canada: Capital from various years of *Canada's international investment position,* GNP from *Historical Statistics* and *Canadian Economic Observer.* This measure of capital does not include agriculture, financial institutions, residential nor governmental buildings. For Mexico: GDP from Solís (1988: 92), and INEGI *Cuentas nacionales.* Capital stocks from Table 5.5a. Capital output ratios from Reynolds (1970: 50)—first year is 1925, and Goldsmith (1985: 39)—for the years 1930, 1940, 1948, 1965, 1978.

Note: While coverage varies among authors, each maintains consistency over time. Note also that Goldsmith does not include his previously published estimates for earlier years. With regard to earlier trends of the capital output ratio in Canada, we do not know of published estimates of the corresponding capital stock. However, letting a = K/O, b = rate of growth of GNP, and c = the (net) investment ratio, then the capital output ratio will decline if c-ab<0. For the early decades of this century, b = 0.04, and c = 0.05 (Firestone, 1958), hence for any reasonable a, the condition for a declining K/O would have been met.

less capital intensive activities. In addition, mining and petroleum were significantly more capital intensive than was manufacturing so that the growth of the latter also contributed to the falling overall K/O ratio. While it is clear that the capital/land ratio grew in Canada and Mexico during the first half of this century, "technological progress" may also have reduced agriculture's K/O ratio.

In a sense, therefore, half of the drop in the top two figures in Figure 5.1 is an optical illusion; if total capital falls with respect to total output, then foreign capital is observed to decline with respect to output even if foreign capital is a fixed share of total capital. Indeed, our data suggest that the ratio of foreign investment to GDP fell in Mexico during the early years of the century, when the foreign share of total capital may have increased. The latter indicator has often been utilized in the literature as indicating an increase in foreign dependence (recently by Womack, 1978), while the former index would presumably argue the opposite. As a matter of arithmetic, these two trends can both be true if the K/O ratio is falling sufficiently.[15]

The two graphs at the bottom of Figure 5.3 compare foreign-owned to total capital, the latter being estimates of nonresidential fixed reproducible capital. From our previous discussions we know that the data for Canada are more reliable than those for Mexico. Nevertheless, there are two or three points that may be confidently asserted. First of all, before the 1930s Depression, the fraction of foreign ownership was only slightly higher in Mexico (~45 percent) than for Canada (~40 percent). That ratio fell drastically in Mexico to less than 15 percent in 1970. The corresponding fluctuations in Canada were much smaller, not changing more than 10 percent since 1926.[16] Looking at the sectoral subtotals, we see that the changes were much larger in Mexico, particularly in transport and the raw material export sectors. Foreign ownership of manufacturing varies in both countries, only slightly more in Mexico than in Canada.[17]

We turn now to a simple exercise comparing a disaggregation of the changes in foreign ownership of the two economies. An overall view of the trends in Canadian capital can be seen in Table 5.10. As discussed earlier, foreign ownership there traces a ∩ shape in both manufacturing and mining, with the declines coming rather more quickly after the mid-1970s. As can be seen in the table, the sectoral distribution of capital remained relatively constant over the century, with the exception of an increase in petroleum and mining, which mirrored the decline in railroads. Using a standard shift/share analysis, the table shows that the overall change in the weight of foreign investment is roughly split evenly between changing foreign ownership in each sector and the changing weight of capital stock of the individual sectors.

While the available data on capital stock in Mexico is not nearly as good as that for Canada, an attempt at depicting broad trends can also be attempted on the basis of the data in Table 5.5 and is also presented in Table 5.10. As in Canada, the decline in railroads in Mexico is a major occurrence, affecting both the sectoral weights and the foreign ownership ratio. While both sets of factors are important, it would appear that the major factor "explaining" the overall change in foreign ownership in Mexico is changes in foreign ownership of individual sectors, and that changes in the relative weights of the sectors were rather less significant.

Table 5.10
Disaggregation of Changes in Foreign Ownership of Capital in Canada and Mexico

CANADA

	1926-1954	1954-1970	1970-1986		1926-1954	1954-1970	1970-1986
Change in Foreign Ownership	-5	3	-4				
	Due to Sectoral Changes in Foreign Ownership				Due to Changing Sectoral Weights		
Manufacturing	3	2	-2		2	-1	-1
Petrol., Mining, & Gas	2	0	-4		3	3	1
Petroleum & Gas	NA	0	-2		NA	3	3
Mining & Smelting	NA	0	-1		NA	0	-1
Services & Merchandising	-11	-1	3		-2	-1	-0
Railroads	-3	-3	4		-6	-3	-1
Other Utilities	-3	1	2		1	1	1
Merchand. & Construction	-0	1	-1		0	0	-0

MEXICO

	1910-1930	1930-1950	1950-1970	1970-1985	1910-1930	1930-1950	1950-1970	1970-1985
Change in Foreign Ownership	-3	-21	-17	4				
	Due to Sectoral Changes in Foreign Ownership				Due to Changing Sectoral Weights			
Agriculture	-0	-2	0	0	0	-1	0	-0
Mining	0	-3	-1	-0	-6	-7	-0	0
Petroleum	0	-2	0	-0	0	1	0	-0
Industry & Construction	0	-3	-0	-0	3	4	0	4
Services	0	-12	-15	1	-0	6	-6	0
Transport	0	-18	0	-0	-2	-14	0	-0
Light, Gas, Telef., & Teleg.	0	-3	-15	0	2	24	-9	0
Commerce	0	0	0	0	0	-0	-0	0
Others	0	0	0	1	-0	0	-0	-0

Source: Author's calculations, based on *Canada's international investment position,* various years, and Table 5.5.

Note: The estimate for agriculture for Mexico does not include the value of land.

Designating k_i as the share of sector i in total capital, and f_i as the foreign share of capital in sector i, then the total foreign share of capital equals $\Sigma(f_i k_i)$. Changes over time in the foreign share can be disaggregated into two components. That corresponding to the change in foreign ownership is $\Sigma(k_i \Delta f_i)$, and that for the change in sectoral weights is $\Sigma(f_i \Delta k_i)$.

FINAL COMMENTS

Do Canada and Mexico have more in common than trying to live in harmony with but distinct from the United States? Their experiences with foreign investment provide a number of fruitful points of departure for comparative analysis. The previous section argued the analytical comparability of the evolution of FDI in the two economies, even with differences in the timing and magnitude of shifts of ownership. The use of the OLI paradigm certainly facilitates a search predicated on commonality—in the road markers, if not the terrain. Both the third chapter and this chapter have indicated differences in the policy approach toward FDI, although there is an important parallel in the reversal of nationalist attitudes towards FDI, which indeed, at least according to some criteria, reached their respective zeniths in the 1970s. Two other phenomena stand out as important shared experiences. First, both countries are engaged in outward FDI, which is concentrated in resource-intensive activities as well as certain services. Second, in both countries the relative participation of the United States in their inward FDI has been declining.

NOTES

1. According to data in the August 1992 *Survey of Current Business,* the distribution of the capital stock in the United States is very similar.

2. One important inconsistency relates to the differences between census data on capital stock and the estimates of the Banco de México, which are much lower. Unfortunately, that source is the only one providing annual estimates of capital stock, nominal or deflated. Their use in studies of technological change creates doubts as to the worth of those investigations.

3. For example, in Goldsmith (1966), which served as a reference for many post-World War II authors, such as Fremantle (1974). It might be noted that the highest percentage foreign ownership reported by Goldsmith is 50 percent, citing A. Navarette in *México 50 Años de Revolución,* Volume 1, p. 521. That number does not appear on the cited page. Womack (1978) also presents the Alanís Patiño data.

4. Ceceña reports an estimated total capital in 1911 at 1,650 million pesos, which is less than a third of the nonagricultural totals presented by Alanís Patiño for either 1902 or 1930. Because of these doubts about the representativity of the data Ceceña used, his estimates were not included in the table in the text. One suspects that the ultimate source for Vernon's figure is the same as that of Ceceña. D'Olwer (1965) discussed two earlier estimates of foreign ownership in 1910, of 67 and 73 percent, but rejected them, judging either the numerator or the denominator to be seriously in error.

5. Note that Alanís Patiño's results can therefore be read to emphasize the importance the growth of petroleum investments. While this has obvious interpretations in terms of the zeitgeist of his period, no such attribution is implied here.

6. We have not seen an estimate of the monetary value of foreign owned land before the revolution. One frequently cited estimate is that foreigners owned 25 percent of farmland. While most of that was nonproductive desert, some of it was obviously very profitable. (Aguilera Gómez, 1982: 94)

7. Meyer (1977: 10), who notes that the companies claimed that their firms were worth $450 million, including reserves underground. The amount of the eventual cash payments to the companies was very small, but this occurred during World War II, when the home governments may have rewarded them in other ways. U.S. firms accounted for 30-40 percent of the total in Meyer's table, reflecting the disinvestment mentioned in the text.

8. Sources: for Brazil, the *Boletim Mensal* of the Banco Central do Brasil, September, 1986; for the other countries, Dunning and Cantwell, 1987. According to the 1990 *Revista del Banco de la República* of Colombia, U.S. firms own 71 percent of that country's FDI stocks.

9. See Banco de México, *Informe Anual, 1991* and various years of the *Anuario Estadístico*.

10. See Sklair (1989) and González-Arechiga (1989) for useful discussions. There is a rapidly growing literature on the maquilas by researchers on both sides of the border as well as from other continents. One suspects that the major impact of the maquila is not its macro effect on one or the other economy but rather its strengthening and integration of the border zone relative to the rest of both countries.

11. Of course, privatization of steel and other activities will leave some of these activities in foreign hands.

12. The capital inflow refers to portfolio and direct. For Canada, these estimates are those of Viner and are available in *Historical Statistics of Canada*. For Mexico see Table 5.5. Estimates of Mexican GDP are from Cárdenas (1987), converted at 2 pesos/dollar. Canadian GNP from Ankli (1980: 267).

13. Some related items, discussed for example in United Nations (1955), are: 1) the strong short-term instability of U.K. investments; 2) the fact that, in addition to Mexico and Canada, the only other country in the hemisphere to receive significant investment from the United States prior to World War I was Cuba; 3) the decline in French and German investments as a result of that war; 4) the stagnation of British investments during the interwar period and their abrupt collapse afterwards, apparently through the sale of assets to nationals—rather than other foreigners; 5) French investments followed the British pattern in emphasizing railroads and government bonds, while the German investments were more concentrated in manufacturing and primary production. For U.S. portfolio investments, see Stallings (1987).

14. For the parallel argument applied to the case of investment in Canadian railroads, see Edelstein (1982: 36).

15. Although it does not directly relate to the discussion in the text, it is curious that our estimates show a decline in the K/O ratio after 1960, while the last estimate of Goldsmith is for an increase. It is unlikely that this is solely due to our underestimating the two items on which no data are published, agriculture and government property.

16. In the graph and in the corresponding discussion in the text we have omitted the period of the Depression itself. The Canadian data relate a large jump in the value of foreign holdings compared to the total value of the capital stock. It would appear that this reflects prices and exchange rates and not massive transactions.

17. Without pretending an analysis of ownership of capital in Canada prior to 1926, we will report that Dunn (1926: 59) cites United States *Commerce Reports* to the effect that in 1920, 65 percent of Canadian "industrial capital" (including lumber, smelting, and electricity generation as well as manufacturing) was in the hands of Canadians.

6

FDI, GROWTH, AND TECHNOLOGY TRANSFER

The public statements of officials from the three governments have tended to describe the benefits of a free trade agreement in terms of increasing economic growth. In the case of Mexico, in particular, this has frequently involved explicit mention of foreign investment; its perceived role for U.S. policymakers is also important, although at times less explicit. This chapter approaches that issue by reviewing both the theoretical and empirical literature on this subject. The expectation is that there will be synergies in the attempt; that the effort of juxtaposing the disparate literatures will yield new insights.

There are a number of channels by which the interactions of multinational companies and a Free Trade Agreement could affect the levels of income and growth: via savings and investment, via exports and/or imports, by achieving economies of scale, by improving efficiency and competitiveness, and by increasing technology. Traditionally, treatments of exports and investment correspond to aggregate demand, and the latter three are supply. However, much of the discussion on FDI and exports is clearly of a supply nature; a firm goes to a host country because the firm wishes to utilize its organizational advantages in production. Additionally, secondary effects are specifically demand; displacement of the home country's exports by MNC sales abroad or reduction in domestic purchasing power due to overseas payments of capital. While no corresponding general model will be attempted here, it is helpful to note from the start the differences in approach and to comment that the statements of public officials are frequently inconsistent mixes of them.

ECONOMIES OF SCALE AND TRADE LIBERALIZATION

In order to prepare the way for a discussion of MNCs and technological change, we will focus first on economies of scale in the context of trade liberalization. Let us begin with Canada, where this analysis has proceeded farthest and where its link to the question of foreign ownership is clearest. We noted in Chapter 2 the widespread acceptance among Canadian economists of the Eastman-Stykolt hypothesis regarding the existence of untapped economies of scale due to the market-limiting effects of protectionism. Extensive subsequent research should provide us with some insight. There are two separate but related lines of investigation: that focusing on economies of scale and that on trade liberalization.

Although the U.S. economy is roughly ten times the size of Canada's, the latter's disadvantages due to nonachievement of economies of scale are not nearly that high. The more appropriate size comparison is that of the average of individual plants in the two countries, which Baldwin and Gorecki (1986: 18) estimate to average "only" 20-40 percent smaller in Canada. Note that an increase in output may not necessarily raise average plant size by the same amount because of the possibility of new entrants. They also estimate (p. 149) that a fourfold increase in market size will eliminate the plant size differential. However, the total productivity differential between the manufacturing sectors of the two countries is estimated to be 25-40 percent (p. 134). Baldwin and Gorecki estimate that the degree of returns to scale (the elasticity of output to inputs, minus unity) is of the order of 15 percent (p. 58).[1] Thus, increasing average plant size in Canada to the U.S. level would only eliminate one-third of the total differential in productivity.[2]

What are the other factors differentiating productivity?   Diversity of production in individual plants associated with low scale receives some attention. They reject the "miniature replica" or "branch plant" economy argument that was summarized earlier due to their finding that the presence of foreign investment has positive effects on scale or total factor productivity. Baldwin and Gorecki's results in their Chapter 7 highlight the importance on x-efficiency of greater import penetration and reduced tariff protection. Although not the subject of their study, they note that the comparison of data for 1970 and 1979 shows a relative improvement in Canadian performance, accompanying the period of trade liberalization in the GATT. Baldwin and Gorecki clearly support the Eastman-Stykolt hypothesis, and favor trade liberalization.

How might these results be applied to Mexico? Different considerations pull in opposite directions. The gap in total productivity is probably much higher for Mexico, paralleling the larger difference in income levels. However, it is less clear that differences in average plant sizes would be nearly as large, which would imply that potential gains for Mexico due to untapped returns to scale are also small. Moreover one expects that, just as in Canada, factors other than scale would be more important in affecting productivity; for Mexico these include educational levels, R&D, infrastructure, and so forth. In summary, this reading of the results of Baldwin and Gorecki would imply that the effect in Mexico of trade liberalization will be less due to scale than to technological improvement.

Other studies of trade liberalization place more emphasis on potential gains to scale. As background, recall that in 1965, Canada and the United States signed an accord, commonly known as the Auto Pact, that eliminated the former country's tariffs on imports of motor vehicle parts and equipment from the latter. The situation involved the same firms (the U.S. "big three"), which must have facilitated negotiations as well as guaranteeing that the benefits of employment and production were shared between the two countries. It is clear that the Canadian production has benefited from the economies of producing for a much larger market.[3]

With that experience fresh in mind, the Wonnacotts argued in favor of free trade between the United States and Canada, estimating that the benefits to Canada of bilateral free trade would be of the order of 7 to 10.5 percent of GNP (1967: 300), rather evenly split between gains to producers (greater efficiency) and to consumers (lower prices). Subsequent estimates for Canada have not exceeded that upper bound and have tended to place greater emphasis on gains on the side of production. An analytical breakthrough was the work of Harris and Cox (1984), which analyzed the gains from economies of scale in the context of trade liberalization, and calculated the country's total gain at 8-10 percent of GNP. It should be recalled that previous estimates of the gains from free trade that ignored scale effects had typically been from one-half to only one-tenth of this magnitude, and that estimates of the gains to partial liberalization, such as in the case of the EEC or LAFTA, were not necessarily even positive.

The results of Harris and Cox quickly found their detractors. Many international economic theorists were reluctant to accept an assumption of increasing returns to scale, although that opposition has been declining. Daly and Rao (1986) asserted that there was grave inconsistency between the implicit order of magnitude of economies of scale in Harris and Cox, and the historical experience of Canada under the GATT trade liberalization. Their analysis also questioned whether Harris and Cox had exaggerated the level of increasing returns to scale at the expense of technological change. Wigle (1988) presented estimates on potential income gains using a similar model, but with results that were low or even negative. Stern (1985) noted that much of the gain to liberalization in Harris and Cox occurred in the Canadian motor vehicle industry and found that result difficult to accept.

. At the end of the 1980s a number of researchers attempted this analysis again, with the FTA and later the NAFTA in mind.[4] The predicted benefits tended to be smaller, although the models were more sophisticated and the initial conditions were obviously different. Nevertheless, what is important for our purposes here is the general result that potential economies of scale were not so large as to permit a prediction of a gain in income or utility more than a couple of year's growth.

Such a result, for Mexico, would represent only a small part of the income gap separating her from her neighbors.

SAVINGS AND INVESTMENTS

One of the easiest ways of discussing the importance of FDI is to compare its size to that of domestic savings/investments. According to UNCTC (1991: Table 2), that ratio is about 3 percent for developed countries and 6 percent for developing countries. Recent ratios for Canada, Mexico, and the United States fall within that general range. The obvious conclusion is that because FDI flows are small fractions of savings and/or investments, changes in FDI will have little influence on the macroeconomy via this channel. While we believe this conclusion to be correct, some qualifying remarks are in order. About one-third of investment is residential construction in Canada and the United States, and it seems inappropriate to include that in the denominators. Depreciation expenses are also problematic.

A more basic question is, what model do we have in mind for such a comparison? Textbook Keynesianism discusses investment and savings from the point of view of injections and leakages. Note, however, textbook models treat marginal propensities and assume that savers and investors are different groups, two aspects not considered in the preceding paragraph. While FDI increases injections, its associated interest payments and repatriated profits reduce aggregate demand. Calculations of the net balance of payments of multinationals, as in CNIE (1988: 71) are motivated by this perspective. However, while the accumulated net outpayments over time will always be larger than the initial investment if a given project is profitable, this does not imply that FDI reduces income, because it will also increase supply.

EXPORTS AND IMPORTS

While FDI inflows are arguably small compared to national totals of investment, it is clear that the exports associated with multinationals are large. In Canada nearly half of industrial exports are produced by multinationals (McFetridge 1989: 40). Over half of nonoil exports from Mexico come from multinationals (Peres Nuñez 1990: 59) apart from the very dynamic maquila sector, which of course is inherently international, independently of the nationality of the owners of the firms.

The strength of FDI in Canada and Mexico—their provision of exports—is also a principal weakness because those exports are predominantly tied to the U.S. market. Statistical information on this is incomplete, being limited to data on exports by U.S. multinationals in the two countries, accounting in each case for about two-thirds of total foreign investment. In both countries, of the total sales by affiliates of U.S. MNCs, exports to the United States account for roughly one-fourth of the total, while exports to third countries are around 5 percent of total sales (see Table 6.1). This weak diversification of an important part of these

Table 6.1

Geographical Distribution of Sales of Affiliates of U.S. MNCs in Canada and Mexico

	1966			1977			1982			1989		
CANADA												
Total Value	23876			84659			10803			17213		
Percentage Breakdown	Local	US	NonUS	Local	US	NonUS	Local	US	NonUS	Local	US	NonUS
Total	84	12	4	78	17	4	77	19	4	74	23	3
Petroleum	94	6	0	91	9	0	84	15	1	82	17	1
Manufacturing	84	13	3	70	26	4	65	29	5	62	35	3
Trans. Eq.	74	25	2	49	49	2	35	60	5	42	56	2
Other Mfg.	87	9	3	82	13	5	82	12	5	77	18	5
Wholesale Tr.	88	4	8	90	3	7	89	5	6	90	5	4
"Others"	67	23	11	85	6	8	92	5	3	97	2	1
MEXICO												
Total Value	1992			5860			11269			16476		
Percentage Breakdown	Local	US	NonUS	Local	US	NonUS	Local	US	NonUS	Local	US	NonUS
Total	92	3	5	90	6	4	90	7	3	69	26	5
Petroleum	100	0	0	100	1	0	NA	NA	NA	98	1	1
Manufacturing	97	1	2	90	7	4	89	8	3	68	NA	NA
Trans. Eq.	NA	NA	NA	86	13	1	85	NA	NA	50	NA	NA
Other Mfg.	NA	NA	NA	90	5	5	90	NA	NA	79	NA	NA
Wholesale Tr.	78	NA	NA	90	NA	NA	NA	NA	7	63	NA	NA
"Others"	64	NA	NA	94	NA	NA	NA	NA	0	97	NA	NA

Sources: Benchmark Surveys.

Note: Total values are in million current U.S.$; other data are percentages. Data refer to majority owned affiliates of nonbank U.S. parents. In the case of Mexico, majority-owned affiliates accounted for only about 55 percent of total affiliate sales. Data are arranged according to industry of affiliate. Wholesale trade includes all trade in 1977 and 1966.

countries' exports implies a high degree of dependence on the U.S. business cycle, although this is characteristic of nationally-owned businesses as well. More subtly, it may also tie the countries' production and export potential to configurations of the U.S. firms' OLI advantages which are not necessarily longlived. However, in his analysis of this subject for Canada, McFetridge (1989) reaches conclusions basically favorable for that country as host to U.S. MNCs.

It is interesting to note the experience of foreign investment inside the United States with respect to foreign trade. Currently, exports by foreign MNCs account for only 6.5 percent of total sales (see Table 6.2), paralleling the finding for Canada and Mexico that investment in North America is not export creating, at least in terms of non-NAFTA countries. However, that total had been higher in previous years due to exports of raw materials (agriculture and mining) as well as exports from branches of foreign wholesale firms. That these exports would have declined is easily explainable in terms of product cycle phenomena.

Another aspect of MNC exporting deserving mention is its import content, which, ceteris paribus, reduces the income-generating effects. There are at hand two examples where this effect is abundantly clear. Imported inputs for the maquila program currently average three-quarters of the total value of production; the use of Mexican manufactured inputs is almost nil.[5] The Canada-U.S. Auto Pact (loosely) ties the growth of imports of parts by the U.S. firms to their exports, and because exports have been the limiting factor, their increases will

Table 6.2
Exports and Imports as Percentage of Sales, U.S. Affiliates of Foreign Companies

Year	1974		1982		1987	
Total Sales	146.8		412.7		744.6	
	Exp/S	Imp/S	Exp/S	Imp/S	Exp/S	Imp/S
All Sectors	16	21	13	18	6	19
Petroleum	8	17	2	19	2	11
Manufacturing	6	10	10	11	6	10
Motor Vehicles	3	5	19	NA	6	29
Agriculture	22	4	7	2	7	0
Mining	28	6	23	1	16	6
Wholesale Trade	29	34	21	27	10	38
"Other Services"	2	2	1	1	1	2

Sources: Benchmark Surveys.

Note: Total sales in billion current U.S.$; other data expressed as percentages. Data are arranged according to industry of affiliate. Nonbank affiliates only.

Exp/S - Exports as a percentage of sales; Imp/S - Imports as a percentage of sales.

also produce growth in imports.

In Mexico there are a number of other examples of export platform products that suffer the same drawback as those officially designated as maquilas. For example, the production of Ford Escorts and Tracers in Hermosillo (based on the Mazda 323) is estimated to incorporate only about 25 percent Mexican components (Wong-González 1989: 14). For computers, the average import content in 1986 was 50 percent (Peres Nuñez, 1990: 96).[6] Thus, while the MNCs promise strong growth of exports, the two dangers of *maquilización* and controlled export growth in the context of the NAFTA tend to dampen that hope.

TECHNOLOGICAL CHANGE IN CANADA

In Chapter 2 we discussed a number of motives for FDI originating in industrial organization factors, almost all of which reflected constraints on the market and competition, and so are in some sense judged negative. The one factor that, while having the negative effect of potentially limiting market access, also provides clearly recognizable gains, is expenditures on research and development (R&D). This section will review the major findings with respect to technological change, relating it to both R&D expenditures or transfers of existing knowledge, either intra- or interfirm. Once again we will see that the Canadian experience has yielded a number of insights relevant for both the United States and Mexico.

Over the years, a major concern of many observers in Canada has been that the high presence of U.S. subsidiaries tends to lower Canadian R&D, technological progress, and overall growth. This is part of "truncated" or "stunted" growth, a syndrome of a "miniature" or "branch plant" economy. One reason that the loss of this part of production would be especially troublesome is that R&D is often believed to provide externalities; the activity in and of itself has economies of scale (underutilized assets such as libraries or special lab equipment), and creative people often stimulate each other to be more successful.

A continuous flow of attention has yielded a number of stylized facts about technology in Canada, beginning with the assertion that Canadian productivity is one-third lower than that of the United States (Baldwin and Gorecki, 1986; Conklin and St-Hilaire, 1988: 115).[7] Canada spends relatively less on R&D than does any other major industrial country (see Table 6.3) and the private sector finances a smaller fraction of those expenditures than most any other country (OECD, 1986). The country's productivity growth performance has been less vigorous than that of its major trading partners, and the combination of a productivity slowdown and trade liberalization has led to widespread apprehension that its industrial sector is fast losing its competitiveness. The principal solution is seen to be "technology;" which can be produced at home as R&D or obtained from abroad either by direct purchase or through transfers via

Table 6.3
Indicators of Research and Development, Late 1980s

	R&D/GNP	Percent Funded by Businesses	Manufacturing R&D /Value Added 1981
Canada	1.4	41.8	2.6
Mexico	0.6	5.0	0.1
United States	2.6	50.2	8.1
United Kingdom	2.3	49.5	6.6
Germany	2.8	63.6	5.4
Italy	1.2	3.9	1.7
Portugal	0.5	6.8	0.3
Spain	0.6	48.8	0.1
Sweden	3.0	61.1	6.3
Switzerland	2.8	NA	NA
Japan	2.8	80.0	4.9
South Korea	1.9	81.9	1.7
Brazil	0.4	19.8	NA
Argentina	0.5	8.0	NA

Source: UNESCO *Statistical Yearbook,* 1990 and 1991, and OECD *Science and Technology Indicators* No. 2.

Note: UNESCO's category is "productive enterprises," which presumably includes parastatals. The data for R&D/Value Added for Korea, Portugal, and Spain involve calculations based on UNESCO data for R&D, and manufacturing value added from UN *Yearbook of National Accounts.* The respective years are 1986, 1983, and 1986. Korean R&D does not include defense.

MNCs. The issue is complex, and its components deserve to be looked at with care.

One direct indicator of technological capability is the generation of patents. The recent trend toward strengthening of intellectual property laws permits more attention on this, and the World Intellectual Property Organization assembles the data. Thus, Canadians were disturbed to find that the fraction of patents granted to foreigners in their country is higher than in other OECD countries, while Canadians obtain a relatively small fraction of patents in other countries (Ellis and Waite, 1985).

With regard to econometric studies, an early paper arguing the statistical insignificance of sector level R&D on sectoral growth (Globerman, 1972) also found a negative effect running from foreign ownership to either R&D or growth. A similar result was reported by Saunders (1980). Positive influences between foreign ownership and productivity and/or growth were subsequently reported by Globerman (1979), Caves et al. (1980), and weakly in Hewitt (1983). Fueling this debate is the incompleteness of data, the difficulty in distinguishing between "basic," "applied," or "adaptive" research, and the evolution toward a service economy, in which technology plays a different role. Nevertheless, advances have been made in creating internationally comparable data bases, and a positive link between R&D and technological change now seems clearly established (Englander et al., 1988). Bernstein's review (1985) of the Canadian evidence strongly supports that verdict, with two addenda. One is that there are some indications that government expenditures on R&D have relatively lower productivity, but that this deserves more research. The second is that there is good evidence of spillover or free-rider effects (see also Bernstein, 1988) that also muddies the policy prescription. The fraction of total productivity growth "explained" by R&D varies considerably among the authors reviewed, clustering closer to half than to all, but clearly these facts are not yet stylized.[8]

Turning to MNCs, it has long been known that subsidiaries of U.S. companies in Canada perform relatively less R&D than their parent companies do at home. However, that is also true of U.S. MNCs in other countries, as shown in Table 6.4. About one-tenth of R&D done by U.S. MNCs is performed overseas, most of it in Europe.[9] The ratio of R&D to sales is higher in Europe than in Canada; a somewhat larger gap separates Canada from Mexico.

Furthermore, the numbers indicate that both domestic and foreign firms have "low" R&D ratios in Canada (compare Table 6.5 with Table 6.3). This finding undermines the nationalist position, although the data in Table 6.6 suggest that Canada (along with Australia) is at the top of the spectrum in terms of foreign-sponsored R&D. Note also that there are indications of an upwards trend in R&D in Canada. Expenditures on R&D as a percentage of total sales vary greatly among manufacturing subsectors, as shown in Table 6.5. Once again, the fundamental industrial organization approach would argue that nationality of owner is of lesser importance than specific characteristics of the industrial subsector, in this case with respect to technology expenditures. Additionally, shifts in the composition of production will also change R&D averages for all of industry. This also returns us to a basic issue for Canadians; should they be content with specializing in raw-material-based industries ("hewers of wood and drawers of water" is the disparaging phrase), or should they attempt the riskier and more expensive route of developing hi-tech industries. As is noted elsewhere, Canadian MNCs basically come from resource based industries, and are definitely characterized by sophisticated technology (Rugman, 1990). Greater specialization in technology-intensive manufacturing sectors will come at a high cost.

The alternative to producing one's own technology is obtaining it from abroad at what might well be a lower opportunity cost. Many have argued that MNCs are a suitable intermediary in this process. Based on case studies, it has been shown that the rate of diffusion of innovations through MNCs is much faster than through "arm's length" transactions, and that diffusion inside MNC branches in Canada is about as fast as that in subsidiaries of MNCs in other developed countries (Mansfield, 1985).

One aspect of technology policy in Canada—and elsewhere—that we feel has

Table 6.4
R&D Percentages for U.S. MNCs in the United States and Abroad,
1966-1989

	1966	1977	1982	1989
U.S. Parent Firms				
Total	NA	1.4	2.5	2.6
Manufacturing	NA	2.4	4.8	4.7
All Overseas Affiliates				
Total	0.6	0.4	0.5	0.7
Manufacturing	1.1	0.9	1.2	0.9
U.S. Affiliates in Canada				
Total	0.7	0.3	0.5	0.5
Manufacturing	1.0	0.4	0.7	0.7
U.S. Affiliates in Mexico				
Total	0.3	0.3	0.3	0.2
Manufacturing	0.3	0.4	0.4	0.2
U.S. Affiliates in Europe				
Total	0.9	0.7	0.7	0.9
Manufacturing	1.5	1.3	1.6	1.5

Sources: Benchmark studies

Note: All data refer to nonbank operations. Data for U.S. overseas affiliates refer to majority-owned affiliates. R&D figures are for expenditures for research and development performed for affiliates. R&D data for U.S. parent firms correspond to total performed *by* the firms; reported amounts performed *for* the firms were about 30 percent lower in 1982 and 1989.

not received sufficient analytical attention is expenditures on licensing and royalties, sometimes referred to as technology payments. This variable is certainly a two-edged sword; although basically it should increase productivity if that is appropriately measured. Controversy arises when viewing technology payments as alternatives to R&D, particularly when the provider of the technology resides in another country. Table 6.7 provides some relevant information. That the United States is practically "self-sufficient" in terms of payments abroad for technology is seen as being the exception. Canada's level of outpayments places it in a middle group, among OECD countries. As with some OECD countries, Mexico clearly spends much more on purchasing technology from abroad than in generating it at home via R&D. Note that omitting licensing expenditures would thus lead to the econometric result of overestimating the benefits of R&D on total

Table 6.5

Current Intramural R&D Expenditures as a Percentage of Company Sales in Canada, by Country of Control, 1973-1988

	1973	1979	1983	1985	1988
Total	0.9	0.8	1.2	1.3	1.4
Canadian	0.9	0.9	1.4	1.5	1.6
United States	0.8	0.7	0.9	1.0	1.2
Other Foreign	1.1	0.5	1.0	1.3	1.4

Current R&D Expenditures as Percentage of Sales, by Industry and Country, 1988

	Total	Canada	Foreign
Total All Industries	1.4	1.6	1.2
Manufacturing	1.5	1.7	1.3
Total Mining	0.5	0.6	0.4
Mining	0.5	0.6	0.5
Petroleum & Gas	0.6	0.8	0.4
Total Services	1.4	1.5	1.1
Transportation	0.4	0.4	0.5
Electrical Power	1.1	1.1	0.0
Computer Services	12.3	12.5	10.0
Engin. Services	16.5	14.5	42.0
Other Nonmanuf.	1.1	1.7	0.7

Source: Basic data from Statistics Canada, *Industrial Research and Development* (1988: 77).

factor productivity, which may have affected those seen above for Canada.

It also further complicates the analysis of the role of MNCs in technology transfer. On average, the overseas affiliates of U.S. MNCs spend slightly more on licensing than they do on R&D, as seen in Table 6.8. Comparison with Table 6.7 shows that U.S. affiliates abroad tend to purchase more of their technology from outside their host countries compared to domestically owned firms. The ratio of licensing to R&D expenses varies considerably by countries, with Canada having relatively more R&D, probably because geographical, infrastructural, and cultural considerations encourage the U.S. MNCs' R&D in Canada. Blomström cites an unpublished paper by Ari Kokko that notes that U.S. MNCs do more R&D in host countries that have higher incomes, greater competitive pressure, and fewer performance requirements. While the terms of the trade-off with regard

Table 6.6
U.S. MNC Affiliate R&D as Percentage of Domestic Business R&D
(Data are million U.S.$)

	U.S. MNC Affiliate R&D 1982	BERD 1981	Affiliate ÷ Total
Canada	545	1,903	29
Belgium	181	950	19
France	263	6,305	4
Germany	893	10,686	8
Italy	136	2,563	5
Netherlands	101	1,336	8
Portugal	1	48	2
Spain	36	443	8
Sweden	29	1442	2
Switzerland	51	1,325	4
United Kingdom	805	7,030	11
Japan	104	15,517	1
Korea	0	442	0
Australia	120	344	35
Argentina	23	NA	NA
Brazil	96	337	28
Mexico	38	29	131

Source: U.S. Department of Commerce 1982 Benchmark, *OECD Science and Technology Indicators*, No.2. For Mexico, Brazil, and Korea, R&D data from UNESCO *Statistical Yearbook.*

Note: BERD is Business Enterprise Research and Development. The data on Mexico's BERD refers to 1984; for Australia and Germany the year was 1981. The UNESCO data refer to the "productive sector" which presumably includes parastatals, and are generally comparable to the OECD data.

to MNCs and technology are clear—more imported technology versus a more slowly developing domestic scientific apparatus with its inherently beneficial spinoffs—the magnitudes of that tradeoff are not at all clear.

In light of all these findings, we may be advised to accept Globerman's (1985) conclusion that the relationship going from foreign ownership to technological change in Canada is positive and modest.

Let us turn briefly to some comments on government policy. One of the responses to the perception of Canada's technological lag has been an increase in government support embodied in a National Science and Technology Policy approved in 1987. Dufour and Gingras (1988), and Leiss (1988) describe various actions during the 1980s, building on initiatives reaching back to the "golden age" of science policy in the late 1960s: the government directly spent more money on R&D, firms were helped by grants and tax breaks,[10] universities and research

Table 6.7
External Technology Payments Compared to Domestic R&D Expenditures

Licensing and Royalty Payments as a Percent of Business R&D

	1971	1981		1971	1981
Payments			Receipts		
U.S.	1.3	1.3	U.S.	13.0	13.2
Japan	15.0	7.2	Japan	3.0	4.8
U.K.	14.8	10.5	U.K.	16.3	1.7
Canada	23.7	24.6	Canada	6.7	7.3
Netherlands	26.3	41.9	Netherlands	23.9	27.3
Portugal	136.7	154.1	Portugal	11.2	25.2
Spain	235.2	158.2	Spain	26.0	50.4
	1977	**1987**			
South Korea	26.0	23.0	royalty payments only		
	1984				
Mexico	about 40,	considering royalties and commissions			
	about 100,	considering royalties, commissions and repatriated profits			

Source: OECD countries from OECD *Science and Technology Indicators*, No. 2, 1986; p. 56. For South Korea, Kiroshi Kakazu, "Industrial Technology Capabilities and Policies in Selected Asian Developing Countries," Asian Development Bank Economic Staff Paper #46, 1990. Mexican R&D from UNESCO *Statistical Yearbook;* technology payments from Peres Nuñez (1990: 28), which include royalties, commissions, and license fees.

Note: Initial year for the United Kingdom and Portugal is 1972; for receipts in Spain, it is 1973. Terminal year for Portugal is 1982.

parks were encouraged, and certain government institutions were reorganized and strengthened. While there have been some successes, these policies have been limited by increasing strife between the national and provincial or territorial levels and the associated policy insecurity. In addition, there have been the usual problems of deciding on the appropriate balance between pure and applied work, incorporation for political reasons of non-R&D objectives, and the lack of a convincing vision of the role for government support of R&D, especially in a resource-rich "small open economy." Naturally enough, these policies have been subject to considerable debate, which, perhaps oversimply, can be conceptualized as a free market/interventionist dichotomy. In the Canadian context, these two factions have been identified with the government's Economic Council and Science Council, respectively.

Table 6.8
Technology Expenditures by U.S. MNC Overseas Affiliates
(Million U.S.$)

	1982			1989		
	R&D	Licenses & Royalties	(ratio)	R&D	Licenses & Royalties	(ratio)
Total	3647	3954	108	7133	9247	130
Canada	545	517	95	911	821	90
Europe	2591	2630	102	5241	5975	114
Belgium	181	161	89	320		
France	263	458	174	556		
Germany	893	533	60	1507		
Italy	136	239	176	318		
Netherlands	101	220	218	363		
Spain	36	64	178	114		
Switzerland	51	99	194	71		
United Kingdom	805	573	71	1684		
Japan	104	306	294	498		
Korea	0	6	8			
Australia	120	160	133	188		
Latin America	179	171	96	157	248	158
Argentina	23	31	135	10		
Brazil	96	13	14	93		
Mexico	38	73	192	37		

Source: 1982 Benchmark, preliminary 1989 Benchmark, and August 1991 *Survey of Current Business.*

Note: The preliminary version of the 1989 Benchmark does not provide data on payments of royalties and license fees.

MNCs AND TECHNOLOGICAL CHANGE IN MEXICO

This chapter has noted a number of ways in which MNCs can affect productivity in the host country. There may be an increase in amount of R&D in the host country, or new techniques may be brought in under licensing. There may be spillovers from new technology, both intra- and interindustry. There may be an increase in x-efficiency due to the greater competition.

Mexico's recent record in technological progress, as summarized in Table 6.9, is certainly passable. The country's average TFP growth of 1.1 percent over the period 1960-1980 was fully two-thirds that of its major trading partner, the United States. Labor productivity grew faster than TFP, as would be expected in a country undergoing capital deepening. Undoubtedly, things could have been

Table 6.9

Technological Change in Manufacturing: Mexico Compared with OECD Countries, 1960-1980

	Total Factor Productivity	Labor Productivity
OECD Average	2.7	4.7
Canada	2.2	3.4
United States	1.6	2.3
Japan	4.8	9.5
Germany	3.5	5.1
United Kingdom	1.6	3.0
Mexico	1.1	3.4
Large Firms	NA	6.6

Source: Hernández Laos and Velasco Arregui (1990), Cuadro 1.

Data are annual average growth rates.

better. Some Asian NICs certainly had higher TFP growth (Dollar, 1991). Moreover, the 1980s was not successful economically for Mexico. While there are serious econometric problems in measuring TFP during a recession, given the decline in R&D and excess capacity in industry, one assumes that TFP growth fell.

The literature provides two lines of investigation of the link between MNCs and technological change; one studies directly the correlation between the two variables, and the second concentrates on ownership and R&D expenditures, assuming that the link between R&D and the more difficult-to-measure technological change does not need to be demonstrated. As was mentioned in the discussion on Canada, licensing and royalties have received little attention as contributors to productivity improvement. Note also that what is called x-efficiency is difficult to quantify and has not been the subject of analysis in Mexico.

Let us look first at the relation between TFP and foreign ownership. Comparison of two sets of relatively carefully constructed estimates of growth of sectoral TFP for Mexico—Hernández Laos and Velasco Arregui (1990) and Samaniego Breach (1984)—with the foreign ownership percentages in Peres Nuñez (1990) does indeed suggest a positive correlation between MNC share of production and TFP growth. Regressing the log of the foreign ownership percentages (FOR) from Peres Nuñez on the TFP data in Hernández Laos and Velasco Arregui yields TFP = -1.25 + 0.9 FOR. The R^2 is only 0.16 with a sample of eight observations, and so this result can only be considered suggestive. An important variation on this theme is the ambitious paper by Blomström and Wolff (1989), who argue that there has been occurring a convergence of their roughly calculated version of TFP between Mexico and the United States, and that the rate of convergence is higher in those sectors showing larger participation by foreign affiliates.

The relation between technology and foreign ownership has been studied more thoroughly with respect to levels and rates of change of labor productivity. That the foreign-owned firms had higher labor productivity along with greater capital intensity was shown for Mexico by Fajnzylber and Martínez Tarragó (1976). In a series of papers, Blomström and his co-authors have analyzed this relationship in more detail, using models explicitly or implicitly derived from some version of the OLI perspective, showing, for example, that there is a positive influence even after accounting for the standard industrial organization variables.[11] It is unfortunately the case that the most extensive study to date of industrial organization in Mexico, Casar et al. (1990), did not estimate the effect of foreign ownership on the level of labor productivity but only on its rate of change. While these coefficients, in their Cuadro 11.4, are negative, this can easily be explained as a catching-up phenomenon, as indeed has been argued in Canada.[12] In light of previous comments, it is noteworthy that they did not find a statistically significant relationship between license and royalty fees and the growth of labor productivity. Nevertheless, because almost all licensing is done through MNC affiliates (Fajnzylber and Martínez Tarragó 1976: 325-326), the doubt remains that this negative finding results from a specification error when foreign ownership is also included as an explanatory variable.

Turning to R&D expenditures, recall that in our earlier review of analyses for Canada and other OECD countries about half of TFP growth was attributed to R&D expenditures. With regard to Mexico, several tables indicated that relative levels of R&D there have been much lower than in the OECD countries, or indeed of some of the faster growing NICs. The level of domestic patenting was similarly much lower. In an absolute sense, there is little R&D done in Mexico or many developing countries by MNCs or anyone else. Moreover, as shown in Table 6.10, most of the registered R&D in Mexico is performed by the government and may be routine lab tests in hospitals or agricultural stations.

With regard to business R&D, the meager statistical information is unfortunately quite inconsistent, and there are no comprehensive official data. One important work, Unger (1983), analyzed questionnaire data for over 100 firms in Mexico. His measured ratio of R&D to sales is quite comparable to what is reported in Canada. This is true in terms of the fraction of firms performing R&D, their ratio of R&D to sales, and for the small difference between foreign and domestically owned firms.[13] However, as Unger clearly states, the firms included in his study were definitely not randomly sampled.

The other bit of information is the comparison, noted earlier, between the UNESCO's estimate of business R&D and that reported for U.S. MNCs by the

Table 6.10
Indicators of R&D Expenditures in Mexico

	1970	1975	1980	1984	1985	1986	1988	1989
Total R&D/GDP (%)					0.6	0.4	0.2	0.2
Government expenditures for R&D as Percent of GDP	0.60	0.83	1.12		0.83	0.68		

1984 Total R&D: 159.4 billion pesos (0.6% of GNP)

Current Expenditures	84%	
Capital Expenditures		16%

Breakdown by Performing Sector:

Productive Sector	30%
Higher Education	51%
General Service	19%

R&D in the Productive Sector by Sector in 1984 (million pesos)

Total	48,277	100%
Agric., Fish, Forest.	10,911	23
Extractive Industries	9,211	19
Manufacturing	4,871	10
Utilities	4,630	10
Construction	1,688	3
Transp. & Commun.	579	1
Other	16,387	34

Source: First line: from UNESCO *Statistical Yearbook*, various years. Second line from Lustig et al. (1989), which is based on official Mexican data. Other data are calculations based on UNESCO *Statistical Yearbook*, 1989 and 1991.

Note: Whiting (1981: 328) cites a study which estimated total R&D as a percentage of GNP in 1967 at 0.13 percent.

U.S. Department of Commerce. While the years of reference are different, the indication would be that most business R&D in Mexico is performed by U.S. firms. Because foreign firms account for less than a third of manufacturing sales, and given that we know (from the annual lists in *Expansión*) that some of the largest firms are domestically owned (private or parastatal), these two results cannot be entirely compatible.[14] We interpret that difference to the underestimation of business R&D by UNESCO, which of course merely reports the official data it receives. Nevertheless, it is unlikely that the degree of underreporting is large enough to cover the observed gap between Mexico and other countries, which, as was shown in Table 6.3, is of the order of magnitude of one or almost two decimal points.

Some Canadians associate their country's lower levels of R&D with the presence of MNCs. The position argued above is that the evidence is not strong that in the absence of the MNC subsidiaries, Canadian firms are doing, or will do much more. We believe that this argument should be made more emphatically in Mexico; indeed, there are very few who have argued that restricting MNCs would increase the country's technological progress. In light of the low level of manufacturing R&D, permitting the establishment of affiliates will probably increase technological growth via both R&D and licensing.

A final comment will be much more speculative in the sense that it is unsupported by previously presented data. Lacking a coherent national science policy, it does not make sense that Mexico would base decisions on foreign investment primarily on a perceived benefit in terms of technology transfer. For one thing, it can be argued that a greater change in technical capability could be generated by improvements in other areas, such as the educational system. Given the country's rudimentary technology infrastructure, some international firms will simply not be able to transfer their sophisticated techniques. Moreover, the OLI analysis continually refers us back to the differences in technical dynamism between industrial sectors (i.e., shoes versus computers). The OLI-informed industrial policy would search for those areas in which growth is possible, knowing that both national and foreign firms will of necessity utilize competitive technology.

MULTINATIONALS, TECHNOLOGY, AND THE UNITED STATES

The government of the United States does not have an explicit policy relating to technology *per se*, much less to the areas of intersection between technology and MNCs. Nevertheless, there are numerous modes of intervention in technology-sensitive areas. The country's political culture places these under the umbrella of national defense. High-performance aircraft and computers are obvious examples of commercial activities whose production has received important subsidies because of their defense linkages. In both of these areas there have developed conflicts involving MNCs, both IFDI and OFDI. One noteworthy case involved the attempted purchase of the U.S. semiconductor firm Fairchild by the Japanese company Fujitsu, which was effectively vetoed by the Defense Department. A joint venture for the production of the FSX fighter in Japan was also criticized as leading to technology leakages, with both defense and economic implications.[15]

In the judgment of Friedberg (1991), the executive branch of the U.S. government was relatively successful in the 1980s at maintaining a laissez faire attitude towards MNCs and technology, thereby resisting pressures from industry, Congress, and the media. It is clear that a president with a different ideological orientation might reverse that orientation. Moreover, U.S. defense policy will be affected both by the end of the Cold War and by the loss of the country's technological autonomy in defense procurement. While it is easy to imagine the emergence of a more explicitly industrial policy as the solution to these conflicting forces, Friedberg's prediction is that "changes at the margin are more likely than truly dramatic departures from the liberal policies of the past" (p. 86).

NOTES

1. This level is consistent with previous work done in Canada, cited by Baldwin and Gorecki, and more than double the more recent estimates of Robidoux and Lester (1992), which are closer to those found by Tybout et al. (1991) for Chile, as well as unpublished estimates by Tybout and Westbrook for Mexico.

2. Green's review of the Baldwin and Gorecki book in the May 1988 *Canadian Journal of Economics* noted that it is not clear exactly where and how this figure, which is after all the book's title and presumably its main finding, is derived. Either of the differences between the authors' versions of TFP1 and TFP4 (weighted averages of reduced sample; Table 6-4, page 135) are indeed about one-third; this is one way of making the calculation. In principle, the explained part of the productivity differential should equal the degree of returns to scale multiplied by the differential in plant sizes. The calculations we show in the text have difficulty stretching to cover a third of the difference between TFP1 and unity. Much of this perceived inconsistency arises from econometric problems originating in incomplete data sets, weighing of averages, and handling of outliers. However, it is reassuring that the estimated coefficients on relative plant size on page 164 are similar to the independent estimates of the degree of return to scale (p. 58). It might also be commented that Baldwin and Gorecki do not attempt simultaneous estimations.

3. Baldwin and Gorecki still find underutilized scale (p. 19) and lower productivity (p. 137) in this sector.

4. See, for example Brown et al. (1992) and Cox and Harris (1992). We have probably read or seen reference to at least two dozen articles and working papers on this subject, most of them utilizing CGE models. A broad sample is provided in the January, 1992 issue of *The World Economy,* and U.S. International Trade Commission (1992). For an example of estimates not utilizing CGE models, see Adams et al. (1992).

5. This has caused some confusion in comparisons of the trade statistics of the two countries because the United States does not separate maquila from other production. It appears that Mexico is gradually eliminating the distinction in official documents, which will bias upward growth estimates made by uncareful researchers.

6. The computer industry provides important examples of the failure of major international producers to reach government-imposed trade goals. See Peres Nuñez (1990) and Whiting (1991).

7. This figure is frequently cited by Canadian authors, whose methodology varies tremendously. We saw above that the Baldwin and Gorecki estimate was one of total factor productivity, i.e., included capital. Note that changes are much easier to estimate than are levels of total factor productivity.

8. R&D is measured as an accumulated stock of annual national expenditures, appropriately discounted, but little consideration is given to inflows from abroad. One line of further research involves the creation of a technology input-output matrix (using, incidentally, Canadian data), following the hypothesis that there are differential benefits to the originators and the users of technology. Similarly, the distinction is made between process and product technology. An interesting case relates to everybody's current favorite NIC, South Korea. As described in Dollar (1991), that country has high R&D level and very high technological progress. However the mode of impacting productivity varies considerably across industries, depending on the degree of embodiedness of the new technology.

9. Note also in that table the preponderance of R&D performed by manufacturing firms.

10. Leiss (1988: 57) cites a study that found that the level of Canada's incentive programs was higher than all but one of nineteen other nations. One noteworthy program explicitly extended benefits to MNCs that designated their Canadian affiliates as the major supplier of a certain product to the world market; the so-called World Product Mandate.

11. See Blomström and Persson (1983), Blomström (1986a, 1986b, 1988, 1989). Note that Blomström (1985) uses industrial organization variables to explain the findings of Fajnzylber and Martínez Tarragó (1976) of differences in productivity by nationality of owner.

12. Fajnzylber and Martínez Tarragó (1976: 269) present a table with a positive relationship, covering only the short time period 1965-1970.

13. A similar finding of small differences between transnational and domestic firms' technological activity is presented by Fairchild and Sosin (1986).

14. It is also clear that domestic firms do engage in R&D; in addition to the obvious cases of PEMEX and exporters such as VITRO and CEMEX, smaller firms have been highlighted in the new magazine *TecnoIndustria,* which is published by the national technology commission, CONACYT.

15. These and other cases are discussed in various articles in the Fall 1991 issue of *Daedalus.*

7

THE FREE TRADE AGREEMENTS

THE CANADA—U.S. FREE TRADE AGREEMENT

Neighboring countries long at political peace, Canada and the United States have been separated by economic barriers for nearly as long. The experience of the rise of foreign investment in Canada, partially as a result of that protectionism, was reviewed above in Chapter 3. The 1960s witnessed a significant increase in nationalist sentiment critical of FDI.[1] During the following decade many concrete and controversial actions were undertaken that aimed at reducing the foreign presence. The subsequent judgment of the Canadian electorate was that these policies had been unsuccessful, and in 1984 the Conservative Party under Brian Mulroney was given the opportunity to attempt an entirely different approach. The cornerstone to the new policy became the Free Trade Agreement with the United States.

At some level, free trade has always been "in the air" as a possible mode of linking Canada and the United States, although as noted before, during the previous century and a half, such initiatives never had been successful. During the early 1980s the McDonald Commission was formed to review possible orientations of Canadian trade policy, and its hearings, and subsequent recommendations—released after negotiations with the United States on FTA had begun—certainly facilitated eventual acceptance of free trade.

Chronology

1965 Canada-U.S. Auto Pact
1982 McDonald Commission formed
1984 Brian Mulroney becomes prime minister of Canada
1985 March. "Shamrock Summit" between Mulroney and Reagan, who agree
      to explore avenues of freer trade

1987   October. Agreement initialed by negotiators
1988   January. President and prime minister sign agreement
       September. Agreement approved by U.S. Senate
       November. Canadian election victory for Mulroney
       December. FTA approved by House of Commons
1989   January 1. FTA enters into effect

Canada initiated the process that led up to the FTA. What were the country's expectations in the negotiations?[2] Perhaps foremost was the search for expanded trade opportunities. Canada wanted better access to the U.S. market both in terms of fewer official trade barriers and greater security against the seemingly arbitrary application of regulations via countervailing duties. The country's newly elected government hoped that the FTA would support the new, continentalist orientation.

For its part, the U.S. negotiators also perceived in the FTA an opportunity to strengthen the renewed openness of their major trading partner. More-concrete potential conquests included expanded access to Canadian energy resources as well as a reduction in protection of cultural industries. Canadian negotiators were subsequently to complain of the lack of a coherent policy on the part of their U.S. counterparts, whose government did not consider the FTA a high-priority item and did not invest political capital in coalescing negotiating positions.

Setting the stage for the negotiations was a long history of successful binational agreements, such as the St. Lawrence seaway, accords on defense procurement, and the Auto Pact of the 1960s. Both countries faced weak internal macroeconomic contexts, with Canadians focusing on high unemployment, while in the United States the problems of the "twin deficits" did not disappear.

The process of approval in the United States was uneventful, with only isolated groups raising dissenting voices. The opposite happened in Canada. Although under its parliamentary system the government had a majority in the House, implementation of the accord would be blocked by the Senate, whose membership was appointed, not elected, and was controlled by the opposition. An election was called, which soon became dominated by the sole issue of the FTA. The Conservatives won 170 seats to 82 for the Liberals and 43 for the New Democrats. The government's majority declined from 211 in the previous House, and represented only 43 percent of the popular vote—a united opposition would have defeated free trade. In Ontario, arguably the province most benefited by protectionism, the result was forty-seven Tories, forty-two Liberals, and ten New Democrats. Explaining this result, the *Economist* commented, "In the last two weeks of the campaign business organisations there spent millions advertising the merits of free trade, and drowned out the voice of the unions. Some of the agreement's critics went overboard in their attacks on it. Their virulence failed to persuade the wavering voters" (November 26, 1989: 43).

The accord itself has over 300 pages of text; twenty-one chapters in eight parts, whose details belie the simplicity of the term *free trade* and reflect compromises to political demands on both sides of the border.[3] To be sure, tariffs on binational trade are to be eliminated. However, a ten-year span is allowed for reductions on some items, and a large number of nontariff barriers remain. Agricultural trade was not affected. Textiles and clothing were still subject to many controls; overall, quotas provided maximum amounts of trade allowed duty-free. In these two sectors, in particular, greater progress will probably only happen under the umbrella of the GATT negotiations. The Auto Pact remained in force, and a 50 percent rule of origin used to identify products as brought in from third countries. With regard to foreign investment, the FTA commits the countries to a policy of national treatment—in most areas. This should preclude the conflicts of the 1970s in Canada and protects Canadian firms from the growth of nationalistic sentiment in the United States. In particular, the limit on size of investments not subject to review was raised to $150 million (from $5 million), and trade-related performance requirements were prohibited. Restrictions on the finance and insurance sectors of Canada were relaxed, although the powerful Canadian banks did not improve their access to the United States.

The most important theme on which no progress was made was subsidies and measures the other side uses to counteract them, known as countervailing duties or antidumping. Subsidies are implemented in different ways in the two countries in terms of the level of government applying them (national, state/provincial, municipal), the means utilized (tax breaks, unemployment and health benefits, subsidized loans, direct expenditures), and even the basic supporting rationale, so that Canadians claim that while they recognize theirs as being a policy to strengthen production, the United States hides behind myths of defense and security.[4] The basic issue is whether a disputed measure affects the economy as a whole or whether it indeed impacts specifically on industries involved in trade.

The opposite side of that coin is the dispute settlement mechanism, which Canadian supporters of the FTA have claimed was the greatest success of the negotiations. Initially conceived as a temporary measure to operate until the issue of subsidies was ironed out, this process created a binational commission to function as the ultimate judge on trade conflicts, empowering it to issue binding decisions on both countries. Because trade is so much more important in the Canadian economy and because of the perception of increased protectionist sentiment in the United States, the protection against arbitrary measures by the latter was felt to be a positive achievement of the former. One early Canadian evaluation of the dispute settlement mechanism is cautiously positive (Crawford, 1992) in spite of a widespread perception that trade disputes have become increasingly noisy.

Two controversial parts of the agreement, on which both sides subsequently hoped to improve their respective positions in the NAFTA negotiations, were cultural industries and energy. The cultural industries include film and video, music recordings, publishing, and television and cable broadcasting. Reservation of these areas as a means to protect Canada's cultural identity was a commitment about which United States negotiators were unsympathetic, while judging their Canadian counterparts to be irrationally defensive. Fairness requires us to note that Canadian ownership of radio and TV stations in the United States also remained restricted.

The agreements with regard to energy policies include the negative commitment not to impose restraints on trade and a positive one to assure supplies to the other party in times of emergency. One can view these as backward-looking policies designed to avoid sources of conflict of the previous decade while missing the chance of breaking the power of local governmental bodies in both countries, which administer trade in oil, gas, and electricity (Verlager, 1988). The United States is a major energy importer, and Canada has major untapped supplies, whose exploitation will require advanced technology and tremendous amounts of capital. Energy continues to be the area of greatest divergence between trust in the market and the perception of national security.

Overall, the number of compromises suggests that the benefits and costs of the agreement were split between both countries. As described in Crawford (1992), Canada won in agriculture (maintaining protectionism on dairy and poultry products), dispute settlement (obtaining a commitment from the United States for arbitration), and energy (a regional victory for the energy-rich western provinces, because a free market is promised). Victories for the United States were adjudicated in autos (duty-remission scheme to be phased out), energy (a promise of continued sales in times of crisis), foreign investment (a relatively high level of the threshold for foreign investment review), and wines (Canadian protectionism reduced). While this listing may reveal the professional orientation of its authors, political scientists at Carleton University, the underemphasis on reduction of tariffs and nontariff barriers as well as the long phase-in of various measures accurately reflect the perceived need to share adjustment costs as well as the continuing influence of so-called vested interests on both sides of the border.

MEXICO STEPS IN

There are clear parallels in the timing and motivation of the decisions by Canada, and subsequently by Mexico, to enter into free-trade negotiations with the United States.[5] Both countries had recently experienced a period of nationalist fervor, and both were coming out of economic recession. However, on each of these counts, the situation in Mexico was more extreme and therefore deserves a careful overview.

Macroeconomic Background

The period of the late 1950s through 1970 in Mexico is often recalled fondly by economic commentators today. The growth of GDP was strong, inflation was low, and the balance of payments was healthy.[6] Things changed in the 1970s, with increasing deficits under President Echeverría leading to a devaluation in 1976, the first since 1954. The disruption caused by the subsequent austerity policies was relieved by the discovery of oil, and the end of the decade saw the country preparing to enter middle-income status, riding on this wave of new-found wealth. The collapse of oil prices together with very high international interest rates forced the country to admit its inability to meet its debt payments, and the debt crisis was ushered in during August 1982. One of the emergency actions taken to stop the hemorrhaging of foreign exchange was the nationalization of the banks.

The term of President De la Madrid was characterized by a succession of economic plans designed to remedy the balance of payments problems associated with the debt crisis. In late 1987 an Economic Solidarity Pact was approved, which imposed wage and price controls, while the government severely reduced its budget deficit. In 1985-1986 the country entered the GATT.

President De la Madrid was succeeded by one of his chief ministers, Carlos Salinas de Gortari, who pursued these policies even more fervently under a free market banner christened "social liberalism." Main elements of this program have been privatization, reduction of government expenditures, continued intervention on key prices and wages, and a small crawl of the exchange rate. For our purposes, specific importance should be attached to the recent liberalization of the foreign investment regulations, greatly opening the space for foreigners in the Mexican stock market, privatization of most of the government parastatals, and the decision to seek a free trade agreement with the United States.

Political Context

Since at least the 1930s, Mexico's political system has been dominated by one party, the Institutional Revolutionary Party, or PRI, which has maintained within its ranks the presidency, almost all governorships, and most congressional seats. Many presidents have promised electoral reform, but it was the case that the official outcome of the 1988 elections was strongly questioned, even though the winning candidate received barely over half of the votes.

In any political system there will be uncertainty over the identities of the candidates in upcoming elections, what policies they will promise to pursue, and so on. Within the PRI, the process of selecting the PRI's presidential candidate has traditionally taken place behind closed doors, although the process for 1988 did involve some public debates among designated pre-candidates.

For a time, many observers compared the openings of Mikhail Gorbachev in the Soviet Union and President Salinas in Mexico. It became clear, however, that the Mexican experience would be characterized by little political openness and a radical economic liberalization, while the Soviet experience would reverse those priorities. It is now fashionable to ask to what degree there will be a political opening in Mexico. For our interests, such an opening involves the major economic risk of the selection of candidates opposed to the current policies, which by all accounts need another presidential term, or *sexenio,* to become fully established. While this is obviously true for the presidency itself, it would not be surprising to see concerns over the electoral process affecting the stability of financial markets.

Another aspect of the political situation that must be noted in terms of its importance on the economic environment is the rapid pace of institutional reforms that the Mexican government maintained during the negotiations. Fundamental reorientations of constitutional provisions such as the nonalienability of *ejido* lands and the isolation of the Church, together with basic changes in areas such as the social security system, the educational system, and the structure of PEMEX, came with a frequency that left commentators of whatever political orientation rather breathless. A pertinent example is the relative absence of commentary on the change of the regulations on foreign investment, announced in May 1989. At that time, the country was immersed in attempts to escape the worst conditions of the crisis via refinancing of the debt, and few commented on this issue.[7]

Finally, it might be commented that Cuauhtémoc Cárdenas, the major candidate of the left, considered by many to have won the presidential elections in 1988, did not reject the idea of a Free Trade Agreement per se, while recommending inclusion of other themes such as ecology, labor rights, and so forth. A piece published in his name in *Nexos* (June 1991), stated, "We are in favor of a broad continental pact of trade and development. . . . It is necessary to encourage the growth of a progressive, modern and vigorous entrepreneurial class which Mexico has never developed. . . . Capital movements, particularly direct foreign investment, are a central component in the new continental society which we wish to construct."[8] The more traditional party of the opposition, the PAN, has always espoused free market economic policies and should be seen as supportive of the goals of a Free Trade Agreement.[9]

Privatization

The current surge in liberal policies, of which privatization is one of the boldest, has origins that go back for some time. Nevertheless, the major change in policy occurred with the arrival of President De la Madrid in 1982, spurred on, as it was, by the economic crisis and the pressures international actors were bringing to bear on the country's decision-makers. It is often claimed that there were 1,155 state-owned companies in 1982, and that by late 1991 this number was reduced to 257.[10] Of course, much of this reduction consisted of the consolidation of dispersed firms into a larger conglomerates; for example, the number of banks was reduced from over sixty to twenty. Nevertheless, the comprehensiveness of the privatization, or disincorporation, as it is literally called in Spanish, cannot be underestimated. Almost all government-owned manufacturing enterprises, the commercial banks (which had been nationalized at the end of President Lopez Portillo's term), and a number of other services, in particular, most of the government's previously dominant share of the national telephone company TELMEX, have been sold to the private sector. Some companies have not been sold; the state oil company PEMEX, the electrical company CFE, and the federal railroads FERRONALES are the most important.

Before reviewing the magnitudes of these sales, it is perhaps of interest to comment on the process of privatization and on the characteristics of the purchasers. Government representatives have continually assured the public that the process will maintain its transparency: that is, clear rules followed impartially without political or personal considerations intervening in the decision to award the company to the highest bidder. While it is not in this author's ability to verify the accuracy of that assertion, it can at least be noted that there have been few criticisms in the Mexican media of the fairness of the process, and nothing approaching a scandal.[11] This does not guarantee that problems will not subsequently emerge, but should rather be seen as an interim report.[12] One particularly important characteristic is that the banking system appears to enjoy the full confidence of the rest of the private sector.

One of the results of the privatization process has been a dispersion of economic power away from the capital, with the largest recipient being the northern city of Monterrey (*El Financiero,* February 4, 1992). Another outcome has been that the new owners of the banks are not the previous owners (with the exception of Banoro), but rather younger entrepreneurs often associated without in the brokerage houses in the early 1980s. In addition, the banks have been purchased by consortia of investors, leading to a so-called democratization of ownership. One presumes that government officials welcome and encouraged these outcomes. One problem has been the undercapitalization of the newly purchased banks, due to the high prices paid for them, which will impede modernizing investments in computer systems and other areas.[13]

The amounts of the purchases are staggering. The banks were sold at about three to four times their book value and over fifteen times their profits; the eventual income for the government should total U.S.$11 billion.[14] The government's share of TELMEX has been sold in stages, and has yielded about U.S.$5 billion.[15] A number of purchases explicitly involved commitments of future investments in the companies, including TELMEX and the two aviation companies Aeroméxico and Mexicana. It is clear that enterprises not in good financial condition received low prices or were not sold at all, and indeed the sale of all the other parastatals will provide an income of less than U.S.$2 billion. The sale of the Cananea mine was hindered by unresolved labor disputes. Sugar mills were not doing well when owned by the state and have not improved in the private sector. It is likely that the government wishes to sell the railroad company, but that there would be no purchasers, at least for the major part of the lines. Thus the sales during 1991 and 1992 of TELMEX stock and the banks will be seen as the high point of the privatization process, in part because the good financial standing of these institutions helped boost prices.[16]

The Mexican Stock Market

Another part of our story is the growth of the Mexican Stock Market. Founded in 1894, this institution had led a quiet existence as an exclusive social club for many years. Heyman (1991) comments that it did not become a serious element in Mexico's development until the passage of the Securities Market Law in 1975, which provided important regulatory and other institutional foundations. Since the early 1980s, this market has grown rapidly, with annual increases, in dollar terms, of 50 or even 100 percent. This growth is perhaps the most visible part of the Mexican miracle and provides a handy comparison between that country and various East Asian NICs.

Heyman (1991) argues that the market is not particularly overvalued in terms of such standard ratios as price/earnings or price/book value. According to that author, the major strengths of the Mexican Stock Market are: 1) a strong, well-capitalized brokerage sector; 2) competent regulators and a government that supports the role of the market in the country's development; 3) a sophisticated, paperless settlement system; 4) a strong mutual fund sector; 5) adequate disclosure requirements and practices; and 6) rapidly increasing foreign investment. Furthermore, two weaknesses are noted: 1) lack of liquidity, so that (in 1991) only twenty stocks would trade more than U.S.$100,000 per day, and a declining number of brokerage accounts; 2) a failure to fulfill its main economic role of being a source of new equity capital to the economy (Heyman, 1991: 132). These criticisms are typical of those leveled at developing country markets and can be found, for example, in Banamex's *Examen de la situación económica de México* (April, 1992), which also highlights concentration, both of brokerage houses and of firms that are attracting investment funds—the value of TELMEX stocks sold locally is roughly 30 percent of the total market capitalization.[17]

The market has increased another 50 percent since Heyman wrote that article and has expanded in terms of the variety of papers that it offers clients. Nevertheless, it is also the case that its role as a provider of new capital has taken second place to that of facilitating the privatization of especially TELMEX and providing a source of entry for foreign investors in Mexican stocks and bonds. Currently, the total capitalization of the Mexican stock market is U.S.$140 billion, of which it is estimated that 20 percent is owned by foreigners, just under half of that from the United States.[18] Given that foreign investment in the market was permitted only in 1989, it is clear that its growth has had substantial effects both in terms of pushing up the value of the market and, as we shall see below, in terms of the country's balance of payments.

Pessimists also note that there was a significant collapse of the market in 1987 under circumstances that led to a major brokerage house owner being put into jail. Whether the historical precedents of the "Dance of the Millions" of the late 1920s or the euphoria in Mexico of 1980-1981 are relevant today is an important if unanswered question. What is clear is that the current modernization of the financial sector very directly puts the Mexican stock market into immediate competition with global economic forces, with Mexican companies raising capital abroad and foreigners investing in the local market, through local brokerage houses or indirectly through American Depository Receipts, ADRs.

THE NAFTA NEGOTIATION PROCESS

Chronology

1965   Maquiladora program; Auto Pact
1985   United States and Canada agree to negotiate an FTA; talks begin 1986
1986   Mexico enters GATT, having declined to do so in 1980
1987   Negotiations completed on Canada-U.S. FTA
1987-89 General discussions between Mexico and the United States on
         strengthening ties, especially in trade and investment
1988   January. Canada-U.S. FTA signed by Mulroney and Reagan
1990   March. *Wall Street Journal* reveals (March 27, 1990) existence of
         exploratory discussions on U.S.-Mexico Free Trade Agreement
         September. President Bush notifies Congress of intent to begin
         negotiations
         May. U.S. Congress approves extension of "fast track" procedures for
         two more years
1992   August. Initialing of proposed agreement by negotiators.

The negotiations took place over a period of fourteen months, organized around nearly twenty themes. There were numerous meetings in several cities in all three countries, with the final ones taking place in Washington, D.C. Signing the agreement were Carla Hills, U.S. Trade Representative, Jaime Serra Puche, Secretary of Commerce in Mexico, and Michael Wilson, Canada's Minister for International Trade. These three had been in charge of statements to the press and other publicity and had ultimate responsibility for the accord; those in charge of the day-to-day negotiations were Herminio Blanco of Mexico, Jules Katz of the United States, and John Weekes of Canada. Additionally, the private sector was represented in the negotiations by "room next door" committees. In Mexico, the head of the private sector information group was Juan Gallardo Thurlow, representing COECE, which apparently had been created for this particular purpose.[19]

The issues around which the negotiations were organized were:

1) tariffs and NTBs	10) services, in general
2) rules of origin	11) financial services
3) government purchases	12) financial services
4) agriculture	13) land transport
5) automobile industry	14) telecommunications
6) other industries	15) other services
7) safeguards	16) investment
8) unfair trade practices	17) intellectual property
9) standards	18) resolution of controversies.

It would appear that, although petroleum was in principle originally included in group (6), "other industries," this theme eventually became the subject of its own group.[20]

Very broadly, the negotiations took as a starting point the agreement between the United States and Canada on which both countries' negotiators would presumably not backtrack, although interest was occasionally expressed in improving the previously agreed arrangements. Thus, tariffs and NTBs, controversy resolution, automobiles, and government purchases were again expected to be important. As pointed out by Hart (1991) and Ritchie (1991), some of the most difficult areas had not been satisfactorily resolved in the earlier negotiations, such as agricultural subsidies, government purchases, and intellectual property. There were some new emphases due to the presence of Mexico. The country's different stage of development led at times to requests for special consideration (maintenance of GSP—trade—privileges, longer phase-in times), or the insistence on lack of such treatment (e.g., the Cavallo doctrine, under which national law treats foreign investors). The Mexican negotiators unceasingly reiterated that the country's Constitution would not be violated, in reference most pointedly to the question of the petroleum industry. Agriculture had an entirely different role in these negotiations, given that it had been generally ignored in the Canada-U.S. FTA,[21] and because any increase of grain exports from the northern two countries would hurt farmers in Mexico, who are among the poorest in the country.

The negotiations took place behind closed doors, and for a long time little information leaked out to the press. A stir was created in March 1992 when a somewhat dated draft was simultaneously made available to critics of the treaty in all three countries. It appeared that the Mexican newsmedia started to contain a larger volume of rumors about the negotiations around May 1992, an interpretation of which would be that the outside media were now being used consciously as part of the bargaining process. This was less true of newsmedia in the United States.

Some key elements in the negotiating positions and strategy of each side were relatively clear. Mexico, which had given up much of its protectionism in order to qualify as a suitable suitor, was expected to liberalize further the financial sector.[22] The United States offered access to its very large market; it was not clear *a priori* how much that country would be willing to change other restrictions to trade and investment, such as banking laws, merchant marine, or agricultural subsidies. Oversimply, one can speak of lower protectionism in the United States being traded for lower investment barriers in Mexico. Canada was usually seen as wishing to maintain the status quo; at times rumors were floated of the country's withdrawal from negotiations. In agriculture, there was an obvious potential *quid pro quo* in terms of the United States improving access for fruits and vegetables in exchange for a reduction of Mexican protection in basic grains.

It was clear that Mexico's insertion involved a possible springboard for non-North American investors; rules of origin were to be centrally important. Indeed, in industries such as automobiles and computers, the Mexican negotiators were essentially deciding which group of multinational firms would be benefited; U.S. or Japanese and German. Greasing the negotiations was some flexibility in the phase-in time for reductions of tariffs and other restrictions. One topic that was excluded from the start was migration. Although the Mexican authorities had prepared the way for negotiations on a number of topics by prior liberalization or restructuring, one area in which this had not occurred sufficiently, and which continues to threaten approval of the eventual agreement, is ecological concerns.

An issue that seemed to gain in potential importance while the negotiations were proceeding was Mexico's trade relations with countries to its south. Free trade agreements were discussed with Chile, Costa Rica, Venezuela, Brazil, at least, and the possibility of cross-trading would complicate agreements made with the United States and Canada. At the same time, the United States had trade/diplomatic initiatives with several other countries in the region that threatened Mexican gains.

Initially, it was hoped that negotiations would be finished by the end of 1991, or at most, early 1992, which would have been most convenient in terms of the confirmation processes. On the U.S. side there had been an unexpectedly nasty fight over the approval of fast-track provision, in 1991. For the Canadians, an unofficial deadline for submission to Parliament is the need for elections, which must be called in 1993. In Mexico, where approval by the PRI-dominated

Congress is assured, the jousting for the presidential campaign—and the PRI's nomination—will be in full swing in 1993, having seen initial skirmishes already in early 1992, rather sooner than normal.

One aspect of the Mexican strategy that has received comment is the increased amount of lobbying and public relations efforts that the government has pursued.[23] This is not surprising from a group that prides itself on its modern outlook, and is quite familiar with U.S. culture; one long-term impact open to question will be its impact on the Latino population in the United States. The degree to which Mexican Americans might feel loyalty to Mexico is open to doubt, particularly because of the fact that many recent migrants work in sectors quite exposed to competition from imports.

Sensitive Areas in the Mexican Productive Structure

Which areas of the Mexican productive system were most at risk in the negotiations, and which have the most to gain? One way to answer this question is by reference to statistical economic models, of which quite a few have been prepared, some of them used directly by the negotiating teams. Rather than review them, which would entail lengthy discussions of how different predictions result from different sets of assumptions, a brief description of key points in major sectors will be presented.

Agriculture. Mexico's weakness is also a major strength—cheap labor and lots of farmland. Increased grain imports directly threaten the livelihood of up to 3 million families. At the same time, as the United States reduces its protection on certain fruits and vegetables, Mexican agroindustry will undergo significant expansion. Specialty crops such as flowers and other tropical products will also flourish. It is not an exaggeration to assert that this sector represents the largest number of workers affected by NAFTA and the widest range of estimates as to the net effect on employment.[24]

Automobiles. This sector epitomizes a certain set of options for the three countries. Almost three decades ago Canada linked the fate of its automotive production to that of the "big three" of the United States, thereby giving up any pretension of autonomous growth while securing a major source of employment. Mexico has been moving in the direction of wholesale acceptance of multinational's dominance of the sector, which is an accomplished fact in vehicle assembly but not in the production of certain parts. This has been referred to as the *maquilización* of Mexico, not least by a former presidential contender.[25] However, two of the five major producers are not North American; Volkswagen and Nissan, and their strength, especially in the domestic market, reflects the competitive weakness of the big three. To the extent that this portends future trends, Mexico should cultivate non-North American companies—and indeed there are indications that Mercedes Benz, Honda, and perhaps others will wish to enter. The motivation for those companies is not necessarily to gain an edge in Mexico's domestic market; rather, it would be to establish a base for exporting to the rest of the North American market, which was the reason behind the U.S. pressure for a relatively high local content rule. While the flow of trade between the United States and Canada tends to be that of parts into Canada and assembled vehicles south, it is rather likely that production and employment there will also be hurt by competition from Mexico. It might also be mentioned that, although motor vehicle sector wages in Mexico are perhaps only one-fifth of those to the north, there are indications that other considerations dominate the decision to relocate; tax reductions, cost of inputs such as energy and water, adaptability of the labor force (see Berry et al., 1992).

Petroleum. This sector attracts the most interest on the part of the counterparts in the U.S. business community, while historical factors guarantee the strongest resistance on the part of the Mexican populace. While initially not a part of the negotiations, this facade could not be maintained. A longstanding desire on the part of certain sectors of the Mexican business and political communities to break up PEMEX became realized in mid-1992,[26] with the announcement that the company would be split into a central corporate "holding" and four autonomous subsidiaries; in exploration, refining, basic petrochemicals/gas, and secondary petrochemicals.[27] The Mexican constitution prohibits alienating subsoil rights; as of this writing there will be no private (domestic or foreign) ownership of the PEMEX subsidiaries. One might expect backsliding on this issue with time because this is exactly what has occurred with respect to the dividing line between primary and secondary petrochemical products, where the number judged to be protected by the constitution has been reduced in stages from over sixty-six in 1988 to nineteen at the start of 1992, and two in the August agreement.

Textiles. Textiles would seem to be an area where much change would be expected as the result of an FTA, given its relatively higher labor content, widespread market, and lack of barriers such as transport costs. As a rule of thumb, the production process becomes less capital intensive as one proceeds from yarn to cloth to apparel assembly, and this logic has led some to foresee a relocation of production according to Mexico's cheaper labor and less abundant capital, that is, a continuation of the maquila phenomenon, with greater content in Mexico. Three considerations qualify that expectation. First of all, some apparel is quite sensitive to fashion shifts, and its production will stay in the United States. Second, the U.S. firms already produce a significant amount overseas, including the Caribbean basin. Finally, the United States is not the technological leader in textiles; according to the UNCTC (1987), that role is currently held by Korea and other Asian NICs, who have displaced Japan in that role. It is intriguing to see that producers in all three countries fear competition from a FTA. Perhaps they are all correct, and that true free trade would lead to a massive shakeout, the elimination of small firms, and other problems. It is clear that there will continue to be much intraindustry trade. However, one item mentioned frequently in the negotiations was that Mexico has not been able to fill its export quota.[28] Another source judging that neither this sector nor agroindustry will experience much new investment is Banamex's *Examen de la situación económica de México* (April, 1992: 99).

Mining. In spite of Mexico's mineral wealth, very little interest has been shown in mining. Reasons for this include oversupply in world markets, a strongly negative legacy of government intervention against foreign ownership, and greater competitive strength of Mexican mining groups. This lack of interest merits comment because of the past importance of the sector in the national economy and its exports, and also because the reasons giving rise to it might well change within a span of a half a decade.

Banks. During the period when the banks were nationalized, two important changes occurred. The government merged a number of banks and otherwise worked to strengthen their financial position. In addition, ex-bankers, using the payments received from the government for their banks, together with new, younger entrepreneurs, established brokerage houses that functioned as "nonbank banks," eventually having total assets equal to half those of the official banks. As noted elsewhere, the banks were reprivatized at prices quite favorable to the government. With the exception of Citibank, foreigners are not allowed participation in banks above 30 percent. This has not stopped the major international banks from maintaining "hotel room offices" for attending major corporations in Mexico.[29] In a general atmosphere of liberalization, one might expect banks and the rest of the financial sector also to be opened up to full foreign ownership. The Mexican response has been twofold; a claim that some time is necessary for the dust to settle on the bank sales, together with complaints that Glass Steagall and the prohibition against interstate banks should also be changed to provide the same treatment in the United States as Canada and Mexico offer at home. In any event, most Mexican commentators assert that foreign banks will only find certain niches in the local economy, such as that of large corporations, because local branch banking has too many local peculiarities. A similar opinion holds for brokerage houses and insurance companies.

Maquila Plants. The question of what will happen to this dynamic sector of the Mexican economy has several partial answers. First of all, North American-owned maquilas[30] should presumably not be directly affected by these changes. Some remaining taxes on exports from these factories will be eliminated, while they will now also be able to sell in the Mexican market without paying import duties. There are other maquilas, from both Europe and Asia, whose future will depend on their ability to meet local-content requirements. Thus, the motives for establishing maquila factories have changed. Finally, as emphasized by a number of studies, many maquilas have been evolving, using more skilled labor. These plants are no longer the fly-by-night operations that originally dotted the map. Many observers believe that the second-generation factories are the wave of the future for Mexican industrial exports.

Franchises. Visitors to Mexico currently are struck by the number of familiar marketing chains in the country. This is not only true of the ubiquitous fast-food outlets but also optical shops, consumer electronics stores, aerobics studios, photocopy shops, rent-a-car agencies, and real estate agencies. Apart from how one might wish to evaluate the cultural impact of this phenomenon, the economist would add that its balance-of-payments effect is probably small (certainly compared to its visibility), the productivity impact is difficult to measure (as it always is in services), and the *direct* effect on it of the NAFTA will be small. Indeed, it is probably the case that the only way these different chains will be affected by the NAFTA is in terms of patents and copyrights.

Transport. This service involves three separable modes; air, marine and land. The Mexican airline companies have been privatized, and intracountry routes will stay with them (no "open skies"). The country's merchant marine is small, and the United States will not expose its shippers to international competition. That leaves land transport, which had been highly regulated (until 1989) and closed to foreigners. Consideration should be further divided into buses, trucks, and railroads. The bus companies are well developed, quite decentralized, and do not fear an opening of competition, although it is likely that foreign companies such as Greyhound will enter into joint ventures with firms that service areas of interest to U.S. passengers. Trucking is quite different. The stock of trucks in Mexico is old and would not be competitive on U.S. interstates. Infrastructural bottlenecks limit passage across the U.S.-Mexican border, and perhaps road quality would continue to discourage large trucks from venturing southward, but this is a clear area of potential expansion by U.S. interests, as indeed happened after the FTA. The Mexican railroad system is also old; its modernization would be extremely costly, and would be greatly hindered by political considerations, not only the constitutional provision reserving it to the state, but also the local impact of removing inefficient lines.

THE NAFTA AGREEMENT

The countries' representatives announced the agreement on August 12, 1992. This was more than half a year later than had been expected by "informed opinion" at the start of negotiations, and threatened that the approval process in the United States would get entangled in that year's electoral battles. Information on the terms of the agreement had been leaking out over the previous two or three months, and, on the above date, only a forty-page summary was made available to the public (Governments of Canada, et al., 1992), whose informational content was basically to certify the accuracy of the leaked and rumored details. Legal experts went to work on preparing an official text of the agreement, which was not completed and made available in Spanish and French as well as English until the following month. Approval of NAFTA had not been considered by the corresponding representative bodies from any of the three countries at the time of this writing (September 1992).

The agreement clearly builds off the Canada-U.S. FTA, with frequent references to provisions and objectives of the GATT. Our discussion of it here will be divided into trade restrictions, foreign investment, operational aspects, and an overall evaluation.

"The NAFTA provides for the progressive elimination of all tariffs on goods qualifying as North American under its rules of origin" (Governments of Canada, et al., 1992: 4). Three parts to this sentence deserve comment. First of all, the fundamental philosophy is indeed the elimination of all tariffs. However, it turns out that subsidies to producers can remain, which indeed reflects the basic weakness of the current GATT arrangements. Trade of certain agricultural products is not liberalized. Secondly, the issue arises as to which goods are North American. Several valuative schemes are indicated, depending on the product, ranging from a change in tariff classification to an estimate of the percentage of "local content" in total value or the restriction of that calculation to "yarn forward" for certain textiles. Thirdly, the trade liberalization will be phased in over time. Itemization of these details quickly becomes tedious, and indeed full information is not yet available. It would appear that the issue of the time period for liberalization of a given product reflects the perception of the adjustment costs of labor and, perhaps, capital in protected countries, and the political influence of those groups inside their countries in addition to the obvious factor of the bargaining ability of the negotiating teams.[31]

While the agreement is described as freeing "trade," much interest attends how it affects investment. This centers on Mexico, because Canada's cultural industries are left alone, as is U.S. banking, which some observers thought might be renegotiated. Mexico further opened up its financial sector and certain parts of petroleum processing, as expected, and FDI in land transportation will be allowed. The point was made in Chapter 5 that Mexico had been liberalizing foreign trade for some time; the biggest change in volumes of direct investment will probably come as a result of reductions of protectionism in the United States and Canada. In this regard the rules of origin become key determinants of how much investment from Europe or Asia will be generated, and the early evaluations are that those rules of origin are rather restrictive. Thus, the NAFTA will encourage investing in Mexico by citizens to its north but discourage those from the east or west, who might consider Mexico as an export platform. The rules of origin are only important in determining whether a product from one country ought to enter another country without tariffs; since NAFTA does not involve common tariffs, production by European and Asian firms in Mexico for sale inside Mexico is not affected.

There are two brief comments about operational aspects of NAFTA. First of all, the philosophy of the dispute-settlement mechanism is maintained, and its operation is expanded to include Mexico. Time will tell how effective this is.

Secondly, both in the negotiations and in the published description of the agreement, significant attention was given to various technical standards, from phytosanitary regulations to licensing truck drivers to environmental requirements. It is important to recognize that this absorbed significant attention of the negotiating teams. While not directly related to "free trade," lack of clear understanding and procedures in these areas can easily lead to manipulation by protectionist interests. Moreover, a broader concept of integration requires homogenization along these lines, which has negative as well as positive connotations.

What about the big picture—is it a good agreement? Those judgments are finally made by historians, and not even the legislatures of the countries have spoken yet. Rather than hazard an overall evaluation of the accord, some comments will now be presented, on its form rather than on its content. The NAFTA builds effectively off the FTA and would have taken much longer to negotiate without it. However, there are in NAFTA several cases of bilateral accords rather than multilateral ones; examples are in automobiles, textiles, agriculture, government procurement, land transport, and finance. This will make accession to the agreement by other countries more difficult. Secondly, this round of negotiations highlights the dispersion of power to state/provincial and local levels, especially in Canada and the United States. These groups did not participate in the negotiations and still retain the ability to hinder the trend towards liberalization. The final comment on its structure refers to environmental issues. Although the government of Mexico made gigantic strides in creating credibility for its new free-market orientation, no similar conversion is apparent with regard to the environment. Not only will this issue hinder the approval process in the United States and Canada, but the fear is widespread that under the NAFTA, Mexico will be forced to vary environmental laws and their enforcement to suit pressures of business groups, both foreign and domestic.

NOTES

1. A representative treatment of these issues here is beyond our means. One consideration would be that the increased Canadian nationalism was not responding solely to FDI but to the U.S. presence more generally. By the end of World War II the relative balance of U.S. and U.K. influences over Canada had been lost. The Defense Procurement Agreement of 1958, and Prime Minister Diefenbaker's ill-fated project of reducing trade dependency on the United States underlined the changing balance of power and independence. See Ritchie (1991), and, for a classic statement, see Grant (1965).

2. One telling indicator of the perceptions by Canadian policymakers at the time is the oft-repeated retort to the question of how the FTA scenario would compare to the status quo—"There is no more status quo."

3. There are also 1,100 pages of tariffs. An official draft of the NAFTA accord, dated September 15, 1992, appears to be of similar size, although the pages are not numbered consecutively.

4. One simple example, probably not mentioned specifically in the negotiations; your author's fellowship for graduate study was financed by the National Defense Education Act.

5. The best discussion, by far, of NAFTA is Hufbauer and Schott (1992).

6. However, it is interesting from a current perspective to note carefully what people today say about that period. For example, Córdoba (1986: 318) refers to the exhaustion of that growth experience while also noting that some would have the economy return to that model. Similarly, people of a nationalist persuasion who rejoice in the successful import substitution that occurred then, often fail to remark on the dependence of industrial growth on foreign investment.

7. At the time of this writing (mid-1992), the government is preparing an initiative that will greatly open up mining to foreign investors. While this is frequently discussed in the media, there has been little debate on it. One reason is that with international prices of minerals at low levels, due to the relaxation of Cold War armament expenditures, there is less interest in this activity.

8. My translation. Of course, one can find more typically nationalistic quotes in this and many other statements by Mr. Cárdenas and other leftist opposition leaders; the point is that for whatever reason they did not reject free trade negotiations out of hand.

9. See the discussion in Alvear Acevedo and Ortega Venzor (1991: 245ff) for an elaboration of these ideas.

10. For example, by Finance Secretary Pedro Aspe (1991).

11. In the privatization of the banks, for example, there was a question about "hidden" loans that eventually would finance the purchase of another bank (Banca Serfin to Inverlat), of high public employees being involved in a buyers' consortium (*La Jornada* February 8, 1992), of a winning bidder withdrawing his bid under unusual circumstances (Grupo Creel and Banco Somex). Aspersions about the process of resolutions of effectively equal bids appear in *Proceso* of March 9, 1992, with regard to Banca Confía and Bancomer. In terms of foreign press, the sharpest criticism appeared in an article in *Business Week* of July 22, 1991, entitled "The Friends of Carlos Salinas." The sale of TELMEX to the Grupo Carso appeared to benefit from a six month loan (at market rates) from the government, while Carso attempted to raise money on the international markets (*Este País*, December 1991, p. 9). A major purchase receiving significant international financing was that of Bancomer, for which Vamsa had received a short-term credit of U.S.$1 billion (*La Jornada* November 9, 1991). Presumably the purchase of most of the banks received external financing, but very few details are made public. With regard to Banoro, see *La Jornada*, April 8, 1992; Banca Promex in *El Financiero*, April 8, 1992; the different positions of the competitors for Banco Mercantil del Norte in *La Jornada*, June 12, 1992;

Banamex sought a billion-dollar financing package in June, 1992.

12. A perceptive friend commented that, were a scandal to arise, the normal timing would be during the next *sexenio*.

13. The liquidity crisis of September 1991 may have been partially responsible for the decision to eliminate the required reserve ratio on peso deposits in banks.

14. Finance undersecretary Guillermo Ortiz, who has led the process of sale of the banks, claims that these prices are typical of such sales. In addition to the fact that government action during the 1980s of consolidating and otherwise helping the banks strengthened many of those banks, another factor making the banks attractive purchases has been the retirement accounts, SAR, modeled after a similar program in Chile, in which individual workers' (obligatory) savings accrue in accounts in private banks instead of the Social Security System. There will be an estimated ten million such accounts. The elimination of the Social Security System's mortgage bank, INFONAVIT, has a similar effect on the attractiveness of the purchase of the banks.

15. The series AA stocks, sold to an international consortium led by Carlos Slim, cost about $1.8 billion. The Series L stocks were worth $2.2 billion, and the subsequent sale in May 1992 of other stock yielded $1.4 billion. See *Este País*, February 1992, and *El Financiero*, May 13, 1992.

16. While providing folklorically bad local telephone service, TELMEX has also been quite profitable. This situation will apparently continue. In a published interview, the manager of the company promised slow changes in household service, as the company would concentrate on countering international competition by investing in fiber optics. *El Financiero*, December 2, 1991.

17. See *La Jornada*, June 19, 1992. It is also claimed (*El Financiero*, June 17, 1992) that the volume of sales of Telmex Series L stock is 3.5 times larger abroad than in Mexico, providing a globalization of the country's stock market with both benefits and costs. These latter arise when a "cough" in the New York market (related to the presidential candidacy of Ross Perot) caused a "cold" in Mexico, as occurred in June 1992. The importance of the example is the political nature of the factor changing investor confidence in the United States.

18. The stock market—Bolsa Mexicana de Valores—comprises stocks, bonds, and various mutual funds. Data from *El Financiero*, June 5, 1992.

19. See Alvear Acevedo and Ortega Venzor (1991: 217). Thurlow is a successful businessman, who during the negotiations continued to be active in such events as the privatization of the banks.

20. In other areas there was an evolution in the number of negotiating groups. An early list contained seventeen groups (*El Mercado de Valores*, August 1, 1991); the list in the text comes from *El Mercado de Valores*, May 1, 1992.

21. Reflecting the generally parallel structures of both production and government intervention.

22. While nationalist groups complained that Mexico had thereby given up its bargaining chips, the obvious response was that the Mexican negotiators could say to the others, "Now it's your turn."

23. See *New York Times,* December 30, 1991, and *Este País,* June 1992.

24. The figures of 3 million families and 4.5 million workers, are the estimates of Calva (1991). Of course this would have devastating consequences on the Mexican economy and flood the border with illegal immigrants. Yúnez-Naude (1991), Levy and van Wijnbergen (1991), and Hinojosa-Ojeda and Robinson (1992) present NAFTA scenarios covering a very broad range of estimates from an increase in demand for agricultural workers to an outmigration of almost 1 million. A careful study of fruit and vegetable export farming estimates the increase in farm labor associated with NAFTA to be only 67,000 jobs (Runsten and Wilcox Young 1992; 12).

25. Interview with Jesús Silva Herzog, reported in *Proceso,* May 4, 1991.

26. This move was made easier because of an industrial accident resulting in the deaths of hundreds of people in Guadalajara, for which PEMEX was perceived to have been primarily responsible and to have responded in a high-handed manner.

27. A precedent is the creation in 1988 of Petróleos Mexicanos Internacional, which is responsible for the international sales of PEMEX's products, as well as the legal holder of PEMEX's stock in other companies, such as the Spanish Repsol (*El Financiero,* June 15, 1992).

28. See BANAMEX, May 1991. The quotas are specified in detail so that some Mexican exports are limited by quotas while other products are simply not competitive in foreign markets.

29. Calculated to account for 20 percent of the business with the 100 largest Mexican firms. *El Financiero,* September 30, 1991.

30. See *El Financiero,* March 12, 1992 for the assertion that some 43 percent of maquilas are 100 percent owned by Mexicans, and less than 5 percent are held by non-North Americans. Because of the institution of *prestanombres* ("name lenders"), it is clear that the foreign influence over maquilas is much higher, although what the geographic breakdown would be is an open question.

31. Bargaining ability is not something easy to measure. Recall that the general evaluation is that the benefits of the FTA were divided between both countries. Early in 1992 when the negotiations seemed to be bogged down, one perceived in Mexico a certain fear that the country's representatives were going to give up most anything to get an agreement, together with a subsequent sigh of relief when it later became apparent that this had not occurred. Such perceptions are completely subjective and in no way suggest that future debate inside the country will not be very critical of the agreement.

8

FDI, NAFTA, AND ECONOMIC LIBERALIZATION

The major subject of this chapter is the potential effects of NAFTA on FDI flows into Mexico. Various scenarios will be sketched out and evaluated in terms of key macroeconomic variables.

Preparatory to those exercises, we wish to look at the effects of trade liberalization itself on Canada and Mexico. Our interpretation of the data, consistent with standard economic theory, is that the major effect has been a realignment of production more closely along comparative advantage lines, whose net impact on the macroeconomy is neither as negative as many Canadian critics of the FTA allege nor as positive as hoped for by some optimists in Mexico. To the extent that this is accurate, therefore, major economic changes in Mexico will come not from that country's further trade liberalization agreed to in NAFTA. An essentially structural shift in production will occur only if expanded access to the U.S. market results in significant new exports from Mexico. Given the pre-NAFTA structure of protection and raw material trade in the United States and Canada, these new exports would occur as part of a regional reallocation of production by the major MNCs, requiring massive flows of FDI to Mexico. The plausibility of such an outcome is considered in the fourth section.

While one evaluation of the new FDI flows compares them to the current stocks of domestic and foreign capital, another, more immediate one looks at them in the context of the balance of payments. In the fifth section of this chapter we contrast the magnitudes of the flows of fixed versus portfolio capital, finding that the latter have indeed been much larger. This has significant implications for short-run exchange rate stability, whose description ends the chapter.

MNCs AND THE FTA

The signing of the FTA between Canada and the United States was accompanied by significant debate in the former country, and indeed the agreement eventually became the dominant issue in a national election. In the popular mind, increased economic integration posed many threats to Canada due to the larger scale and perceived technological superiority of U.S. producers. Avenues of greater U.S. penetration would be both more exports into Canada and more foreign investment. Needless to say, there were and are many important social issues in that debate that will remain outside the purview of this work, such as the maintenance of distinct national and even regional cultures in Canada, and safeguarding its political independence, threatened by U.S. regulations on the operations of its MNCs abroad.

With regard to foreign investment, the debate in Canada contained two mutually inconsistent fears: that the FTA will bring in more MNCs, and that it will cause them to leave. The former position essentially reflects a belief that the barriers to foreign control of Canadian cultural activities, along with those protecting other service industries, were being reduced. The opposite position was held by those who feel that the tariff continues to be important and judge MNCs' contributions to be positive. While the OLI approach places great importance on the effect of tariffs in attracting industries, investigators believe that the converse is not true for Canada and that lowering tariffs will not lead to a mass exodus. Rugman (1990) and McFetridge (1989) summarize studies based on surveys; they generally conclude that the effect of (further) lowering tariffs on MNCs in Canada will be small. This prediction is supported by the recent data reported earlier in Table 4.5.

That being said, it is still very early to evaluate the overall impact of the FTA on either the United States or Canada. Many critics in Canada blame a significant increase in unemployment on the agreement, which is an issue we take up immediately below. Moreover, it is clear that the initiators of the agreement hoped that some effects would be felt before its actual signing and coming into power, while other aspects of the FTA involve benefits—such as the trade dispute mechanism—to be realized over the long term. These considerations certainly complicate a general evaluation of the FTA. But let us now turn to the specific issue of exports and imports.

TRADE LIBERALIZATION AND PRODUCTION

Basic economics predicts that the reduction of tariffs and other controls on imported goods will probably lower domestic production and employment in these sectors. There should also be a corresponding increase in activities oriented towards exports. In principle, one can investigate the net effect of liberalization on output and employment.[1] Currently, this question has important ramifications in both Canada and Mexico, even though the contexts are quite different—Canada has lowered some barriers as part of the Free Trade

Agreement signed with the United States, while Mexico's adhesion to the GATT required a unilateral tariff reduction, much larger than that of Canada.[2] In both these countries, the tariff reduction has been accompanied by a recession, which has been sharper in Mexico. Neither case is an ideal test of liberalization. Canada has been lowering tariffs for some time, while Mexico's recession had begun before the GATT accord, as a result of the debt crisis.

Responding to the slower growth of the mid-1980s as well as to the nationalist policies of his predecessor, the newly elected government of Brian Mulroney initiated discussions with the United States on greater economic integration, which eventually led to the signing of the FTA in 1989. Three years later, the Canadian economy was suffering a prolonged recession, partially caused by the recession of its major trading partner, and domestic policies, particularly a tight, anti-inflation monetary policy. Some government critics are fond of claiming that this recession was "made in Canada." However, many also blame the Free Trade Agreement for hurting local industrial production because of expanded imports. These economic problems, combined with political problems over the Constitution and the status of Quebec, caused the Mulroney government to have very low standings in the public opinion polls.

During the 1980s, Mexico suffered severe economic problems associated with adjustments forced by the debt crisis. The government's response was a wide-ranging series of liberal policies, including the 1985 decision to enter the GATT. By the end of the decade, the worst threats of the debt crisis appeared to be receding, and the newly elected president, Carlos Salinas de Gortari, attempted to ensure the permanence of these advances by securing new sources of growth, one of which is the NAFTA. It is fair to expect that the experience of the impact of tariff reductions, in the context of the GATT, will have important lessons regarding the prospect of further trade liberalization in the NAFTA.

In this section we will attempt a comparison of the effects of the two trade liberalizations on manufacturing production and employment. The central task is to separate statistically for each country the results of liberalization and recession, and the methodology utilized involves the implicit assumption that the recessionary effects of liberalization are essentially of a second degree of magnitude. Whatever the accuracy of that assumption, we shall see that other, longer-term issues also cloud the discussion, such as a common trend towards a lowered labor intensity of production. Our focus on manufacturing industry responds to two considerations: 1) in both countries there have been much smaller changes in protection and hence in trade flows for the other two traded good sectors, agriculture and mining; and 2) an economywide approach, studying the net general equilibrium effects on the entire labor market of changes in industrial employment due to trade liberalization, is simply beyond our means. It is hoped that this less-ambitious approach still permits the highlighting of the major elements involved in trade liberalization.

We will use two routes to estimate the impact of trade liberalization. The first might be referred to as an implicit supply function for domestic output, in which a dummy variable reflects the net effect of liberalization. A second approach looks more directly at trade and looks at the effect of liberalization on imports. Implicitly treating all manufactured products as traded goods, we estimate the impact of increased imports both directly, as the increase indicated by the dummy on the import function, and indirectly as the decline in production, implied by the dummy in the output function. The latter interpretation slights the positive contribution of liberalization to exports, but of course the issue being discussed is trade liberalization as a cause of the observed recessions.[3] This factor should have been relatively more important in Canada, although those exports also suffered from the global recession. The use of dummy variables for the periods of greater trade liberalization is a shortcut for an analysis using detailed data on the prices of imports and national output, one that avoids the problem of nonobservability of nontariff barriers.

The total output equation takes the form of $Q_i = f(Q_t, dQ_t, \text{Dummies})$, where Q_i is either total manufacturing output or sectoral output, and Q_t is GDP, all measured in real terms. dQ_t is the deviation of observed GDP from trend, and was hypothesized to have a positive sign, due to an assumed greater weight of industry in (presumably cyclical) investment. Under the assumption that the degree of import expansion would increase with time, a separate dummy was used for each year of the postliberalization phase. The import functions take the form of $I_i = f(Q_t, \text{RER}, \text{Dummies})$, where RER is the real exchange rate, of the form $E*P'/P$, where E is the domestic price of foreign currency, P' is foreign prices, and P is a domestic price index. The Mexican series is a trade-weighted balance of real exchange rates. The output series is gross value for the Mexican data, allowing direct comparability with the import series. Data availability forced the use of value added for Canada. Finally, an equation of manufacturing employment was estimated, of the form $L_i = f(Q_i, W/P, dQ_t, \text{Dummies})$, where L_i is either total or sectoral employment and W/P is the corresponding real wage.

As the equations are estimated with the dependent variable in logarithms, the interpretation of a coefficient on a dummy variable, with an estimated value of z, is that the level of the dependent variable was changed by the amount $(1-e^{-z})$, which, for values of z close to zero, is approximately z.

The time span was 1970-1991 for Mexico, and 1971-1991 for Canada; the liberalization dummies were assigned for the years beginning in 1987 for Mexico and 1989 for Canada.

All data come from official sources. For Mexico, the primary source was the various publications of INEGI/SPP *Cuentas Nacionales* (1970-1978, 1979-1981, 1981-1987, 1986-1989). Data on real wages, employment, and output for 1990-1991 were taken from the survey data presented in several issues of INEGI *Avance de Información Económica*. More recent data on import growth rates was taken from issues of *Comercio Exterior*, and thus is also an approximation to the official INEGI data. The real exchange rate was taken from the Banco de México

Indicadores Económicos.

For Canada, most data come from several issues of the Bank of Canada *Review*, supplemented by data from the *Canadian Economic Observer*. Production data was taken from Statistics Canada's *National Income and Product Accounts* and *Manufacturing Industries of Canada.*

ECONOMETRIC ESTIMATES

A representative set of estimated equations for production, imports, and employment in manufacturing are presented for the two countries in Table 8.1. To save space, only the most important econometric regressions will be reported here. Detailed results are presented in a working paper (Twomey, 1992). We turn first to the results for output.

The elasticity of output with respect to GDP is slightly less than unity in Mexico, which is not surprising. However, estimates of that elasticity vary strongly for Canada, being also less than unity when a time trend is not included, but doubling in size when that trend is included. The variable representing cyclical factors (dGDP) has the expected positive sign, and again is much higher in Canada. With regard to manufacturing and the dummy variables representing the trade liberalization, these are positive in both countries, although small and statistically insignificant in Canada. If the effect of greater imports dominates, the sign of these variables should be negative. Of course, there are obvious problems of an econometric nature involved in this time series analysis.[4] However, alternative explanations will be explored below.

The most important result for the equations on imports in Table 8.1 is the high and statistically significant values for the dummies representing liberalization in both countries. Generally, the size of the estimated coefficients on the dummies increased over time, as expected, reflecting the growing impact of this policy. That the coefficients were higher in Mexico than in Canada also responds to conventional wisdom about that country's greater steps towards trade liberalization in the latter 1980s. One uncomfortable result was the hypothetically wrong sign on the coefficient on relative prices for Canada, although it was not statistically significant.

Turning finally to the labor equations in Table 8.1, we see in each country that the output elasticity of demand for labor was less than unity, that the time trend and the cyclical effect were both negative as hypothesized, and that the coefficients on real wages have the expected negative sign. The coefficients on the dummy variables were not significant in either country, although that for Canada was negative and larger than its standard error.

In summary, the effect of trade liberalization on imports is clear, but its impact on production and employment is not yet apparent. A richer and presumably more accurate appreciation of the effects of liberalization can be

Table 8.1
Regression Results for Canada and Mexico

(Independent Variables)

(Dependent
Variable)

Manufacturing Output

	Constant	GDP	dGDP	Year	Dum87	Dum88	Dum89	Dum90	Dum91	R^2
CANADA	51.60	1.73	0.96	-0.03			0.02	0.01	0.01	0.97
	(4.83)	(8.48)	(4.00)	(4.72)			(0.84)	(0.52)	(0.32)	
MEXICO	6.19	0.95	0.40	0.001	0.003	0.02	0.05	0.06	0.06	0.99
	(0.68)	(10.9)	(2.52)	(0.01)	(0.16)	(0.02)	(1.56)	(1.79)	(1.78)	

Manufactured Imports

	Constant	GDP	RER	Year	Dum87	Dum88	Dum89	Dum90	Dum91	R^2
CANADA	-65.9	1.49	0.05	0.03			0.01	0.05	0.15	0.99
	(5.26)	(8.73)	(0.24)	(4.19)			(0.24)	(0.90)	(2.36)	
MEXICO	245.	3.32	-0.52	-0.13	0.49	0.87	1.03	1.24	1.44	0.83
	(3.38)	(4.60)	(1.30)	(3.21)	(2.16)	(3.61)	(3.92)	(4.41)	(4.74)	

Manufacturing Employment

	Constant	Q	dQ	W/P	Year	Dum87	Dum88	Dum89	Dum90	Dum91	R^2
CANADA	17.90	0.59	-0.18	-0.37	-0.01			0.05	0.02	-0.05	0.87
	(5.05)	(6.92)	(1.82)	(2.08)	(2.69)			(2.19)	(0.59)	(1.24)	
MEXICO	44.90	0.89	-0.25	-0.20	-0.02	0.03	0.03	0.03	0.03	0.01	0.99
	(4.25)	(8.05)	(2.50)	(2.80)	(3.56)	(1.71)	(1.59)	(1.76)	(0.97)	(0.27)	

Note: The following variables were transformed to logarithms; Manufacturing output, GDP, Imports, Manufacturing Employment, and the Real Exchange Rate. Dum87 takes a value of 1 for 1987, Dum88 equals 1 in 1988, . . ., Dum91 takes a value of 1 for 1991. The manufacturing output variable for Canada is real value added, for Mexico it is real value of gross output.

R^2 is the adjusted R squared. Absolute values of t-coefficients in parenthesis.

obtained by estimating separately each equation for disaggregated sectors. The corresponding estimated equations, not listed here, repeat many of the above messages. For example, with regard to what was called the implicit supply, its equations generally have an income elasticity close to one, a positive cyclical response, and increasing coefficients on the time dummies. The signs of the time trends differ, presumably identifying dynamic and stagnant industries.

The disaggregated estimates should help clarify the interaction of trade liberalization and production. Some basic calculations are provided in Table 8.2, where the cumulative effect of liberalization, represented by the coefficient of the dummy D91, is compared to its impact on production. First, note in columns (1) and (2) that imports represent a higher fraction of total manufacturing production in Canada so that increases in this variable represent a proportionately larger amount of supply in Canada. Secondly, columns (3) and (4) of that table show that in Mexico the percentage growth of imports was much higher than that of production, as we saw earlier. The more relevant comparison, however, is to a common denominator, for which we use total demand, approximated by summing production plus imports. These numbers are presented in columns (5) and (6).

In Mexico, the behavior of two export sectors, nonmetallic minerals and (especially) metal products, is quite different from the others. That metal products would show a positive response during the liberalization period should not surprise us, for the growth of automobile production and exports is well known.[5] The opposite side of the coin is equally important; excluding the metal products sector, the rest of manufacturing has a negative coefficient on the liberalization dummy, implying that its production has declined as a consequence of this policy. Tapia Maruri and Cervantes González (1992: 62) also estimated the net effect of trade liberalization on Mexican industrial production to be small, up through mid-1988.

The results for Canada also reflect the distinction between export and import competing sectors. Production improves in beverages, paper, primary metals, transport equipment, and petroleum, all of which belong to the former group. Moreover, imports tend to be negatively correlated with production, as theory predicts. The experiences of leather and textiles, having negative coefficients on both variables, are not consistent with the simple model of liberalization, nor is that of wood products, a major export.[6] That observation, plus the weaker relationship between import growth and production decline, leads us to suspect that other factors had important effects in Canada. Prime candidates would be the behavior of exchange rates and interest rates; treatment of these factors would necessitate a more ambitious macroeconomic model. Unfortunately, pursuit of this topic would take us too far afield.

What can be said about manufacturing employment? In the disaggregated equations for both countries, the time trend is usually negative and statistically significant. For the specific case of Mexico, the coefficient on the liberalization dummy is vaguely positive, which is to say small and not statistically significant. More noteworthy are the two cases where it is negative, namely basic metals and metal products, with the latter being the major growth area in Mexican manufacturing. In the specific case of metal products, our estimated effect of

Table 8.2
Mexico and Canada: Estimated Percentage Changes in Production, Imports, and Total Demand, as a Result of Trade Liberalization, 1991

	(1) Production	(2) Imports (observed levels)	(3) % Change Attributed to Liberalization Product	(4) Imports	(5) Change in Item as Percentage of Total Demand Product	(6) Imports
CANADA	(billion 1986 C$)					
Manufacturing	202.6	127.5	1	7	1	3
Food	29.0	8.2	-5	13	-4	3
Beverages	4.0	0.5	5	-6	4	-1
Rubber	2.1	0.4	-5	7	-4	1
Plastics	3.9	2.8	-17	10	-10	4
Leather	0.7	0.7	-60	-15	-31	-7
All Textiles	8.3	4.3	-22	-21	-15	-7
Wood Industries	10.7	0.8	-7	3	-7	0
Furniture Industries	2.5	2.4	-8	30	-4	14
Paper & Allied	16.1	0.3	16	-7	15	-0
Printing & Publishing	7.7	2.0	-28	21	-23	4
Primary Metals	15.0	4.6	26	6	20	1
Metal Fabricating	12.0	14.7	5	16	2	9
Machinery	5.9	11.5	-7	1	-2	1
Transport Equipment	38.1	37.1	9	1	4	0
Electrical Products	16.0	21.5	-3	19	-1	11
Nonmetallic Minerals	4.6	0.1	13	1	13	0
Petroleum & Coal Products	12.0	1.7	10	-22	9	-3
Chemicals & Products	13.2	5.9	-11	4	-7	1
Miscellaneous	4.1	7.9	-3	13	-1	9
MEXICO	(billion 1980 Pesos)					
Manufacturing	3014	611	7	76	6	13
Food and Beverages	894	47	-3	83	-3	4
All Textiles	262	27	-9	95	-9	9
Wood Products	80	6	-17	85	-16	6
Printing & Paper	148	21	-2	71	-2	9
Chemicals	577	133	-3	53	-2	10
Nonmetallic Minerals	138	9	7	90	6	6
Basic Metals	196	38	-6	78	-5	13
Metal Products	659	303	39	81	27	25
Other Industries	54	20	6	56	4	15
Total Mexican Manufacturing, without Metal Products					-3	8

Columns (3) and (4) are 100*(1-exp(-z)), where the z are the coefficients of Dum91, in the first two sets of equations in Table 8.1. Column (5) = [(1)*(3)]/[(1)+(2)]; column (6) = [(2)*(4)]/[(1)+(2)].

liberalization on employment is reduced by over half, due to increased capital intensiveness of production.

With regard to Canada, the tendency is that more of the coefficients on the liberalization dummy variables in the labor demand equation are large and statistically significant. This is the case for the following sectors; food, leather, textiles, wood, printing, transport equipment, and electrical equipment. This finding is robust to changes in the specification of the equation. Thus, even given the level of production, there still was a strong tendency for labor use to fall. In other words, a good part of the employment problem in Canada is completely independent of trade liberalization.

Let us return briefly to the case of Mexico. While these estimates and calculations suggest a negative impact of liberalization on production and employment, arguably the more relevant comparison is not liberalization versus the prior protectionist regime, but rather pertains to a quite different scenario involving the recession associated with the debt crisis and its aftermath. Specifically, had total output continued to grow in Mexico during the 1980s as it had in the previous two decades, real GDP would have been roughly 65 percent higher in 1991 than it actually was, and manufacturing output would have been more than 60 percent higher. With an output elasticity of demand for labor of 0.9, manufacturing employment would have been more than 50 percent higher than occurred. Both the negative time trend and the loss of demand due to the long recession appear to have had much more severe effects on Mexican industrial employment than did the trade liberalization.

NAFTA AND FDI INTO MEXICO

Let us now turn to some speculative comments about the effects of the North American Free Trade Agreement on the Mexican economy. The first observations is that Mexico has already taken a giant step at reducing its tariffs and NTBs in accordance with its accession to the GATT. This may well have a larger impact on the country's economy over the next five or even ten years than would the NAFTA.

It may be of some use to estimate, however crudely, the potential increase in FDI. Before presenting three projections it is necessary to specify the initial conditions. These depend on two estimates: the actual (1985) values of total and foreign-owned capital stock and the projected percentage increase in foreign ownership. It is clear that any actual increase in the capital stock will occur over a period of years, in the inverted V pattern typical of accelerator models. We turn first to the more straightforward issue of the initial values of domestic and foreign capital.

Available data on the nonresidential capital stock in Mexico was summarized in Table 5.5. Our estimated total value of Mexican nonresidential capital stock is U.S.$ 174 billion for 1985. While the lack of census data after 1985 weakens the estimates to follow, the distribution of fixed investment cannot have changed that much in subsequent years. The biggest gap in our statistical knowledge relates to agriculture. As discussed in Chapter 3, experience in Mexico is that foreign investors prefer to own the industrial phase of food production, leaving the farms in the hands of the direct producers. Therefore, lack of data on agriculture may be less significant for our purposes.

With regard to foreign ownership, we used the percentages for the industrial sector that appear in Peres Nuñez (1990: 19), the values for agriculture, mining, and petroleum reported in Table 5.5, and the percentages reported by Baillet and Cisneros (1988) for the service sector.

How much will foreign investment increase as a result of the NAFTA? This is a key policy question, one on which our theoretical model should have something to contribute. A number of structural variables, emphasized by the OLI perspective as important determinants of FDI, will not change in the short run—R&D, advertising, concentration ratios, economies of scale, and degree of multiplant production. This is also basically true of Mexican real income and wages. Moreover, the reduction of Mexican tariffs should not have a large effect—these tariffs are already low. Thus, there are two major variables which will change; governmental restrictions on FDI, and the size of the market for Mexican products, due to greater openness in the northern economies.

The message of the lengthy discussion of governmental policy in chapters 3 and 5 was that there were few sectors in the economy for which access by foreigners was still restricted before the NAFTA negotiations were initiated. In some cases—including most of manufacturing—this had effectively been true for some time. The foreign investment regulation of 1989 formalized that position. FDI in agriculture was encouraged by the constitutional changes of 1991, although some restrictions still remain. Moreover, certain other areas continue to be off limits; basic petroleum is the most noteworthy. The most dramatic changes in percentage of foreign ownership caused by regulatory changes will undoubtedly occur in the banking, finance, and insurance sectors. While there may well be a significant inflow of capital, it will not be fixed assets. Moreover, the corresponding employment impacts will be small as these activities are not labor intensive and their market will not expand much due its essentially internal orientation.

What many commentators believe will be the most important factor leading to an increase in FDI is of course the increased access that products from Mexico will have in the markets of the United States and Canada. There are limits to this process; restrictions on imports will last for as long as fifteen years in some cases. Moreover, the local content regulations will discourage investors from Europe and Asia, whose products will be directly imported.

Three different scenarios are considered. The first, which will be called the investment liberalization scenario, simply assumes that Mexican productive sectors achieve the ratio of foreign ownership that Canada had in 1987. Although this may be a useful stand-in for an assumed liberalization of foreign investment regulations in Mexico, it suffers from certain biases of opposite signs. First, some FDI in Canada is already there because of that country's nearly unrestricted access to the U.S. market. Secondly, OLI-type considerations would lead us to believe that, if given unlimited access to the domestic Mexican market, foreign investors would dominate it more than they have the domestic market in Canada.

The second scenario analyzes Mexico's unilateral elimination of tariffs in a context of increasing returns to scale and international mobility of capital, utilizing the estimates from version three of Sobarzo (1991).[7]

The third case, referred to as the NAFTA scenario, assumes that all of Mexican industry obtains the level of import penetration into the United States that Mexican automobile sector currently enjoys (1.5 percent), and that there is no corresponding response of domestic investment in Mexico. The underlying hypothesis here is that the access to the U.S. market that will eventually be achieved by producers in Mexico will basically be determined by political forces, and that the automobile case approximates the corresponding upper limit. No attempt is made to model formally the effect on FDI of trade liberalization. The reader will recall that the OLI approach has not yet been incorporated in CGE type models which are currently the preferred technique for trade liberalization analysis.

To a significant degree, the first two scenarios refer to actions that Mexico had taken before the beginning of the NAFTA negotiations, while the third attempts to incorporate the effects on Mexican production and capital stock of a NAFTA-caused partial opening of the U.S. economy. As can be seen in Table 8.3, the three scenarios involve increases in FDI of U.S.$10, 23, and 15 billion, respectively. In principle, the three scenarios attempt to gauge three different effects; that of eliminating controls on FDI, liberalization of trade in Mexico, and attaining a certain level of access to the U.S. market. The numbers presented in the table do not distinguish so cleanly between the three situations, and because of the significant overlap among them it would be assumed that their combined effect would be much less than the sum of the parts.[8]

How important would be these new investments? Several evaluations spring to mind. One obvious point of comparison is the inflow of foreign exchange on the current account. The value of Mexican physical exports in 1991 was around U.S.$27 billion, while services and other items bring the current account total up to about $45 billion. For the sake of discussion, consider an increase in FDI of U.S.$20 billion, occurring over five years, or $4 billion per year. This would imply an annual increase in the availability of foreign exchange of about less than 10 percent. Another comparison is with the estimate of the amount of foreign funds needed for healthy development, which presidential adviser José Córdoba recently estimated at U.S.$15 billion/year.[9] The new FDI flows would cover one-fourth of that gap. It will be noted below that portfolio flows have continued to

Table 8.3
Estimated Changes in Mexican Capital Stock, Different Scenarios

	Initial Conditions		Investment Scenario		Unilateral Trade Scenario		NAFTA Scenario	
			Assumed		Capital		Growth of:	
	Total Stock US$	Foreign Control %	Capital Stock Control %	Stock Inflow $US	Stock Increase %	$US	Capital Output %	Stock $US
Total	174	9	19	10	13	23	8	15
Agriculture	27	1	2	0	7	2	0	0
Mining	2	8	27	0	22	1	0	0
Petroleum Extraction	10	0	0	0	0	0	0	0
Manufacturing	42	27	49	7	19	8	35	15
Construction	6	1	5	0	53	3	0	0
Services	86	4	13	2	11	10	0	0
Breakdown of Manufacturing								
Foodstuffs	3.6	11	27	1	6	0	106	4
Beverages	1.9	30	38	0	7	0	0	1
Tobacco	0.1	78	99	0	8	0	0	0
Textiles	1.9	9	46	1	11	0	22	0
Clothing and Footwear	0.3	8	8	0	9	0	0	1
Wood and Cork	0.9	6	22	0	21	0	114	1
Furniture & Other Prod.	0.2	11	12	0			105	0
Cellulose and Paper	1.9	23	12	0	11	0	76	1
Printing and Publishing	0.5	10	27	0			206	1
Leather Goods	0.1	12	16	0	10	0	0	0
Rubber Products	0.5	67	87	0	15	0	220	1
Chemical Products	5.6	35	76	2	12	1	10	1
Pharmaceuticals & Cosmt.	0.5	73		0			0	1
Oil Byproducts	0.2	56	74	0			0	0
Nonmetallic Minerals	3.7	12	55	2	24	1	11	0
Basic Metals	6.9	14	26	1	29	2	0	0
Metallic Products	1.5	20	18	0	25	0	116	2
Nonelectrical Machines	1.1	49	53	0	37	0	72	1
Electrical Machines	1.7	58	58	0	26	0	59	1
Transport Equipment	3.9	69	85	1	25	1	0	0
Miscellaneous	0.2	40	35	0	14	0	539	1
Basic Petrochemicals	4.8	0	(assumed not to change)					
Breakdown of Services								
Transport	10	1	5	0	10	1	0	0
Light and Gas	16	1	1	0	13	2	0	0
Telephone and Telegraph	12	7	12	1	NA	NA	0	0
Commerce	11	14	20	1	10	1	0	0
Others	8	14	8	0	10	1	0	0
Government	30	0	(assumed not to change)					

Capital Stock adapted from Table 5.5, converted at end-of-year exchange rate. NAFTA scenario utilizes U.S. input ouput table from *Survey of Current Business*. Scenarios are defined in the text.

be the main source of foreign exchange in Mexico's capital account.

A third comparison is to the capital stock. Our hypothesized inflow of U.S.$20 billion would double foreign-held capital, raising foreign ownership of manufacturing from 25 to 50 percent.[10] Its impact on the nation's total nonresidential capital stock would be an increase of almost 10 percent. This would certainly be a very significant change, even if spread over a five- to ten-year period. The reader is reminded that these rough exercises are designed to test the upper bounds of the impact of the NAFTA, not the lower ones. For example, under the investment scenario there might be significant displacement of domestic by foreign capital, without adding to the overall total. Similarly, the scale economies may have been exaggerated in the calculations which were the basis for the unilateral trade liberalization scenario.

Another message in the estimates in Table 8.3 concerns the sectoral distribution of the impact of the different scenarios. Most of the new FDI flows are directed into manufacturing and could increase by half the capital stock in that sector. The largest inflow of capital into the service activities occurs under the unilateral trade liberalization. Moreover, by definition, greater access into the U.S. market will not directly generate any FDI into services in Mexico, as investors will be initially attracted to industry. Furthermore, the differences between levels of foreign ownership of services in Canada and Mexico are not large enough to have the "investment scenario" predict capital inflows that are significant at the macroeconomic level. It is this type of consideration that leads to the conclusion that the eventual signing of a NAFTA might not be as important for the country as the unilateral liberalizations of the 1980s. That the short-term effect on the Mexican economy of a free trade agreement will be smaller than the effects of trade and investment liberalization was a major point made by Mexico's secretary of commerce, Jaime Serra Puche, in an interview published in *Este País*, May 1991.

What about employment in Mexico? Once again, the investment scenario might not have any effect here if there were to be displacement of owners without additions to the stock. The Sobarzo simulation specifically assumed no increase in total employment, and the indications of his Table 8 are of large reallocations of workers inside sectors, with a small net effect even in manufacturing. An opposite extreme would be to consider the direct impact of the NAFTA scenario's U.S.$15 billion in new capital for new exports, ignoring all secondary effects on wages and other productive sectors. Even here there is a significant problem, noted earlier in Table 4.12, that the labor content of U.S. MNC affiliate sales/production in Mexico is more than three times the MNC global average and rising. As discussed earlier, this presumably reflects the growing importance of the maquilas on the overall Mexican averages. It is unlikely that new production for export would be as labor intensive. The assumed new investment would, over a period of years, generate from 150,000 to 500,000 new jobs, depending on the assumed labor content ratio.[11] Total manufacturing employment in the country is about 2.5 million; the labor force is some 22 million and grows by nearly 1 million per year.

Going beyond attempts at quantitative estimates, a few qualitative observations can also be made about the sectoral impact of NAFTA on FDI into Mexico. The major factors in the agreement are tariff reduction in the United States and Canada and local content rules. The motor vehicle sector is a convenient first example. As was noted for the so-called Auto Pact between the United States and Canada, the initial situation was one of the countries splitting up the production of world-class auto firms, each of which came from the United States. Now, both Mexico and Canada have an incentive to invite in investors from other countries who are world leaders, and wish to sell into the United States, whose producers seem to have lost their competitive edge. In automobiles, this is currently happening with Honda in Canada and is effectively occurring with Mitsubishi in Hermosillo, with Ford Motor Co. acting as middleman. The high local-content rules (62.5 percent) will make that difficult for non-North American firms. It must also be recalled that there is a tremendous overcapacity of automobile production in North America, which will dampen the enthusiasm of the U.S. automotive companies for any new investments.

Skeptical comments have also been made with regard to petrochemicals. Production in this sector involves large, very capital-intensive projects. Foreigners remain uncertain about the precise role of Pemex with regard to primary production and marketing (*El Financiero Internacional*, September 21, 1992; *Wall St. Journal*, August 13, 1992). Indications of the government's overall intentions will be inferred from its handling of exploratory drilling by outsiders.

The agreement in textiles is widely acknowledged to be among the most complex. Although Mexico achieved waiving of restrictions from the Multi-Fiber Agreement, numerous arrangements were made to slow down rapid increases in trade that would damage any of the three countries' local industries. While there will very definitely be increased competition in this sector, it will be tempered by the very visible hands of all three governments as well as intergovernmental commissions.

With regard to services, the most important area is banking, which has already been opened up to limited foreign ownership, a process that will continue under NAFTA. This is really part of the larger set of issues regarding capital flows, that are addressed below.

What would be the corresponding impact of these changes on the economies of the United States and Canada? There is an unavoidable urge to preface any answer with a series of qualifications. The potential impact of free trade on Canada and the United States has been subject to many more studies than its effect on Mexico, but very few conclusions have emerged, even as to signs of changes in such variables as employment. One minimal area of agreement is that most changes will be small, especially in the United States. In addition, the impact of NAFTA will probably occur slowly. Outsourcing is a crucial process, on which it is difficult to get basic data, much less develop elaborate models. It is especially difficult to divide the impact on employment between the United States and Canada.

That being said, it is not hard to conceive of the increased capital flow into Mexico leading to the displacement of over 100,000 jobs from the north. Considerably larger estimates would be consistent with the discussion above on the employment impact in Mexico. In her appearance before the Senate Finance Committee, U.S. Labor Secretary Lynn Martin gave 150,000 as an upper limit estimate of job loss, while adding that some studies show a net gain. This would be one-half of 1 percent of total U.S. manufacturing employment of just under 20 million, and less than one-tenth of 1 percent of total U.S. employment. How quickly these workers would find employment elsewhere is an open question. Conventional wisdom has it that the labor groups hit hardest would include unionized and low-skilled workers, and that the regional impact would be concentrated in the rust belt of the U.S. midwest and the corresponding parts of Ontario and Quebec.

In light of the lengthy discussion in Chapter 6, what can be said about the effect of the new FDI on economic growth in Mexico? Answers to this type of question often hinge on the degree to which one wishes to rely on mechanistic models.

For example, new FDI flows of magnitudes such as those discussed in the previous section, will not have a significant impact on national savings and investment totals. The improvement in the capital account would also be small. In part, this reflects the fact that manufacturing—where the FDI would be concentrated—accounts for only a fraction of total GDP and employment. The accumulated increase in exports under the NAFTA scenario would be sizeable, between one-third and one-half, and would certainly represent a major strengthening of manufactured exports.

The area of technology improvement represents the biggest gap between expectations for improvement and demonstrable evidence that these will be fulfilled. For example, consider the regression result presented in Chapter 6, linking total factor productivity growth (TFP) and percentage of foreign ownership. A 25 percent increase in foreign ownership of manufacturing, certainly within the upper limits of the estimates in Table 8.3, would increase TFP by 0.25 percent. This is not insignificant, of course, especially if compared to the two decade average that those authors estimate at 1.1 percent per year. However, it still leaves a significant gap between Mexico and the OECD average, reported above in Table 6.9, not to mention the faster growth that would be needed to catch up with the OECD countries. Moreover, manufacturing only represents a small fraction of the Mexican economy. But even this 0.25 percent estimate is probably biased upwards because it does not include the contribution to TFP of other industrial characteristics. The literature mentioned in Chapter 6 concludes that if these other factors are incorporated, the foreignness of FDI makes only a marginal contribution to technological change. It is ironic that the OLI approach, which tends to downplay the importance of foreign ownership on behavioral characteristics such as profit rates and import propensities, also de-emphasizes the independent contribution of FDI to technological change.

Freeing ourselves from the shackles imposed by rigorous modeling certainly permits larger estimates of the effect of FDI on Mexico's technological growth via spin-offs and changing mentalities. However, it just as easily lets in skeptics who view FDI as hurting growth, *a la* Dependency School. While many believe that technology transfer will indeed be very significant, the search for empirical support for this hypothesis has had limited success.

A final contribution in the nonquantifiable category is the potential of this FDI to jumpstart the economy. The turnaround in business attitudes between 1987 and 1991 is certainly remarkable.

CAPITAL FLOWS AND FINANCIAL LIBERALIZATION

One of the ways of evaluating the importance of FDI is its importance in a country's balance of payments. Data on the amount of the inflow of direct foreign investment can be seen in Table 8.4. As often happens, there are two relevant sources of data, that incorporated in the balance-of-payments data of the Bank of Mexico, and that of SECOFI, through its registers in the CNIE and RNIE. Curiously, the relative size of the series provided by these two sources switches, and currently the CNIE provides rather higher estimates attributed to the time lag between the request for a permission to invest, and the actual flow, which would be registered in the balance of payments as well as to investors deciding not to realize an approved project.[12]

As shown in Table 8.4, both official sources report a recent upsurge in FDI into Mexico. However, to some degree this reflects the reduced levels of FDI flows (and/or stocks) that were maintained during the lean years of the mid-1980s. The level of FDI flows compared to GDP was rather similar in 1991 to what it had been in the mid-1950s; the lowest point of this ratio appears to have been reached in the early 1980s as part of the debt crisis.[13]

Turning now to a detailed report of the balance of payments in Table 8.5, we see some rather drastic fluctuations in a number of key items. The onslaught of the debt crisis brought a very significant change in the capital account, eventually resolved by the corresponding reduction of imports and the current account deficit. Very recently, the situation has again become one of a large current account deficit.

Note that the direct foreign investment has not been the dominant item of the capital account. In particular, the major source of improvements since 1989 has been loans and, in 1991, portfolio flows. While these significant capital inflows are, in principle, beneficial, they have also given rise to some questioning in the

Table 8.4

Mexico: Official Estimates of Annual Direct Foreign Investment Inflows, 1950-1991

(Annual averages in U.S.$ million, and percentages)

	Banco de Mexico data				SECOFI Data Total	FDI Flows /GDP
	Total	New Invest.	Re-Inv. Earning	Inter-Company Debt		
1950-54	78	43	9	28		1.3
1955-59	129	77	12	38		1.4
1960-64	105	78	11	39		0.6
1965-69	198	114	10	90		0.7
1970-74	367	159	46	168		0.8
1975-79	597	269	12	333	326	0.7
1980-82	2216	1051	990	178	1317	1.1
1983-85	447	294	215	-62	1332	0.3
1986-88	2455	2088	544	-178	3152	1.7
1989	3037	2028	643	365	2500	1.4
1990	2633	2018	654	-38	3722	1.1
1991	4762	4606	757	126	3565	1.7

Sources: Banco de México: *Serie Estadísticas Históricas: Balanza de Pagos,* 1950-1969 and 1970-78; and Banco de México, *Indicadores Economicos* and *Indicadores del Sector Externo,* and for 1991, *Informe Anual.* The SECOFI data—from the CNIE—is reported in the third *Informe* of President Salinas, and SECOFI (1992), "Evolución de la inversión extranjera directa en 1991," excluding investment in the stock market ("inversión en el mercado de valores").

Note: For the calculation of FDI/GDP, the FDI figure is always that of the Banco de México. GDP data are the Banco de México estimates reported by Cárdenas (1987), until 1970, after which the source is the official figures of INEGI, converted at annual average exchange rate.

In 1960, there was a outflow of U.S.$ 116.5 million, due to the purchase of the electrical companies.

financial media. By permitting the country to import much more than it earns from exports, there is a possibility that industrial employment is reduced, in a version of what is known as the "Dutch Disease." Of course, this is a major argument of those who downplay the influence of trade liberalization on the recession in Canada.

A different worry relates to the stability of those capital inflows, given that the greater part is highly liquid. Indeed, some commentators point to the rather obvious parallels between the current situation and that of 1981. These criticisms are countered by pointing out that the economic policies now are very different, a point that certainly cannot be denied. The counterargument is that the political process of economic policymaking is still very much the same and that the end of the *sexenio* political cycle will bring along investor nervousness and capital

Table 8.5
Mexico's Balance of Payments, 1980-1991
(Million U.S.$)

Year	1980	1985	1988	1989	1990	1991
Current Account	-6,761	1,237	-2,443	-5,449	-7,114	-13,283
Exports Merchandise	15,308	21,664	20,565	22,765	26,838	27,120
Exports Services	9,714	9,111	12,025	13,820	18,229	18,678
Imports Goods	18,436	13,212	18,898	23,410	31,272	38,184
Imports Services	13,346	16,626	16,134	18,624	20,909	20,897
Capital Account	9,799	-1,527	-1,448	3,037	8,164	20,179
FDI	1,071	491	2,595	3,037	2,633	4,762
Portfolio Investments*				493	1,995	7,540
Other Capital Flow	8,728	-2,018	-4,043	-493	3,536	7,877
Errors & Omissions	-1,961	-2,134	-2,843	2,792	2,183	1,241
Change in Reserves	1,151	-2,328	-7,127	396	3,233	8,137

Source: various issues of the Banco de México, *Informe Anual.*

* Foreign investment in the Mexican Stock market was legalized in late 1989. As discussed in the text, the criteria of the Banco de México for separating Portfolio Investments from FDI are not clear.

outflows, just as it did in 1987/88, 1982, 1976, and even to a small degree in 1970.[14]

The potential volatility of capital flows merits further comment. First of all, the very high capital inflows in 1991 cannot be solely explained as a direct effect of the disincorporation of government enterprises, because the volume of capital inflows in 1991 (U.S.$20 billion) was larger than the value of all sales during this administration (about $17 billion), and of course a considerable part of the funds for those purchases have come from inside the country.

More details may be helpful. The sale of the banks has generated almost U.S.$11 billion.[15] One-third of the value of the banks' shares can be owned by foreigners. As we saw above, it is likely that many owners will finance part of their purchases by borrowing abroad; the magnitude of this process is not public knowledge. The other very big sale was that of most of the government's shares in TELMEX, which netted almost $5 billion, at least half of which was purchased by foreigners. However, the government had owned only 51 percent of TELMEX stock; the opening of the stock market made more stock available to outsiders than did the government's sale. Finally, the rest of the disincorporation will result in about $2 billion, whose distribution between foreigners and nationals is not possible to determine on the basis of publicly available information and indeed has not been a matter of much public discussion. For the purposes of argument, we might place the range of foreign currency entering with the specific intention of purchasing recently privatized companies at $5-10 billion, which would account for very roughly one-fourth to one-half of capital inflows during 1991.

Some U.S.$10 billion of foreign currency has entered through the stock market (*inversión en cartera*), of which perhaps $2-3 billion has purchased TELMEX stock, and was counted above.[16] This accounting suggests that the privatization may well have been less important than the stock market liberalization in attracting foreign funds, although of course privatization helped create an atmosphere congenial to capital inflows.

It is worth noting two broader issues that are basically more important for the short- and medium-term stability of the economy. First of all, is this money being put to productive use? The government has used its funds to reduce its debt, which has obvious beneficial effects. But has the money entering the stock market actually financed an increase of the capital stock? The data from 1991 are not too impressive, but Finance Minister Aspe has spoken of an incredible boom in 1992. The second point is simply to note that, were there to be a crisis of confidence, for example in the exchange rate, the ensuing capital flight would not be bound by the amount of recent capital inflows. This was shown too clearly in 1981-1982 and would be repeated now with a rapid decline of the stock market instead of a quick fall in dollar deposits in the bank.

NOTES

1. The World Bank has been engaged in a number of studies of the effects of trade liberalization. A recent update is Tybout (1992).

2. Unfortunately, neither Mexico nor Canada is covered in the World Bank's case studies on the effects of trade liberalization on production, employment, and efficiency. The summary volume is Michaely et al. (1991).

3. One work on Mexico asking the same question and providing a similar answer is Tapia Maruri and Cervantes González (1992). They estimate equations for imports, exports, output, and inflation, using quarterly data from 1977 thru the first half of 1988. It appears that their results for imports are similar to those presented below in that there is a significant increase due to liberalization. They estimate an equation for imports as a function of the nominal exchange rate, relative prices, income, average tariff, unexpected growth in the money supply, and the percentage of imports requiring permits, a variable representing commercial liberalization. Another related paper is Ize (1990).

4. Equations were also estimated with a lagged dependent variable, estimating the autocorrelation via Cochrane-Orcutt transformations and in first differences. There was no obviously superior specification that produced results different from

those indicated here.

5. Of course, this growth is not solely the result of the liberalization policy, as the automotive sector has been affected by special policies since 1962. Much has been written on this sector; a useful introduction is presented in Peres Nuñez (1990).

6. For a more thorough investigation of "revealed comparative advantage" of Canadian manufacturing, incorporating issues such as trade liberalization and deindustrialization, see Matthews (1985).

7. This is a full-employment model with a fixed real exchange rate, in which, accompanying the large inflow of capital, there is a significant trade balance deterioration, while wages rise 16 percent because of the increased productivity. Sobarzo's reported percentage changes were converted to absolute changes using the capital stock data from Table 5.5.

8. Using a different methodology slightly more complex than that presented here, Koechlin and Larudee (1992) estimate that NAFTA's cumulative net effect by the year 2000 will be a diversion of investment from the United States to Mexico of as much as U.S.$53 billion, and a decline in U.S. employment of up to half a million jobs. They highlight the importance for Mexican employment of the "devastating" effects of liberalization of corn trade.

9. To achieve 6 percent annual growth, $15 billion per year and an increase in domestic savings rate of 3 percent of GDP would be needed. *El Financiero*, April 30, 1992.

10. The reader will recall from Chapter 4 that there is a significant gap between the SECOFI estimates of U.S. FDI in Mexico, and those of the U.S. Department of Commerce, partially because SECOFI reports projects approved but not necessarily realized. If we accept as accurate the US source and assume the SECOFI data overestimates all FDI as much it does U.S. investment (which in any event is some two-thirds of the total), then the accumulated value of FDI in Mexico would only have reached U.S.$15 billion in 1991, not 1985. The uncertainty about these numbers cannot hide the rapid growth of FDI in Mexico in the late 1980s, nor the relatively large impact that would be made by the U.S.$20 billion discussed in the text.

11. Recall from Table 4.12 that the differences between Mexican and global averages for U.S. MNCs diverged when comparing assets and sales. Also, note that there is no pretense of correcting for labor intensity differences in the several industrial subsectors. The numbers in the text are meant as an illustration of the orders of magnitudes involved.

12. There may also be inconsistencies of the handling of noncontrolling purchases of stocks.

13. This type of calculation is affected by non-constancy of the real exchange rate (the nominal rate multiplied by the ratio of foreign to domestic prices). An extreme case is the fall of this ratio by one-third between 1988 and 1991, according to the Banco de México's *Indicadores Económicos*. Indeed, the near

doubling of the ratio between 1985 and 1986 can only be attributed to exchange-rate anomalies. Additionally, it must be noted that the Banco de México's report of an absolute decline of FDI stocks in the late 1970s similarly must be attributed to valuation problems because there is no corresponding negative FDI flow during those years. It is probably not a coincidence that the Banco de México soon stopped reporting an FDI stock.

14. While there are obvious parallels to what happened in 1987, interpreting that crisis as only the (beginning of the) end of the *sexenio* is simply too facile.

15. While the payment schedule corresponding to the purchase of a bank is not announced, news reports have indicated that almost U.S.$10 billion was received by the federal government for the banks during 1991. Some payments for other enterprises would have been made before 1991 while still others would be due in 1992. The process of disincorporation was to be finished in 1992.

16. The newspaper reports are not particularly precise on this issue, but some of the uncertainty lies with the data reporting of the authorities. The Banco de México's balance of payments tables report data separate from direct investment, on portfolio investment (*inversión en cartera*); this category includes certain mutual funds (*Fideicomisos*) and the TELMEX "L" series—see the *Informe Anual* for 1991, pp. 158 and 269. SECOFI reports a total on direct investment which includes investment in the stock market (*inversión en el mercado de valores*—recall that this term incorporates stocks and bonds), as well as ADRs and the NAFINSA *Fideicomiso*. In 1991, Banco de México reports FDI of U.S.$4.762 billion, while the corresponding figure for SECOFI, after subtracting out stock and bond purchases, is only $3.565 billion. Additionally, Table 7 of SECOFI (1992) breaks down the $3.565 billion, indicating that funds (*fideicomisos*) accounted for $1.115 billion. This leaves us with the possibility that in 1991 only $2.45 billion was approved and/or registered, or about half the amount reported by the Banco de México. Part of the issue would seem to be how to categorize purchases of stock that explicitly do not provide voting privileges, the ownership of some of which is quite dispersed. Additionally, one wonders how the SECOFI data handles repatriated flight capital that was destined for the purchase of these funds.

9

CONCLUSIONS

NAFTA defines a major mode of globalization in the last decade of the twentieth century. It is selective in its membership, and in its degree of trade liberalization. Moreover, multinational corporations continue to be important in the foreign trade of the three countries; they may also be the key players in the reallocation of production among the members. Because the growth and evolution of the international economy produces strains, it is not surprising that MNCs are at the center of debate about the overall process. The role of MNCs in the intersecting paths of the three countries' history, government policy, and future prospects has been the focus of this study.

OLI AS A THEORY OF FOREIGN DIRECT INVESTMENT

In any study of such a contentious issue, a major decision involves the choice of an analytical model. We have argued that the OLI paradigm presents a useful framework for the study of foreign direct investment. Its most important implication is the simplest one—FDI is a competitive response to market-created opportunities and fundamentally represents an improvement in economic welfare. Such a baldly unqualified statement does not ignore certain theoretical considerations that could represent important counterexamples—wasteful strategic investment or immiserizing growth using "tariff factories"—nor is it intended to wish away a long century of unsavory political intromissions associated with FDI.

As a theoretical construct, the most significant issue raised by OLI is the duration of the life cycle of a firm's FDI, the answer to which clearly varies by economic sector, as well as the relative weight of organization and location advantages. Another important contribution of OLI is to downplay the importance of demonstrating above-average profit rates, import propensities, and other variables, for firms or sectors dominated by MNCs, because this should be our expectation. In particular, the "branch plant economy" is the natural outcome of using tariffs to stimulate domestic industry, a policy economic nationalists now increasingly view as counterproductive.

The empirical work associated with the OLI paradigm is a significant corpus that is particularly strong with regard to Canada. However, in our review of that work we noted a distinct absence of studies analyzing the comparative contribution of host and home countries to the OLI-type advantages that lead to FDI flows. Particular examples might be the differences between variables in two countries; industrial organization variables such as concentration and R&D as a fraction of sales, or trade variables such as relative wage differences. Such work would be very useful for historical studies utilizing a product-cycle approach. In addition, in spite of the richness of the OLI empirical literature, very little has been done specifically linking FDI to outsourcing strategies.

It is in the area of strategic-trade policy, which has become a popular lodestone for proponents of industrial policy, that the OLI paradigm opens up the proverbial Pandora's box both in terms of theory and policy. To the extent that market imperfections are an important part of the contemporary world, doubts fester as to the optimality of laissez faire, although theoretical arguments point in such diverse directions that a noninterventionist orientation may dominate, winning as if by default. Nevertheless, the questioning by researchers in the OLI school of the empirical importance of dynamic economies of scale and scope has produced a creative tension that has enriched the whole profession.

HISTORICAL EXPERIENCES

The major objective of the historical sections of this book has been to put into perspective the changes in the role of FDI in the three countries in terms of statistical magnitudes and policy orientations. The Canadian situation is viewed as perhaps the classic case of import-substituting tariffs creating a foreign-dominated industry relatively incapable of competing in third-country markets. Although Mexico initially chose to evolve along that route, more-recent decisions made that country the first one in the hemisphere to pursue aggressively a policy of export-led industrialization. Yet the decision by both countries to seek a free trade arrangement with the United States is not necessarily evidence of some common policy position with regard to FDI or tariffs but rather a shared perception that the rules of international trade are changing towards greater protectionism, and both seek to assure their access to their common neighbor.

Any study of long-term changes inevitably looks for cycles, of which a good number became apparent. The importance of portfolio investment declined during the century, reflecting the characteristics of the sectors that received the funds (decline of railroads and utilities, the rise of manufacturing), as well as the shifting importance of the source of funds, away from the United Kingdom, which invested bonds, towards the United States, which preferred direct investment. Investment in the extraction of raw materials lost importance to that oriented towards manufacturing. Cycles passed more quickly in different manufacturing sectors, but rather slowly and with difficulty in petroleum. The data provide hints of the rise of a new phase in which investment will be dominated by multinational service conglomerates, will not involve direct management of production by foreigners, and will be highly information-intensive.

While these cycles appear well defined for the United States and Canada, the Mexican experience can be forced into the mold only with a generous allowance for the impact of policy. This encouraged a more extreme foreign dominance before the Revolution and led to an unusually low level at mid-century, which is still the heritage today. The allusion to discovering the New Mexican Past is particularly appropriate in terms of foreign investment. The economic dimensions of the role of FDI in Mexico have been little investigated, hindering an informed discussion of policy options today. It was interesting to note that the nationalist phase of Canadian intervention against FDI during the 1970s was rather quickly reversed, although its repercussions are still being felt.

Investment into the United States has traced a long, shallow inverted ∩ pattern during this century. The opposite pattern was observed for foreign ownership of Canadian productive capital. In Mexico, nationalist feelings released by the Revolution led to policies reducing foreign ownership during half a century, which are only recently being reversed. Using the simplistic division of factors causing a change in foreign ownership into economic and political, it was argued that the overall influence of economic factors has been greatest in the United States, and that of political factors was greatest in Mexico.

Our discussions of the stagnation or decline of outward investment from the United States, and the increase of FDI into the United States, along with the parallel analysis of U.S. FDI in Canada, suggested a slippage of the technological competitiveness of U.S. firms. To the extent that this is true, Mexico will receive less FDI from its northern neighbor as a result of NAFTA or Mexico's broader liberalization of foreign investment regulations. The subject of U.S. disinvestment has received some attention by Canadian economists; that literature should also be followed by their Mexican colleagues.

The preponderance of investment into the economies of Canada and Mexico should not distract us from the cases of their outward investment. A close parallel exists here in that in both countries outward investment tends to be in sectors that are intensive in natural resources and in which a significant export capacity had been achieved. Indeed, such was the case for the United States at the start of the century.

A suggestive aspect of Canadian research on FDI that was reviewed is the issue of R&D. Branch plants tend to perform less R&D and are thereby perceived as depriving the host country of beneficial spin-offs. However, the literature—and the experience of Canada—provides no indication that governments have policy tools at their disposal that can lead to an effective increase in R&D by local firms. Moreover, the state of scientific development in Mexico is such that all observers agree that the entrance of foreign firms would increase R&D. The issue for the United States is quite distinct. Some foreign firms come to the United States to improve their access to the recognizably world-quality technology produced in the country, leading some to argue that this IFDI is leading to technology leakages from the United States. On the proverbial other hand, certain "tariff factories" in the United States are being studied closely by their hosts in the attempt to learn the purportedly superior management techniques of their foreign owners. This complex of responses typifies the situation, mentioned above, of contradictory outcomes on an issue—R&D—defaulting to a government policy stance of laissez faire.

One standard question from international trade theory—who benefits from free trade—retains some theoretical validity in the OLI approach to foreign investment. The Stolper-Samuelson theory leads to the conclusion that capital and labor receive opposite benefits/costs from free trade (as part of a positive-sum game); a similar prediction is compatible with an OLI analysis of policies permitting or restricting FDI. Casual evaluation of the policy trends in the United States suggests some support, in that large business interests are in favor while labor has on occasion been opposed. The Stolper-Samuelson logic would suggest a reversal of those positions in countries that receive large amounts of FDI, such as Canada and Mexico. This prediction does not appear to be supported by the evidence, and in fact the more general pattern is an opposition by labor, and support—or at least laissez faire—by owners of capital. One might explain this outcome as a result of greater appeal to labor of nationalistic positions, along with a more uniform commitment to nonintervention among business leaders. However, as the United States continues to move into a situation of net recipient of FDI, the possibility of an inversion of policy positions with regard to FDI presents itself. It was argued that the high-local-content rules of the NAFTA agreement is one symptom of such a change. The 1992 presidential campaign provided others.

Such a redefinition of policy in the United States would have significant impacts on Canada and Mexico. Flows of FDI would be affected, of course, but the larger change would be in bilateral trade associated with FDI. This is most true for Mexico, whose government is hoping that NAFTA will expand these exports to the United States.

While our discussion has attempted to focus on a changed attitude toward FDI as a result of a different constellation of OLI factors, a broader view would look for such a change coming as a general response to globalization in its many forms and motivated as much by fear and ignorance as by an economic calculus. As an object of debate, foreign investment is an obvious target for a certain type of irrational analysis. Certainly none of our three countries has a monopoly on jingoistic nationalism, but the threat of a redefinition of policy motivated along these lines is strongest in the United States, with major repercussions for countries seeking closer economic ties with it.

NAFTA AND FDI

The historical analysis consciously pressed the search for parallels in the experiences with FDI among the three countries. The United States had often expressed interest in the free trade agreements, but it was the other countries who finally requested the negotiations. Moreover, in both cases, the timing occurred when the country was in an economic recession and recovering from perceived excesses of nationalism. The negotiations for NAFTA were made much easier by the previous existence of the Canada-U.S. FTA, but the approval process promises to be even more contentious.

Like its predecessor, the NAFTA is composed of a series of compromises towards the ideal of free trade. Certain sectors remain off limits while in others there will be a long period for the reduction of protectionist barriers. The dispute-settlement mechanism remains a singularly important achievement, one that will, however, attract controversy as the arena on which substantive battles over trade adjustment are engaged.

Will NAFTA lead to significant FDI flows into Mexico? The OLI model, at least as applied here, provides only general answers. Basically, Mexico becomes a more attractive host for FDI not because of changes in its internal economy, nor even less because of changes in the industrial organization characteristics of the production technologies, but mainly because of its position as a springboard for supplying the United States. Changing strategies of supply will increase international outsourcing, usually via at least partially owned companies. High-local-content regulations will clearly discourage FDI from non-NAFTA countries. Long phase-in periods for tariff reductions in sensitive industries in the United States and Canada will also reduce Mexico's attractiveness. Two safe predictions are that the increases of FDI into Mexico will be concentrated in a few sectors, and, probably, regions.

The attempt was made to isolate the impact of different aspects of NAFTA on the inflow of FDI. Liberalization of foreign investment regulations, already advanced before the negotiations began, will be important, as will further reductions of Mexican tariffs. Separately, access to the U.S. and Canadian markets for production from Mexico will make that country a highly desirable location for outsourcing. Although in principle Mexican-owned firms could be the major beneficiaries of these new opportunities, it was argued, in part by reference to the Canadian experience, that the more likely outcome is for this export-oriented growth to be foreign dominated.

Traditionally, economic predictions of the gains due to a free trade agreement suggest that these are rather modest. Although no sophisticated modeling exercise was attempted here, some numbers were generated about the possible increase in FDI. It is easy to foresee a doubling of the level of FDI in manufacturing in Mexico. Other areas will not be so strongly impacted because of several different factors: they are still not open (petroleum), the world market is weak (minerals), the domestic market is limited (various services), or not attractive (agriculture). If this prediction is correct, then the impact of FDI on economy-wide growth will not be large, at least when considering the immediate effects that economists traditionally attempt to measure.

The observation that today's outsourcing is an extension of yesterday's maquilas merits various comments. The maquila has been characterized by its intensivity in low-wage, low-skilled labor and is infamous for the associated social and environmental problems. In addition, it is a major source of foreign exchange and employment for Mexico. Some argue that the border zone is entering a new stage of development, corresponding to a more integrated industrialization. It is also asserted that the associated economic growth has altered the political center of gravity. In sum, *maquilización* is a viable strategy even if its negative effects inside the country will continue to attract criticism.

Note was taken that, although FDI inflows into Mexico have grown considerably in recent years, the balance of payments is currently dominated by capital inflows that are much less stable. In the current context of the slowing down of the macroeconomy and the end of the euphoria of privatization of banks and parastatals this may create short-term problems.

Our analysis points towards a view that this outsourcing, and the FDI that facilitates it, will initially be a (nearly) zero-sum game, namely, that employment gained in Mexico will be at the cost of jobs elsewhere. Of course, over the longer run, the displacement of those other jobs will be translated into a sectoral reallocation of labor in the affected countries, together with lower wages. Our upper-bound estimates of the number of workers involved reached into the hundreds of thousands, which would be a notable addition to manufacturing employment in Mexico. However, even if all this were to occur at the expense of jobs in Canada and the United States, the relative impact on the latter two countries is of course smaller. Furthermore, since one-quarter of manufacturing employment in Canada is in U.S. MNCs, there is some apprehension at the prospect that noneconomic factors might lead to Canada's absorbing relatively more unemployment.

The political element that was so strong in Mexico's experience with FDI and had a brief life in Canada has been relatively absent in the United States. Several considerations lead to the prediction that this will change. Complacency will not survive the stresses of globalization. Possible new orientations include a chauvinistic rejection of foreign investors inside the United States, or a neomercantilist call for restrictions on outward investment from there. NAFTA represents the first free trade agreement between the United States and a country with much lower wages. While Canada has successfully avoided being the object of either of these attacks, Mexico may well be the focus of the latter type. The larger the success of Mexico in expanding its exports, the greater the threat of a change of heart in the north.

A very different comment about the success of NAFTA suggests that its evaluation will depend on what happens in the GATT. President Salinas showed decisiveness when opting for the NAFTA negotiations and tremendous political skill in bringing them to a conclusion. If the process of multilateral reduction in protectionism that has occurred under the GATT does break down, he will be further praised for his foresight, even as his northern colleagues may be blamed for their contributions to the strengthening of trading blocks. However, if the Uruguay Round is successfully completed, then President Salinas may well be seen as having needlessly precipitated an agreement by offering more than was really necessary to obtain access to northern markets.

In any event, residents of the two northern countries will look at the economic forces NAFTA unleashes as a preview of further challenges and opportunities in the global economy. The final judgment on NAFTA, for them, will depend on their ability to absorb its lessons and respond successfully.

BIBLIOGRAPHY

Adams, F. Gerard, Byron Gangnes, and Gene Huang. (1991). "Impact of Japanese Investment in U.S. Automobile Production." *Journal of Policy Modeling* 13, no. 4, pp. 467-87.

Adams, F. Gerard, Mario Alanis, and Abel Beltran del Rio. (1992). "The Mexico-United States Free Trade and Investment Area Proposal: A Macroeconometric Evaluation of Impacts on Mexico." *Journal of Policy Modeling* 14, no. 1, pp. 99-119.

Agarwal, Jamuna P. (1980). "Determinants of Foreign Direct Investment: A Survey." *Weltwirtschaftliches Archiv* Band 116, Heft 4, pp. 739-73.

Agarwal, Jamuna P., Andrea Gubitz, and Peter Nunnenkamp. (1991). *Foreign Direct Investment in Developing Countries: The Case of Germany.* Kieler Studien No. 234 Tübingen: J. C. B. Mohr.

Agarwal, Sanjeev, and Sridhar N. Ramaswami (1992), "Choice of Foreign Market Entry Mode: Impact of Ownership, Location and Internalization Factors." *Journal of International Business Studies* First Quarter, pp. 1-27.

Aguilera Gómez, Manuel. (1982). "Las inversiones extranjeras directas durante la revolución 1913-1920." *El Economista Mexicano* (Julio-Agosto), pp. 93-100.

Alanís Patiño, Emilio (1943). "La Riqueza de México." *El Trimestre Económico* 10, pp. 97-134.

Alvear Acevedo, Carlos and Alberto Ortega Venzor. (1991). *TLC: Marco histórico para una negociación.* México: Editorial Jus.

Amsden, Alice H. (1990). "Third World Industrialization: 'Global Fordism' or a New Model?" *New Left Review* 182, (July-August), pp. 5-32.

Ankli, Robert E. (1980). "Canadian Economic Growth, 1896-1920." *Explorations in Economic History* 17, pp. 251-274.

Arno Press. (1976). *Estimates of United States Direct Foreign Investment, 1929-43 and 1947.* New York: Arno Press.

Aspe, Pedro (1991). "The Process of Divestiture and Privatization of State-Owned Enterprises: New Opportunities for Investment." In Banamex, *Inversión extranjera directa/direct foreign investment*. México: Banamex.

Baillet, Alvaro, and Arlette Cisneros. (1988). "La inversión extranjera directa en el sector de servicios en México." El Colegio de México documento de trabajo No. IX-1988.

Baldwin, John R., and Paul K. Gorecki. (1986). *The Role of Scale in Canada/U.S. Productivity Differences in the Manufacturing Sector; 1970-1979*. Toronto: University of Toronto Press.

―――. (1991). "Firm entry and exit in the Canadian manufacturing sector." *Canadian Journal of Economics* (May), pp. 300-23.

Banamex. (1991). *Inversión extranjera directa/direct foreign investment*. México: Banamex.

Banamex. Monthly. *Examen de la situación económica de México*.

Banco de México (BdM). (1969). *Cuentas Nacionales y Acervos de Capital, consolidadas y por tipo de actividad económica 1950-1967*. México: BdM.

―――. (1978). *Encuestas: Acervos y formación de capital 1960-1975*. Mexico: BdM.

―――. (1982). *Inversión extranjera directa. Cuaderno 1938-1979*. México: BdM.

―――. (1991). *The Mexican Economy 1991*. México: BdM.

Bank of England. (1950). *United Kingdom Overseas Investments 1938 to 1948*. London: Bank of England.

Barnet, Richard J., and Ronald E. Müller. (1974). *Global Reach*. New York: Simon and Schuster.

Becker, David G., Jeff Frieden, Sayre P. Schatz, and Richard L. Sklar. (1987), *Postimperialism: International Capitalism and Development in the Late Twentieth Century*. Boulder: Lynne Rienner.

Bergsten, C. Fred, Thomas Horst, and Theodore H. Moran. (1978). *American Multinationals and American Interests*. Washington, D.C.: The Brookings Institution.

Bernstein, Jeffrey I. (1985). "Research and Development, Patents, Grant and Tax Policies in Canada." In D. G. McFetridge, ed. *Technological change in Canadian industry*. Toronto: University of Toronto Press.

―――. (1988). "Costs of production, intra- and interindustry R&D spillovers: Canadian evidence." *Canadian Journal of Economics* 21, no. 2 (May), pp. 324-47.

―――. (1989). "The Structure of Canadian Inter-Industry R&D Spillovers, and the Rates of Return to R&D." *The Journal of Industrial Economics* 37, no. 3, pp. 315-28.

Berry, Steven, Vittorio Grilli, and Florencio López-de-Silanes. (1992). "The Automobile Industry and the Mexico - US Free Trade Agreement." NBER Working Paper No. 4152.

Betcherman, Gordon, and Morley Gunderson. (1990). "Canada-U.S. Free Trade and Labour Relations," *Labor Law Journal* (August), pp. 454-66.

Bhagwati, Jagdish N., Elias Dinopoulos, and Kar-yiu Wong. (1992). "Quid Pro Quo Foreign Investment." *American Economic Review* 82, no. 2, (May), pp. 186-90.

Blomström, Magnus. (1985). "El comportamiento de las empresas nacionales y extranjeras en México: Revisión del estudio de Fajnzylber y Martínez Tarragó." *El Trimestre Económico* pp. 175-194.

―――. (1986a). "Foreign Investment and Productive Efficiency: The Case of Mexico," *The Journal of Industrial Economics* 35, no. 1, (September), pp. 97-100.

―――. (1986b). "Multinationals and Market Structure in Mexico." *World Development* 14, no. 4, pp. 523-30.

―――. (1988). "Labor Productivity Differences Between Foreign and Domestic Firms in Mexico." *World Development* 16, no. 11, pp. 1295-98.

―――. (1989). *Foreign Investment and Spillovers*. London: Routledge.

―――. (1990). *Transnational Corporations and Manufactured Exports*. United Nations: UNCTC.

Blomström, Magnus, and Kakan Persson. (1983). "Foreign Investment and Spillover Efficiency in an Underdeveloped Economy: Evidence from the Mexican Manufacturing Industry." *World Development* 11, no. 6, pp. 493-501.

Blomström, Magnus, and Edward N. Wolff. (1989). "Multinational Corporations and Productivity Convergence in Mexico," NBER Working Paper #3141, October 1989.

Blomström, Magnus, Irving B. Kravis, and Robert E. Lipsey. (1988). "Multinational Firms and Manufactured Exports from Developing Countries." NBER Working Paper #2493, January.

Blomström, Magnus, and Robert E. Lipsey (1989). "US Multinationals in Latin American Service Industries." *World Development* Vol. 17, no. 11, (November) pp. 1769-76.

Bohrisch, Alexander, and Wolfgang König (1968). *La política mexicana sobre inversiones extranjeras*. México: El Colegio de México.

Bornschier, Volker, and Christopher Chase-Dunn (1985). *Transnational Corporations and Underdevelopment*. New York: Praeger.

Brecher, R. A., and R. Findlay (1983). "Tariffs, Foreign Capital and National Welfare with Sector Specific Factors." *Journal of International Economics* 7, pp. 317-22.

Brown, Drusilla K., Alan V. Deardorff and Robert M. Stern. (1992). "A North American Free Trade Agreement: Analytical Issues and a Computational Assessment." *The World Economy* 15, no. 1, (January), pp. 11-30.

Buckley, Kenneth. (1955). *Capital Formation in Canada 1896-1930*. Toronto: University of Toronto Press.

Buckley, Peter J. (1989). *The Multinational Enterprise*. London: Macmillan.

Burbach, Roger, and Patricia Flynn. (1980). *Agribusiness in the Americas.* New York: Monthly Review Press.

Butlin, Noel. (1962). *Australian domestic product, investment and foreign borrowing, 1861-1938/39.* Cambridge: Cambridge University Press.

Calva, José Luís. (1991). *Probables Efectos de un Tratado de Libre Comercio en el Campo Mexicano.* México: Fontamara.

Cárdenas, Enrique. (1987). *La industrialización mexicana durante la Gran Depresión.* México: El Colegio de México.

Cardoso, Fernando Henrique, and Enzo Faletto. (1979). *Dependency and Development in Latin America.* Berkeley: University of California Press. (translation of Spanish original from 1971).

Casar, José I., Carlos Márquez Padilla, Susana Marván, Gonzalo Rodríguez G., and Jaime Ros. (1990). *La organización industrial en México.* México: Siglo XXI.

Caves, Richard E. (1974). "Causes of Direct Investment: Foreign Firms' Shares in Canadian and United Kingdom Manufacturing Industries." *Review of Economics and Statistics* 56, no. 3, pp. 279-93.

———. (1982). *Multinational Enterprise and Economic Analysis.* Cambridge: Cambridge University Press.

Caves, Richard E., Michael E. Porter and A. Michael Spence. (1980). *Competition in the Open Economy,* Cambridge, MA: Harvard University Press.

Ceceña Gamez, José Luís. (1969). "Grupos de poder económico en el porfirismo." *Problemas del desarrollo* 1, no. 1.

Ceceña, José Luís. (1970). *México en la órbita imperial: las empresas transnacionales.* México: Ediciones El Caballito.

Centro de Información y Estudios Nacionales. (1983). *Análisis: Teléfonos de México.* Mimeo.

Chang, Sea Jin, and Unghwan Choi. (1988). "Strategy, Structure and Performance of Korean Business Groups." *Journal of Industrial Economics* 37, (December) pp. 141-158.

Chilcote, Ronald H. (1990). "Post-Marxism: The Retreat from Class in Latin America." *Latin American Perspectives* 17 no. 2 (Spring), pp. 3-24.

Chou, Tein-Chen. (1988). "American and Japanese Direct Foreign Investment in Taiwan: A Comparative Study." *Hitotsubashi Journal of Economics* 29, pp. 165-179.

Clegg, Jeremy. (1987). *Multinational Enterprise and World Competition.* New York: St. Martin's Press.

Clement, Wallace, and Glen Williams, ed. (1989). *The New Canadian Political Economy.* Kingston: McGill-Queen's University Press.

Clemenz, Gerhard. (1990). "International R&D Competition and Trade Policy." *Journal of International Economics* 28, (February), pp. 93-113.

Comisión Federal de Electricidad (n.d.). *Informe de labores, 1986-1987 Anexo.* México: CFE.

Comisión Nacional de Inversiones Extranjeras. (1988). *Informe 1983-1987.* México: CNIE.

Conklin, David W., and France St-Hilaire. (1988). *Canadian High-Tech in a New World Economy: A Case Study of Information Technology.* Halifax: Institute for Research on Public Policy.

Córdoba, José. (1986). "El programa mexicano de reordenación económica." In SELA *El fmi, el banco mundial y la crisis latinoamericana.* México: Siglo XXI.

Cossío, Luís, and Rafael Izquierdo. (1962). "Estimaciones de la relación producto-capital de México, 1940-1960." *El Trimestre Económico* 29, no. 4, (Octubre-Diciembre), pp. 634-60.

Cox, David, and Richard G. Harris. (1986). "A quantitative assessment of the economic impact on Canada of sectoral free trade with the United States." *Canadian Journal of Economics* 19, no. 3, (August), pp. 377-94

————. (1992). "North American Free Trade and its Implications for Canada: Results from a CGE Model of North American Trade." *The World Economy* 15, no. 1, January, pp. 31-44.

Crawford, Michael. (1992). "Who's abusing whom?" *Canadian Business* (August), pp. 32-38.

Crowe, Kenneth C. (1978). *America for Sale.* Garden City: Doubleday & Co.

Culem, Claudy G. (1988). "The Locational Determinants of Direct Investments among Industrial Countries." *European Economic Review* 32, pp. 885-904.

Daly, Michael J., and P. Someshwar Rao. (1986). "Free Trade, Scale Economies and Productivity Growth in Canadian Manufacturing." *The Manchester School* (December), pp. 391-402.

Damus, Sylvester, Paul A. R. Hobson, and Wayne Thirsk. (1991). "Foreign tax credits, the supply of foreign capital, and tax exporting." *Journal of Public Economics* 45, pp. 29-46.

Davidson, W. H., and D. G. McFetridge. (1984). "Recent Directions in International Strategies: Production Rationalization or Portfolio Adjustment?" *Columbia Journal of World Business* (Summer), pp. 95-101.

Diaz Alejandro, Carlos. (1970). *Essays on the Economic History of the Argentine Republic.* New Haven: Yale University Press.

Dollar, David. (1991). "Convergence of South Korean Productivity on West German Levels, 1966-78." *World Development* 19, pp. 253-73.

D'Olwer, Luis Nicolau. (1965). "Las Inversiones Extranjeras." In *Historia Moderna de México* Vol. 8, Daniel Cosio Villegas, ed. México: FCE.

Droucopoulos, Vassilis. (1984). "The Changing Remittance Behaviour of U.S. Manufacturing Firms in Latin America: A Comment and an Update." *World Development* 12, pp. 97-100.

Dufour, Paul, and Yves Gingras. (1988). "Development of Canadian science and technology policy." *Science and Public Policy* 15, no. 1, (February), pp. 13-18.

Dunn, Robert. (1926). *American Foreign Investments.* New York: Arno Press reprint.

Dunning, John H. (1980). "Toward an Eclectic Theory of International Production: Some Emipirical Tests." *Journal of International Business Studies* pp. 9-31.

———. (1981). *International Production and the Multinational Enterprise.* London: George Allen & Unwin.

———. (1988). "The Eclectic Paradigm of International Production: A Restatement and Some Possible Extensions." *Journal of International Business Studies* (Spring), pp. 1-31.

———. (1990). "Changes in the level and structure of international production: the last one hundred years." Chapter 1 in Peter J. Buckley, ed. *International Investment.* Great Yarmouth: Galliard.

Dunning, John H., and John Cantwell. (1987). *IRM directory of statistics of international investment and production.* Houndmills, England: MacMillan.

Dunning, John H., ed. (1985). *Multinational Enterprises, Economic Structure and International Competitiveness.* Chichester: John Wiley & Sons.

Eastman, H. C., and S. Stykolt.(1967). *The Tariff and Competition in Canada.* Toronto: Macmillan.

Economic Council of Canada. (1988). *Adjustment Policies for Trade Sensitive Industries.* Ottawa: Canadian Government Publishing Centre.

Edelstein, Michael. (1982). *Overseas Investment in the Age of High Imperialism: The United Kingdom, 1850-1914.* New York: Columbia University Press.

Ellis, Ned, and David Waite. (1985). "Canadian Technological Output in a World Context." In D. G. McFetridge ed. *Technological Change in Canadian Industry.* Toronto: University of Toronto Press.

Englander, A. Steven, Robert Evenson, and Masaharu Hanazaki. (1988). "R&D, Innovation and the Total Factor Productivity Slowdown." *OECD Economic Studies* no. 11 (Autumn), pp. 7-41.

Ethier, Wilfred H. (1986). "The Multinational Firm," *Quarterly Journal of Economics* 101, (November), pp. 805-33.

Evans, Peter. (1987). "Class, State, and Dependence in East Asia: Lessons for Latin Americanists." In Frederic C. Deyo, ed., *The Political Economy of the New Asian Industrialism.* Ithaca: Cornell University Press.

Fairchild, Loretta, and Kim Sosin. (1986). "Evaluating Differences in Technological Activity Between Transnational and Domestic Firms in Latin America." *Journal of Development Studies* 22, (July), pp. 797-808.

Fajnzylber, F., and T. Martínez Tarragó. (1976). *Las empresas transnacionales, expansión a nivel mundial y proyección en la economía mexicana.* México: Fondo de Cultura Económica.

Feder, Ernest. (1977). *Strawberry Imperialism: an Enquiry into the Mechanisms of Dependency in Mexican Agriculture.* The Hague: Institute of Social Studies.

Fernández Arena, and Herbert K. May. (1971). *El Impacto Económico de la*

Inversión Extranjera en México. México: Editorial Tabasco.

Firestone, O. J. (1958). *Canada's Economic Development 1867-1953*. London: Bowes and Bowes.

Florescano, Enrique. (1991). *El nuevo pasado mexicano*. México: Cal y arena.

Freidberg, Aaron L. (1991). "The End of Autonomy: the United States after Five Decades." *Daedalus* 120, no. 4, (Fall), pp. 69-90.

Fremantle Jackson, Hugo. (1974). *La inversión extranjera en México; la política mexicana sobre la inversión extranjera (1917-1973)* . . ., Unpublished master's thesis, UNAM.

Fry, Earl H. (1980). *Financial Invasion of the U.S.A.: A Threat to American Society?* New York: McGraw Hill.

Galbraith, Craig S., and Neil M. Kay. (1986). "Towards a Theory of Multinational Enterprise." *Journal of Economic Behavior and Organization* 7, pp. 3-19.

Globerman, Steven. (1972). "The empirical relationship between R and D and industrial growth in Canada." *Applied Economics* no. 4, pp. 181-95.

————. (1979). "Foreign Direct Investment and Spillover Efficiency Benefits in Canadian Manufacturing Industries." *Canadian Journal of Economics* (February), pp. 42-56.

————. (1985). "Canada." In John H. Dunning, ed., *Multinational Enterprises, Economic Structure and Industrial Competitiveness*. Chichester: John Wiley.

Globerman, Steven, and Lindsay Meredith. (1984). "The Foreign Ownership-Innovation Nexus in Canada." *Columbia Journal of World Business* (Winter), pp. 53-62.

Gold, Marc, and David Leyton-Brown, eds. (1988). *Trade-offs on Free Trade: The Canada-U.S. Free Trade Agreement*. Agincourt, Ontario: Carswell Co.

Goldsmith, Raymond W. (1966). *The Financial Development of Mexico*. Paris: OECD.

————. (1985). *Comparative National Balance Sheets*. Chicago: University of Chicago Press.

González-Aréchiga, Bernardo, and Rocío Barajas Escalmilla. (1989). *Las maquiladoras: Ajuste estructural y desarrollo regional*. Tijuana: El Colegio de la Frontera Norte and the Fundación Friedrich Ebert.

Gordon, Wendell C. (1941). *The Expropriation of Foreign-Owned Property in Mexico*. Washington, D.C: American Council on Public Affairs.

Gorecki, Paul K. (1976). "The Determinants of Entry by Domestic and Foreign Enterprises in Canadian Manufacturing Industries: Some Comments and Empirical Results." *Review of Economics and Statistics* 4, pp. 485-88.

————. (1990). "Patterns of Canadian foreign direct investment abroad." Research Paper No. 33, Business and Labour Market Analysis Group, Statistics Canada.

Government of Canada. (1972). *Foreign Direct Investment in Canada*. published by the Government of Canada (the Gray Report).

Governments of Canada, The United Mexican States, and The United States of America. (1992). "Description of the Proposed North American Free Trade Agreement," Processed.

Graham, Edward M., and Paul Krugman. (1989). *Foreign Direct Investment in the United States*. Washington, D.C.: Institute for International Economics.

Grant, George. (1965). *Lament for a Nation: The Defeat of Canadian Nationalism*. Princeton: D. Van Nostrand Co.

Green, Christopher. (1990). *Canadian Industrial Organization and Policy*. third edition, Toronto: McGraw Hill.

Grinols, Earl L. (1992). "Increasing returns to scale and trade-related industry enlargement." *Economic Letters* 38, no. 1, (January), pp. 61-66.

Grubaugh, Stephen G. (1987). "Determinants of Direct Foreign Investment." *Review of Economics and Statistics* 61, no. 1, pp. 149-52.

Gunder Frank, Andre. (1966). "The Development of Underdevelopment." *Monthly Review*, 18, no. 4, pp. 17-31.

———. (1992). "Latin American Development Theories Revisited: A Participant Review." *Latin American Perspectives* (Issue 73), 19, no. 2, (Spring), pp. 125-39.

Haber, Stephen H. (1991). "La economía mexicana, 1830-1940: obstaculos a la industrialización (II)." *Revista de Historia Económica* 8, no. 1, pp. 335-62.

Hammer, Heather-Jo, and John W. Gartrell. (1986). "American Penetration and Canadian Development: A Case Study of Mature Dependency." *American Sociological Review* 51, (April), pp. 201-13.

Harris, Richard G., and David Cox. (1984). *Trade, Industrial Policy, and Canadian Manufacturing*. Toronto: Ontario Economic Council.

Hart, Michael. (1990). *A North American Free Trade Agreement: The Strategic Implications for Canada*. Ottawa: Centre for Trade Policy and Law.

———. (1991). "Elementos de un acuerdo de libre comercio en América del Norte." In Gustavo Vega Cánovas, ed. *México ante el libre comercio con América del Norte*. México: El Colegio de México.

Heckscher, Eli F., and Bertil Ohlin. (1991). *Heckscher-Ohlin Trade Theory*. Translated, edited, and introduced by Harry Flam and M. June Flanders. Cambridge: MIT Press.

Helleiner, G. K. (1989). "Transnational Corporations and Direct Foreign Investment." in *Handbook of Development Economics, Vol. II*. Edited by H. Chenery and T. N. Srinivasan. New York: Elsevier.

Helliwell, John F., Mary E. MacGregor, Robert N. McRae, and André Plourde. (1989). *Oil and Gas in Canada: The Effects of Domestic Policies and World Events*. Toronto: Canadian Tax Foundation.

Hernández Laos, Enrique, and Edur Velasco Arregui. (1990). "Productividad y competitividad en las manufacturas mexicanas 1960-1985." *Comercio Exterior* 40, no. 7, pp. 658-66.

Hewitt, Gary K. (1983). "Research and Development Performed in Canada by

American Manufacturing Multinationals." In Alan M. Rugman ed. *Multinationals and Technology Transfer: The Canadian Experience.* New York: Praeger.

Heyman, Timothy. (1989). *Investing in Mexico.* México: Editorial Milenio.

————. (1991). "Direct Foreign Investment and the Mexican Stock Market." In BANAMEX *Inversión extranjera directa/direct foreign investment.* México: Banamex.

Hiemenz, Ulrich. (1987). "Foreign Direct Investment and Industrialization in ASEAN Countries." *Weltwirtschaftliches Archiv* Band 123, Heft 1, pp. 121-39.

Hines, James R., and R. Glenn Hubbard. (1990). "Coming Home to America: Dividend Repatriations by U.S. Multinationals." In Assaf Razin and Joel Slemrod, *Taxation in the Global Economy.* Chicago: University of Chicago Press.

Hinojosa-Ojeda, Raúl, and Sherman Robinson. (1992). "Diversos escenarios de la integración de los Estados Unidos y México: Enfoque de equilibrio general computable." *Economía mexicana* 1, no. 1 (Nueva época), Enero-Junio, pp. 71-144.

Hood, Neil, and Stephen Young. (1979). *The economics of multinational enterprise.* London: Longman.

Horst, Thomas. (1972). "Firm and Industry Determinants of the Decision to Invest Abroad: An Empirical Study." *Review of Economics and Statistics* 54, no. 3, pp. 258-266.

Howes, Candace. (1991). "Transplants No Cure." *Dollars and Sense* Issue 168, (July-August), pp. 16-19.

Hufbauer, Gary Clyde, and Jeffrey J. Schott. (1992). *North American Free Trade: Issues and Recommendations.* Washington, D.C.: Institute for International Economics.

Hymer, Stephen. (1976). *The International Operations of National Firms: A Study of Direct Investment.* Cambridge: MIT Press. Reprint of author's 1960 Ph.D. thesis.

Instituto Nacional de Estadística, Geografía e Informatica (INEGI). (1988). *Estadística Industrial: Información por tipo de empresas e indices de concentración.* México: INEGI.

Ize, Alain. (1990). "Trade Liberalization, Stabilization and Growth: Some Notes on the Mexican Experience." Washington, D.C.: IMF Working Paper WP/90/15.

Juhl, Paulgeorg. (1979). "On the Sectoral Patterns of West German Manufacturing Investment in Less Developed Countries: The Impact of Firm Size, Factor Intensities and Protection." *Weltwirtschaftliches Archiv* Band 115, Heft 3, pp. 508-21.

Julius, DeAnne. (1990). *Global Companies and Public Policy.* London: Royal Institute of International Affairs.

Koechlin, Timothy, and Mehrene Larudee. (1992). "The High Cost of NAFTA."

Challenge (September-October), pp. 19-26.

Kojima, Kiyoshi. (1973). "A Macroeconomic Approach to Foreign Direct Investment." *Hitotsubashi Journal of Economics* 14, no. 1, pp. 1-21.

———. (1989). "Theory of Internalisation by Multinational Corporations." *Hitotshubashi Journal of Economics* 30, no. 2, (December), pp. 65-85.

Kojima, Kiyoshi, and Terutomo Ozawa. (1984). *Japan's General Trading Companies: Merchants of Economic Development.* Paris: OECD.

Komiya, Ryutaro, and Ryuhei Wakasugi. (1991). "Japan's Foreign Direct Investment," *Annals* AAPS, 513, (January), pp. 48-61.

Kravis, Irving B., and Robert E. Lipsey. (1982). "The Location of Overseas Production and Production for Export by U.S. Multinational Firms." *Journal of International Economics* 12, 201-24.

Krugman, Paul R. (1986). *Strategic Trade Policy and the New International Economics.* Cambridge: MIT Press.

Lamartine Yates, Paul. (1978). *El campo mexicano.* México: El Caballito.

Landefeld, J. Steven, and Ann M. Lawson. (1991). "Valuation of the U.S. Net International Investment Position." *Survey of Current Business* 71, no. 5, (May), pp. 40-49.

Landefeld, J. Steven, Ann M. Lawson, and Douglas B. Weinberg. (1992). "Rates of Return on Direct Investment." *Survey of Current Business* 72, no. 8 (August), pp. 79-86.

Laney, Leroy O. (1991). "The Impact of U.S. Laws on Foreign Direct Investment." *Annals* AAPS 516, (July), pp. 144-53.

Lechuga, Jesús, and Fernando Chávez. (1989). *Estancamiento Económico y Crisis Social en México, 1983-1988.* Tomo 1, Económia. México: UAM.

Lee, Chung H. (1980). "United States and Japanese Direct Investment in Korea: A Comparative Study." *Hitotsubashi Journal of Economics* 20, pp. 26-41.

———. (1990). "Direct Foreign Investment, Structural Adjustment, and International Division of Labor: A Dynamic Theory of Direct Foreign Investment." *Hitotsubashi Journal of Economics* 31, pp. 61-72.

Leiss, William. (1988). "Industry, technology and the political agenda in Canada; the case of government support for R&D." *Science and Public Policy* 15, no. 1, pp. 57-68.

Levitt, Kari. (1970). *Silent Surrender: The Multinational Corporation in Canada.* Toronto: Macmillan Company of Canada.

Levy, Santiago, and Sean Nolan. (1992). "Trade and foreign investment policies under imperfect competition." *Journal of Development Economics* 37, 31-62.

Levy, Santiago, and Sweder van Wijnbergen. (1992). "El maíz y el acuerdo de libre comercio entre México y los Estados Unidos." *El Trimestre Económico* 59, no. 2.

Lewis, Cleona. (1938). *America's Stake in International Investments.* Menasha, Wisconsin: George Banta Publishing Co.

Lipsey, Robert E. (1991). "Foreign Direct Investment in the United States and

U.S. Trade." *Annals* AAPS 516, (July), pp. 76-90.

Lipsey, Robert E., and Irving B. Kravis. (1987). "The Competitiveness and Comparative Advantage of U.S. Multinationals 1957-1984." *Quarterly Review of Banca Nazionale del Lavoro* no. 161 (June), pp. 147-165.

Lustig, Nora. (1992). *Mexico the Remaking of an Economy.* Book manuscript to be published by the Brookings Institution.

Lustig, Nora et al. (1989). "Evolución del Gasto Público en Ciencia y Tecnología 1980-1987." *Estudios* 1 (México).

Mansfield, Edwin. (1985). "Technological Change and the International Diffusion of Technology: A Survey of Findings." In D. G. McFetridge ed., *Technological Change in Canadian Industry.* Toronto: University of Toronto Press.

Mares, David R. (1987). *Penetrating the International Market: Theoretical Considerations and a Mexican Case Study.* New York: Columbia University Press.

Matthews, Roy A. (1985). *Structural Change and Industrial Policy: The Redeployment of Canadian Manufacturing, 1960-1980.* Ottawa: Minister of Supply and Services Canada.

McDougall, John N. (1991). "North American Integration and Canadian Disunity." *Canadian Public Policy* 17, pp. 395-408.

McFetridge, Donald G., ed. (1985). *Technological Change in Canadian Industry.* Toronto: University of Toronto Press.

McFetridge, Donald G. (1987). "The Timing, Mode and Terms of Technology Transfer: Some Recent Findings." In A. E. Safarian and Gilles Y. Bertin eds. *Multinationals, governments and international technology transfer.* Beckenham: Croom Helm.

———. (1989). *Trade Liberalization and the Multinationals.* Ottawa: Canadian Government Publishing Centre.

McMechan, J., J. Lothian, and J. Farnworth. (1992). "Mergers and Acquisitions and Foreign Control." *Canadian Economic Observer* (May), pp. 3.1-3.16.

McNally, David. (1990). "Beyond Nationalism, Beyond Protectionism: Labor and the Canada-U.S. Free Trade Agreement." *Review of Radical Political Economics* 22, no. 1, pp. 179-94.

Meller, Patricio. (1978). "The Pattern of Industrial Concentration in Latin America." *The Journal of Industrial Economics* 27, no. 1, pp. 41-47.

Meredith, Lindsay. (1984). "U.S. Multinational Investment in Canadian Manufacturing Industries." *Review of Economics and Statistics* 66, no. 1, pp. 111-19.

México. Secretaría de la Economía Nacional. (1941). *Resumen general del censo industrial de 1935.* México: Talleres Gráficos de la Nación.

Meyer, Lorenzo. (1974). "La resistencia al capital privado extranjero; el caso del petróleo, 1938-1950." In Bernardo Sepúlveda Amor et al., *Las empresas transnacionales en México.* México: El Colegio de México.

————. (1977). *Mexico and the United States in the Oil Controversy, 1917-1942.* Austin: University of Texas Press.

Michaely, Michael, Demetris Papageorgiu, and Armeane M. Choksi. (1991). *Liberalizing Foreign Trade. Volume 7 Lessons of Experience in the Developing World.* Cambridge: Basil Blackwell.

Mitchell, B. R. (1983). *International Historical Statistics: The Americas and Australasia.* Detroit: Gale Research Press.

Moore, O. Ernest. (1963). *Evolución de las instituciones financieras en México.* México: CEMLA.

Murray, John D. (1982). "The Tax Sensitivity of US Direct Investment in Canadian Manufacturing." *Journal of International Money and Finance* 1, No. 2, (August), pp. 117-40.

Nacional Financiera, S.A. (NAFINSA). (Annual). *La economía mexicana en cifras.* México: NAFINSA.

Navarette R., Alfredo. (1960). "El financiamiento del desarrollo económico." In *México: Cincuenta años de revolución,* Vol. 1. México: FCE.

Newfarmer, Richard S. ed. (1985). *Profits, Progress and Poverty: Case Studies of International Industries in Latin America.* Notre Dame: University of Notre Dame Press.

Organisation for Economic Co-operation and Development (OECD). (1986). "R&D, Invention and Competitiveness." *OECD Science and Technology Indicators No. 2.*

————. (1987). *Recent Trends in International Direct Investment.* Paris: OECD.

Orr, David. (1974). "The Determinants of Entry: A Study of the Canadian Manufacturing Industries." *Review of Economics and Statistics* 56, pp. 58-66.

Ortiz Mena, Raúl, Víctor L. Urquidi, Albert Waterston, and Jonas H. Haralz. (1953). *El desarrollo económico de México y su capacidad para absorber capital del exterior.* México: Fondo de Cultura Económica.

Palma, Gabriel. (1978). "Dependency: A Formal Theory of Underdevelopment or a Methodology for the Analysis of Concrete Situations of Underdevelopment?" *World Development* 6, 881-924.

Paterson, Donald G. (1976). *British Direct Investment in Canada 1890-1914.* Toronto: University of Toronto Press.

Peres Nuñez, Wilson. (1990). *Foreign Direct Investment and Industrial Development in Mexico.* Paris: OECD.

Pitelis, Christos. (1990). "Beyond the Nation-State?: The Transnational Firm and the Nation-State." *Review of Radical Political Economy* 22, no. 1 (Spring), pp. 98-114.

Poder Ejecutivo Federal. (1991). *Segundo Informe de Gobierno: Anexo.* México: PEF.

Pomfret, Richard. (1981). *The Economic Development of Canada,* Toronto: Metheun.

Rama, Ruth, and Raúl Vigorito. (1979). *Transnacionales en América Latina, El complejo de frutas y legumbres en México.* México: ILET, Editorial Nueva Imagen.

Ramírez de la O, Rogelio. (1983). *De la improvisación al fracaso: La política de inversión extranjera en México.* México: Ediciones Océano.

Ramstetter, Eric D. (1991). *Direct Foreign Investment in Asia's Developing Economies and Structural Change in the Asia-Pacific Region.* Boulder, Colo: Westview Press.

Ray, Edward John. (1989). "The Determinants of Foreign Direct Investment in the United States, 1979-85." In Robert C. Feenstra, ed., *Trade Policies for International Competitiveness.* Chicago: University of Chicago Press.

Razin, Assaf, and Joel Slemrod. (1990). *Taxation in the Global Economy.* Chicago: University of Chicago Press.

Reynolds, Clark W. (1970). *The Mexican Economy: Twentieth Century Structure and Growth.* New Haven: Yale University Press.

Rippy, J. Fred. (1959). *British Investments in Latin America: 1822-1949.* Camdon Conneticut: Archon Books.

Ritchie, Gordon. (1991). "Beyond the Volcano: Canadian Perspectives on Trilateral Free Trade." *Columbia Journal of World Business* (Summer), pp. 82-90.

Robidoux, Benoit, and John Lester. (1992). "Econometric estimates of scale economies in Candian manufacturing." *Applied Economics* 24, no. 1 (January), pp. 113-22.

Roett, Riordan ed. (1991). *Mexico's External Relations in the 1990s.* Boulder: Lynne Reinner.

Rosenzweig, Fernando. (1965). "La industria." In Daniel Cosio Villegas, ed., *Historia Moderna de México* Vol. 8, México: FCE.

Ruffin, Roy J. (1984). "International Factor Movements." In Ronald W. Jones and Peter B. Kenen, eds., *Handbook of International Economics.* Volume 1. New York: North Holland.

Rugman, Alan M. (1980). *Multinationals in Canada.* Boston: Martinus Nijhoff.

———. (1987). "Multinationals and Trade in Services: A Transaction Cost Approach." *Weltwirtschafliches Archiv* Band 123, Heft 4, pp. 651-67.

———. (1990). *Multinationals and Canada-United States Free Trade.* Columbia, South Carolina: University of South Carolina Press.

Rugman, Alan M. ed., (1983). *Multinationals and Technology Transfer: The Canadian Experience.* New York: Praeger.

Runsten, David, and Linda Wilcox Young. (1992). "Demand for Labor, Wages and Productivity in Mexican Fruits and Vegetables: Preliminary Estimates and Implications for NAFTA." Paper presented to the 1992 LASA meetings.

Safarian, A. E.. (1985). *Foreign Direct Investment: A Survey of Canadian Research.* Montreal: Institute for Research on Public Policy.

Samaniego Breach, Ricardo. (1984). "The Evolution of Total Factor Productivity in the Manufacturing Sector in Mexico 1963-1981." El Colegio de México

Documento de Trabajo No. 1984-IX.

Sanchez Gamper, Philippe Alphonse. (1989). *Del conflicto al consenso: los empresarios y la política de inversiones extranjeras en México, 1944-1970.* Unpublished Licenciatura thesis, El Colegio de México.

Sandoval Godoy, Sergio A., ed. (1992). *La Industria Alimentaria en Sonora.* Hermosillo: Ediciones CIAD, S. A.

Sariego, Juan Luís, Luis Reygadas, Miguel Angel Gómez, and Javier Farrera. (1988). *El estado y la minería mexicana: Política, trabajo y sociedad durante el siglo xx.* México: SEMIP/Fondo de cultura económica.

Saunders, Ronald S. (1980). "The Determinants of Productivity in Canadian Manufacturing Industries." *Journal of Industrial Economics* 29, no. 2 (December), pp. 167-83.

———. (1982). "The determinants of interindustry variation of foreign ownership in Candian manufacturing." *Canadian Journal of Economics* 17, pp. 77-84.

Sazanami, Yoko. (1988). "Recent Trends in Japanese Trade and Capital Flow - Japan vs Western Europe and Asia." *Keio Economic Studies* 25, no. 1, pp. 21-38.

Scaperlanda, Anthony. (1990). "An Empirical Investigation of the Locational Determinants of Foreign Direct Investment Flows into the U.S." Paper presented to the International Trade and Finance Association, Washington D.C.

Schott, Jeffrey J., and Murray G. Smith eds. (1988), *The Canada-United States Free Trade Agreement: The Global Impact.* Washington, D.C.: Institute for International Economics.

Secretaría de Comercio (1977), *Informe técnico económico sobre energía eléctrica y gas en México, 1976.* Boletín No. 77, Diciembre.

Secretaría de Comercio y Fomento Industrial (SECOFI), Subsecretaria de Industria e Inversión Extranjera, Dirección General de Inversión Extranjera. (1992). "Evolución de la inversión extranjera directa en 1991." Unpublished report, January.

Secretaría de Planeación y Presupuesto (SPP). (1980). *La industria petrolera en México.* México: SPP.

———. (1986). *La Industria Petrolera en México.* Mexico: SPP.

Sepúlveda, Bernardo, and Antonio Chumacero. (1973). *La inversión extranjera en México.* México: Fondo de Cultura Económica.

Shah, Anwar, and Joel Slemrod. (1990). "Tax Sensitivity of Foreign Direct Investment: An Empirical Assessment." WPS Working Paper #434, Washington, D.C.: The World Bank.

Sherwell, G. Butler. (1929). *Mexico's Capacity to Pay,* Washington D. C.: U.S. Department of Commerce.

Sklair, Leslie. (1989). *Assembling for Development: The Maquila Industry in Mexico and the United States.* Boston: Unwin Hyman.

Sobarzo, Horacio E. (1991). "A General Equilibrium Analysis of the Gains from

Trade for the Mexican Economy of a North American Free Trade Agreement." El Colegio de México: unpublished working paper.

Solís, Leopoldo. (1971). *La realidad económica mexicana: retrovisión y perspectivas,* México: Siglo veintiuno. 2a edición.

Stallings, Barbara. (1987). *Banker to the Third World: U.S. Portfolio Investment in Latin America 1900-1965.* Berkeley: University of California Press.

Statistics Canada. (1980). *Industrial organisation and concentration in the manufacturing, mining and logging industries.* Ottawa: Minister of Supply and Services Canada. Catalogue 31-402.

————. (1985a). *Domestic and foreign control of manufacturing, mining and logging establishments in Canada: 1981.* Ottawa: Minister of Supply and Services Canada. Catalogue 31-401.

————. (1985b). *Fixed capital flows and stocks: 1985.* Ottawa: Minister of Supply and Services Canada. Catalogue 13-211.

————. *Annual Report of the Minister of Supply and Services, Canada, under the Corporations and Labour Unions Returns Act. Part 1, Corporations.* Ottawa: Minister of Supply and Services Canada. Catalogue 61-210. (Title and corporate author vary slightly; referred to in text as CALURA Report).

————. *Canada's international investment position.* Ottawa: Minister of Supply and Services Canada. Catalogue 67-202.

————. *Industrial Research and Development Statistics.* Ottawa: Minister of Supply and Services Canada. Catalogue 88-202.

Steed, Guy P. (1989). *Not a Long Shot: Canadian Industrial Science and Technology Policy.* Background Study Number 55, Ottawa: Science Council of Canada.

Stern, Robert M. (1985). Review of *Trade, Industrial Policy and Canadian Manufacturing* by Richard G. Harris and David Cox, in *Journal of International Economics* 19, 189-200.

Stone, Irving. (1987). The Composition and Distribution of British Investment in Latin America, 1865-1913. New York: Garland Publishers. (copy of 1962 Ph.D. dissertation).

Tai, Lawrence S.T., and Dileep R. Mehta. (1988). "Trade and Investment Behavior in U.S. and Japanese Manufacturing Industries: 1962-1981." *Hitotsubashi Journal of Economics* 29, pp. 59-71.

Tannenbaum, Frank. (1929). *The Mexican Agrarian Revolution.* New York: MacMillan.

Tapia Maruri, Joaquín, and Jesús Cervantes González. (1992). "México: Un modelo econométrico de la apertura comercial en la balanza comercial, actividad económica y precios." In Federico Rubli K. and Benito Solís M. eds., *México: Hacia la globalización.* México: Diana.

Teece, David J. (1986). "Transactions Cost Economics and the Multinational Enterprise." *Journal of Economic Behavior and Organization* 7, pp. 21-46.

Teichova, Alice, Maurice Levy-Leboyer, and Helga Nussbaum. (1988).

Multinational enterprise in historical perspective. Cambridge: Cambridge University Press, reprint.

Tsai, Pan-long. (1987). "The Welfare Impact of Foreign Investment in the Presence of Specific Factors and Non-Traded Goods." *Weltwirtschaftliches Archiv* Band 123, Heft 3, pp. 496-508.

Twomey, Michael J. (1992). "Macroeconomic Effects of Trade Liberalization in Canada and Mexico." El Colegio de México Documento de Trabajo Número I-1992.

Tybout, James R. (1992). "Linking Trade and Productivity: New Research Directions." The *World Bank Economic Review* 6, no. 2, pp. 189-211.

Tybout, James, Jaime de Melo, and Vittorio Corbo. (1991). "The effects of trade reforms on scale and technical efficiency: New evidence from Chile." *Journal of International Economics* 31, 231-50.

Unger, Kurt. (1983). "Transfer of Technology, Trade and Industrial Structure in Mexico." unpublished paper, El Colegio de México.

Unger, Kurt. (1990). *Las exportaciones mexicanas ante la reestructuración internacional: La evidencia de las industrial química y automotriz.* México: El Colegio de México.

Unger, Kurt, and Luz Consuelo Saldaña. (1989). "Las economías de escala y de alcance en las exportaciones mexicanas más dinámicas." *El Trimestre Económico* 56, no. 2, #222, (Abril-Junio).

United Nations. (1955). *Foreign Capital in Latin America.* New York, E/CN.12/36 ST/ECA/28.

————. *Industrial Statistics Yearbook.* New York: UN (annual).

United Nations Centre on Transnational Corporations (UNCTC). (1985). *Transnational Corporations in World Development: Third Survey.* London: Graham & Trotman.

————. (1987). *Transnational Corporations in the Man-Made Fibre, Textile and Clothing Industries.* New York: UNCTC ST/CTC/63 IIA.1987.11.

————. (1988). *Transnational Corporations in World Development: Trends and Prospects.* New York: UNCTC, ST/CTC/89.

————. (1989). *The Process of Transnationalization and Transnational Mergers.* New York: UN.

————. (1989). "Transnational Service Corporations and Developing Countries: Impact and Policy Issues." *UNCTC Current Studies* Series A, No. 10.

————. (1991). *World Investment Report: The Triad in Foreign Direct Investment.* New York: UNCTC E.91.II.A.12.

United Nations Economic Commission on Latin America (CEPAL). (1957). *The Economic Development of Colombia,* Geneva: UN E/CN.12/365.

————. (1965). *External Financing in Latin America.* New York: UN 65.II.G.4.

————. *Statistical Yearbook for Latin America and the Caribbean,* (annual).

United States Department of Commerce. (1955). *Investment in Mexico: conditions and outlook for United States investors.* Washington D.C.: U.S. Government

Printing Office (USGPO).

———. (1957). *U.S. Investments in the Latin American Economy.* Washington, D.C.: USGPO.

———. (1960). *U.S. Business Investments in Foreign Countries.* Washington, D.C.: USGPO.

———. (1975a). *U.S. Direct Investment Abroad, 1966: Final Data.* Washington, D.C.: USGPO.

———. (1975b). Historical Statistics of the United Sates, Colonial Times to 1970. Washington, D.C.: USGPO.

———. (1976). *Foreign Direct Investment in the United States.* Washington, D.C.: USGPO.

———. (1981). *U.S. Direct Investment Abroad, 1977.* Washington, D.C.: USGPO.

———. (1983). *Foreign Direct Investment in the United States: 1980 Benchmark.* Washington, D.C.: USGPO.

———. (1986). *U.S. Direct Investment Abroad: 1982 Benchmark Survey Data.* Washington, D.C.: USGPO.

———. (1989a). *U.S. Direct Investment Abroad: Operations of U.S. Parent Companies and Their Foreign Affiliates 1986.* Washington, D.C.: USGPO.

———. (1989b). *Foreign Direct Invesment in the United States: 1987 Benchmark Survey, Final Results.* Washington, D.C.: USGPO.

———. (1991). *U.S. Direct Investment Abroad: 1989 Benchmark Survey, Preliminary Results.* Washington, D.C.: Bureau of Economic Analysis.

United States International Trade Commission (USITC). (1992). *Economy-Wide Modeling of the Economic Implications of a FTA with Mexico and a NAFTA with Canada and Mexico.* USITC Publication 2508, Washington, D.C.: USITC.

Urquhart, M. C., and K. A. H. Buckley. (1965). *Historical Statistics of Canada.* Cambridge: The University Press. Also second edition, 1983.

Vega Cánovas, Gustavo, ed. (1991). *México ante el libre comercio con América del Norte.* México: El Colegio de México.

Verlager, Philip K. (1988). "Implications of the Energy Provisions," In Jeffrey G. Schott and Murray G. Smith eds. *The Canada-United States Free Trade Agreement.* Washington, D.C.: Institute for International Economics.

Vernon, Raymond. (1963). *The Dilemma of Mexico's Development.* Cambridge: Harvard University Press.

———. (1979). "The Product Cycle Hypothesis in a New International Environment," *Oxford Bulletin of Economics and Statistics* 41,; pp. 255-67.

Villarreal, René. (1976). *El desequilibrio externo en la industrialización de México (1929-1975),* México: Fondo de Cultura Económica.

Whiting, Van R. (1981). *Transnational Corporations and the State in Mexico: Constraints on State Regulation of Foreign Investment, Technology Inventions and Trademarks.* Unpublished Ph.D. dissertation, Harvard University.

————. (1991). "Mexico's New Liberalism in Foreign Investment and Technology." *Columbia Journal of World Business* (Summer), pp. 138-51.

Wigle, Randy. (1988). "General equilibrium evaluation of Canada-U.S. trade liberalization in a global context." *Canadian Journal of Economics* 21, (August), pp. 539-64.

Wilkins, Mira. (1989). *The History of Foreign Investment in the United States to 1914.* Cambridge: Harvard University Press.

Willmore, Larry N. (1986). "The comparative performance of foreign and domestic firms in Brazil." *World Development* 14, pp. 489-502.

Womack, John. (1978). "The Mexican Economy During the Revolution 1910:1920 Historiography and Analysis," *Marxist Perspectives* 1, no. 4, pp. 80-123.

Wong-González, Pablo. (1989). "International Integration and Locational Change in Mexico's Motor Industry: Regional Concentration and Desconcentration." manuscript, CIAD-Hermosillo.

Wonnacott, Ronald J., and Paul Wonnacott. (1967). *Free Trade Between the United States and Canada: The Potential Economic Effects.* Cambridge: Harvard University Press.

Woodward, Douglas P. (n.d.). "Locational Determinants of Japanese Manufacturing Start-ups in the United States." Unpublished manuscript, University of South Carolina.

World Intellectual Property Organization (WIPO), *Industrial Property Statistics* Geneva: WIPO (annual).

Wright, Angus. (1986). "Rethinking the Circle of Poison: The Politics of Pesticide Poisoning Among Mexican Farm Workers." *Latin American Perspectives* 51, (Fall), pp. 26-59.

Wright, Harry K. (1971). *Foreign Enterprise in Mexico: Laws and Policies.* Chapel Hill: University of North Carolina Press.

Young, R. A. (1989). "Political Scientists, Economists and the Canada-U.S. Free Trade Agreement." *Canadian Public Policy* 15, no. 1, pp. 49-56.

Yoshihara, Kunio. (1982). *Sogo Shosha: The Vanguard of the Japanese Economy.* New York: Oxford University Press.

Yu, Chwo-Ming J., and Kiyohiko Ito. (1988). "Oligopolistic Reaction and Foreign Direct Investment: The Case of the U.S. Tire and Textiles Industries." *Journal of International Business Studies* (Fall), pp. 449-59.

Yúnez-Naude, Antonio. (1991). "Hacia un tratado de libre comercio norteamericano: Efectos en los sectores agropecuarios y alimenticios de México." Documento de trabajo No. IV-91, México: El Colegio de México.

Zagaris, Bruce. (1980). *Foreign Investment in the United States.* New York: Preager.

Zeitz, Joachim, and Bichaka Fayissa. (1992). "R&D Expenditures and Import Competition: Some Evidence for the U.S." *Weltwirtschafliches Archiv* Band 128, Heft 1, pp. 52-66.

INDEX

About the Author

MICHAEL J. TWOMEY is Associate Professor in the Department of Social Sciences of the University of Michigan at Dearborn. He co-edited (with Ann Helwege) *Modernization and Stagnation: Latin American Agriculture into the 1990s* (Greenwood Press, 1991).

ISBN 0-275-94617-7

EAN

HARDCOVER BAR CODE